D1179381

CUPID AND THE JACARANDA

List of Chief Works by Sacheverell Sitwell

Poetry

THE PEOPLE'S PALACE (1918)
THE HUNDRED AND ONE HARLEQUINS
THE THIRTEENTH CAESAR
THE CYDER FEAST
TWO POEMS : TEN SONGS
EXALT THE EGLANTINE
DR. DONNE AND GARGANTUA (in Six Cantos)
CANONS OF GIANT ART : Twenty Torsos in
   Heroic Landscapes
COLLECTED POEMS
SELECTED POEMS : Old and New
BALLADS AND POEMS (*in preparation*)

Prose

SOUTHERN BAROQUE ART (1924)
FAR FROM MY HOME (short stories)
A LIFE OF LISZT
MOZART
A BACKGROUND FOR DOMENICO SCARLATTI
LA VIE PARISIENNE
VALSE DES FLEURS
MORNING, NOON AND NIGHT IN LONDON
POLTERGEISTS
OLD-FASHIONED FLOWERS
CONVERSATION PIECES
NARRATIVE PAINTINGS
THE ROMANTIC BALLET (with C. W. Beaumont)
AUDUBON'S AMERICAN BIRDS ⎫
TROPICAL BIRDS   ⎪ In Batsford's
THE ROMANTIC BALLET   ⎬ Colour Series
HEIDELOFF'S 'GALLERY OF FASHION' ⎭
BRITISH ARCHITECTS AND CRAFTSMEN
ENGLISH CHURCH MONUMENTS (with Mrs. Arundell Esdaile)
RUMANIA
MAURETANIA
THE NETHERLANDS
SPAIN
THE HOMING OF THE WINDS
ALL SUMMER IN A DAY
THE GOTHICK NORTH (in three volumes)
DANCE OF THE QUICK AND THE DEAD
SACRED AND PROFANE LOVE
PRIMITIVE SCENES AND FESTIVALS
SPLENDOURS AND MISERIES
THE HUNTERS AND THE HUNTED

CUPID AND
THE JACARANDA

BY

SACHEVERELL SITWELL

LONDON
MACMILLAN & CO. LTD
1952

PRINTED IN GREAT BRITAIN

CONTENTS

v

BOOK III

THE JASMINE KINGDOM

BOOK IV

DREAM OF THE TWO SISTERS

GYLDENLØVE

I HAVE been reading in an old book of the burning of a royal castle upon a cold foggy day in December when there was thick snow upon the ground, and of how the writer drove quickly as post-horses and the high-booted postilion could carry him and was in time to see the whole building, roofless, blackened, burning in the snow. The last of the glorious towers had just fallen, making the earth tremble as it fell, while volumes of black smoke curled and eddied in the winter mist. The riddersaal with its gilt and fretted roof had fallen in. As he arrived, the castellan was ordering the pictures to be brought out, one by one, battered, singed, but few uninjured. The most splendid of the series of royal portraits had perished in the flames, and the writer, returning to Elsinore when it was already dark, and driving past the castle which shone bright with its entire empty shell still illumined by the fire, turned his head away and would not look. It was too painful for one who had spent so many happy days studying the history of the country in the portraits of her rulers. He had known the castle in its glory, and in the excitement of its flames, and he vowed never to return to it.

"Do not imagine I slept that night : no — I lay tossing on my bed ; the spectres of that gallery were for ever before my eyes ", he continued ; and there passed before him the strange, yet familiar ghosts whom he had known ; a queen, in particular, with her pale blue Northern eyes ; and Anne of Denmark in starched ruff and monstrous farthingale, on which

1

sits perched a small black terrier dog. She wears a red powdered wig, and on a ribbon in the sky is written her motto, *La Mia Grandezza Viene Dal Eccelso* ; her sister Augusta of Holstein-Gottorp with a spotted carriage dog couched at her feet, " the only proof we now possess of these dogs being of this origin " ; and an earlier queen wearing on her head a strange headdress formed of linen, with a sort of mask of the same material across her mouth to protect her against the ' flying sand ', a black mask, he goes on, such as is still worn by the peasant women in parts of Jutland, similar to those worn at the *bal masqué*, minus the *bavolet*. " They have quite an Oriental type of countenance — long eyes, dark, *fendu à l'amande*, aquiline nose, fine and delicate mouth, a dark and brilliant complexion ; even the fashion of the masks (though our grandmothers of the eighteenth century never walked or ' rode out ' without wearing these ' *loups* ' as they were then termed) give the impression as if they were some remnant of customs imported from an Eastern land ; and what with the Varangian Guard and early connexion with Byzantium it is not at all impossible it may be so. Anything more ludicrous cannot be imagined ", he concludes, " than a troop of these black-masked creatures returning home, driving their cows from the dunes. It seems to affect the ewes, too, for we met several new-born lambs white as the driven snow, with black masks exactly like their mistresses'." [1]

More portraits pass before him as he lies, half awake, half dreaming. Anne of Denmark, once more, in a flaxen wig, almost albino, and carrying a feathered fan ; a Stuart prince with an orange surcoat and a splendid *panache* of orange-coloured plumes upon his helm ; another foreign prince in

[1] The black masks are still worn on the island of Fanø, opposite the port of Esbjerg.

monstrous galligaskins ; others " with long *effilé* fingers and transparent hands ". He sees, again, the royal stables and the cream horses, true albinos, with roseate eyes and ears, used in state processions. More princes, with the receding forehead, the *front fuyant* of the eighteenth century ; but he returns, in memory, to earlier and greater times, to the huge King and his marlok ; to the portrait of his mistress, " a fine young woman with milkmaid face and gold-powdered hair ", and I had thought, on first reading his account, that ' marlok ' was another word for ' mistress ', but it appears the meaning is quite different and that Christian IV, who in his early days wore his hair " frizzed up something in the Valois style ", later wore it in a pigtail hanging down on the right side of his head, and ending in a red bow. For he suffered from a hair disease, the *plica polonica*, could not cut his hair or he would bleed to death, and therefore allowed it, perforce, to grow longer while his courtiers, in flattery, wore the marlok like their master and marloks became the fashion.

And the holocaust continues. Those lost portraits are personalities whom he will never see or know again. In imagination, in his darkening room while the fire still flickers in the grate, there pass before him Adolf of Holstein and his giant race, the handsomest in Europe, from whom, and his son's sons, the Czar Nicholas I derived his demigod-like beauty and terrifying eyes ' of pewter ', as described by Herzen in his memoirs ; the Arveprinds in black armour ; Tycho Brahe, the blue-blooded astronomer, with the joint showing in his golden nose ; Queen Caroline Matilda and her lover Struensee, hunting their separate packs of hounds through the woods of Hirschholm along the dead waters of the Sound ; Frederick IV, the bigamist King, with his two living queens at white, swan-like Fredensborg under the leafless trees ; a

3

prince in red jacket and silver buttons " something like that worn at a Spanish bull fight " ; and a great room of portraits of early Kings, all on horseback, each horse following that of his predecessor like the horses of a royal carrousel or merry-go-round, a King, among them, who began life as Archbishop of Bremen, on horseback like the rest, armed cap-à-pie, but wearing the starched ruff of the Lutheran clergy.

He will have seen again, in the fitful firelight, the old castles of Jutland, inland from Elsinore, among the woods and lakes ; crossing a moat, with swans in numbers, and cygnets too, which were the heraldic bearings and supporters of the family, and finding long corridors hung with portraits, and below them, black wood brass-bound chests, full of old and faded dresses, old beds of needlework, old mirrors, old powder and pomade boxes, and in the garden, gigantic orange trees in full blossom and perfume standing in green '*caisses*'. The castle of the Rosenkrantz (crown of roses), of immortal fame in poetry ; with echoes from the sister country, across the narrow Sound, of such family names, in a literal translation, as Lily Root, Lobster Helm, Lily Hawk, Rosy Sunbeam, Rose Leaves, Bunch of Acorns, Northern Falcon, Reindeer Shield, Laurel Sunbeam, Laurel Mountain, Night and Day, with another family who have for crest three black waterlilies ; and so, crossing the Sound again, to Clausholm the castle of the Reventlow Queen, of the ' conscience marriage ', for the King had his other wife living, and to its gardens of roses and tulips, sweet-williams and candytufts, and the old double yellow cabbage rose. Here were dairies where the yellow butter in the presses was as large and round as cartwheels.

Then, to the whitewashed ' convent ' Gisselfeld, but it is a ' convent ', not of nuns, but noble ladies, and the eldest daughter of the Danneskjold family is hereditary ' Abbess '.

At the back there are great beech-woods and the park is white with mushrooms. Near by there is another ' convent ', Vemmetofte, and in the great saloon there hang portraits of the ten first elected ladies of the ' chapter ', pretty young women dressed in black, with the badge and star of the ' order ' upon their breasts, while the rooms are " full of tapestries and ancient furniture, Chinese scent bottles of Princess Hedvige, and queer old gilded stones ". Next, to Vallø, the most beautiful of the lay ' convents ', founded by Sophia Maddalena and opened by the Queen in person.[1] " We see the Dames de Vallø dancing and waltzing about the world in white tarlatan with grand cordon and badge of the ' order ' ", and the ten sisters highest on the list have their own apartments. They say their prayers in the chapel " in a sort of peeresses' pew, with the retainers of the ' convent ' — a second pew under the pulpit being put aside for the deaf ones — the drawing-rooms are lighted up of an evening ", and they dine together, have their own chaplain, own doctor, own carriages, a beautiful garden, hothouses, and a deer park.

And he returns past the woods and lakes to where the royal castle that he loved is still burning. The castellan has the last of the portraits carried out into the snow, but so many are lost and have perished in the flames. Once more, he sees the great King, the builder and music-lover (John Dowland

[1] On 28 November 1737, for an Abbess of royal or princely birth, a Deaconess descended from counts, and twelve Stifts-Froichens with sixteen quarterings, three of whom had to be ladies-in-waiting. The habit was black; except on special occasions, when a white silk dress — that of the Abbess of damask, of the Deaconess of satin, of the Froichens of Gros de Tours — ornamented with black lace was worn, and with it a long veil and a turquoise blue mantle, the Abbess's lined with ermine, the Deaconess's with satin, the Froichens' with ' taffent '. In 1932 some three hundred noble ladies were receiving annuities (for which they were entered at birth with a fee), and there were eleven residents of the Abbey, each occupying a suite of half a dozen rooms. The yellow cabbage rose (cf. above), elsewhere extinct, may still be growing in some Danish garden.

was his lutanist and had a salary equal to the pay of the highest ministers of state), with his marlok, and all the splendid family of Gyldenløves. And what were they ? The Gyldenløves (golden lions) were bastards of the royal family ; a Gyldenløve would be High Admiral, Knight of the Elephant, or Field-Marshal, just as in the sister country with which they were at war, mostly, the royal bastards of the house of Wasa were known as Gyllenhjelms.

For ourselves, in the bleak and tragic times in which we live, there is a particular significance in this procession of unknown, but not nameless phantoms. It was of importance for our purpose that they should have romantic names, and little more ; that, even, they should belong to a country and to a history that may remain mysterious for a little and are not to be known, immediately, in the first sentence. This country of lakes and woods had its Kings and Queens, and ' convents ', its Rosenkrantz and Gyldenstjern. The heyducks line the palace stair upon the King's birthday, wearing Hanoverian uniforms, with nosegays of artificial flowers put in their tall mitre hats. They are wearing pots of artificial flowers upon their heads, and the lions of the country's coat of arms are upon their mitres or half-sugarloafs.[1] The ivory of the Kingdom is the narwhal horn and there are silver lions to guard the throne.

[1] I have been unable to find any detailed account of this most picturesque of all Court ceremonies which takes place every year upon the King of Denmark's birthday. The scene is in that one of the four palaces of the Amalienborg which contains the Coronation and State Rooms. These palaces, placed diamond-wise in an octagonal square, were built by Nic. Eigtved (1740–50), and form one of the finest squares in Europe. In the middle stands the equestrian statue of Frederick V by the French sculptor, Saly. It is in this square that the Danish Royal Guard mount guard in their red tunics, blue trousers, and bearskin caps. All the information I have been able to discover about the ceremony I am describing is a small drawing of one of the heyducks in his flower-pot hat in the book of an English traveller who stopped at Copenhagen on his way to attend the Coronation of Czar Nicholas II in 1895.

Towards the winter morning, at half-past five or six o'clock, he will have fallen asleep, and thinking of that night-gowned or frock-coated phantom of some ninety years ago,[1] we have to admit that with respect to the world in general, and all the past, we are in his position, that we have been born, or are arrived in time, to see it burning. One by one the portraits, not the Kings and Queens and " fine young women ", themselves, but their counterfeit or memory, which is all that is left of them, we see taken out from the collapsing, blazing building, and we know that more, and those the most splendid, have perished in the fire. This is a question that is higher than politics and wise men of all kinds of opinion mourn their loss. There are others, besides ourselves, who thinking of them will pass a restless, tossing night, and will not sleep.

We have to consider, too, and this is, in part, our theme, that Greece and Italy are no longer the mothers of the arts. The Englishman will go no more to Italy, as I did myself when young. It is as though the points of the compass have altered owing to the two wars. More particularly, the South has altered, or it has lost its warmth. It is no longer the " dew-dropping South " of Mercutio. They are no more, " love-whisp'ring woods and lute-resounding waves ". Buildings of pleasure, as I knew them, are dead and gone, and the golden churches will fall slowly into dust. That light and brilliant architecture is dead like laughter. It is too painful to me to think of this, or to try and remember what I spent my youth in learning, and so, like the traveller of a hundred years ago, upon our first page, who passed once more where the castle that he loved lay burning in the snow, but turned his head

---

[1] The source for our account of Denmark is a little known book, *A Year's Residence in Jutland and the Danish Isles*, by Horace Marryat : London, John Murray, 1860. The author was a brother of Captain Marryat.

away and would not look, I must look away and vow never to return to it.

Look out of window ! Snow is falling, and it is beginning to lie deep. Could it be made audible, the sound of three continents would be a shivering and a chattering of teeth. Not for the only reason that it is winter, but there is universal coldness or chilling of the spirit, and in midst of that the raging fire, a fire which burns more furiously because of the deep snow and the heavy weight that loads the roof and breaks the leafless boughs. The inner core is on fire like the hold of a ship burning on the salt, high seas. It is drifting, helplessly, and there are no vessels standing by. The great beech trees have caught fire and are scorched and smouldering. The rooks' nests flare up in little tufts of flame. There are burning rose trees, which had stood asleep, and melting statues ; and we would half expect to see the ghosts of the castle coming out in person. In a few weeks, when the earth wakens, we could see a Gyldenløve, it matters not whom, standing by the white Guelder-rose ; or a young princess, wearing a mask or ' loup ', riding under the Turkish lilac while rain dashes from the white or purple spires upon her face and hands.

Huntsmen practise their fanfares under the trees and we hear the great hounds belling while they exercise. The crowned stags walk in safety on that summer day, for a few weeks more, and then the holocaust. Where are the reindeer sleighs, and the astrologers with long thin beards and high fur caps who have driven across the snows ? Or is it only that we have been looking in an ancient atlas for the Kingdom of Prester John ? But they have the long gowns of astrologers and high pointed caps, and are come from the mammoth-hiding tundras over the ice and snow. They must live in high, conical fur tents among the tethered reindeer. This wizard tribe was an obsession with the draughtsmen of the old Dutch atlases. They are journeying out of the North, always, and we are to imagine that their merchandise consists of precious furs, sables, ermines, that they are hunters or trappers, and at once, magicians and astrologers of the North, tall men, with red beards and hair, and aquiline noses, almost resembling Jewish wizards and necromancers of the Middle Ages in Moorish Spain. Such is the magician of the piece, and arriving at the castle he will come into the ballroom — it is the ridder-saal — dressed as a black swan, to a blare of trumpets, a silvery fanfare, holding his beautiful, glittering daughter by the hand.

For ourselves, there is to be no escape from the haunted lake shore, the mists and sighing reeds. Out on the water, in the middle of the lake, the duck take to wing with much splashing and ' feathering ' of the weeds, and come back a turn higher and make off into the distance, for no reason, but as though knowing what is coming. They are gone entirely, and there is utter silence, a pause that could be the delay or breakdown in some stage machinery, a moment of waiting and of apprehension, then from far off, coming nearer out of the mist, their long necks forward, their great wings clapping in close time, the familiar, silvery, feathered whistling or ringing, and a flight of wild swans passes overhead, and has gone back into the mist.

INVITATION

A CLOCK strikes from across the water on a summer evening.
One . Two . . Three . . . Four . . . . Five . . . . . Six
o'clock . . . . . . But the warning or intimation is a little
foot in a white ballet shoe thrust as in some old Italian fresco
or wall painting by a trick of perspective round a corner of
the door as though to keep the door ajar, or it could even be
that the dancer's shoe has left its imprint on the paper of this
page, but it is a symbol or warning, we see no more of its
owner for the moment than her foot and ankle, it is only, as
it were, to keep the door open leading out of one world into
another. To one side of the door the lights of artifice or lit
airs of the theatre, and to the other the dying sunset ; and in
between them the imminence or promise of this glittering
figure, herald or messenger of the embarcation, which begins
with no more ado than the noise of a number of persons rising
from the grassy bank on which they have been sitting, and
the sound of their starting down from the knoll or mound in
order to set foot in a gilded shell, which is nothing other than
the barge of Venus.

The ladies and cavaliers are rising to their feet, but one or
two of them are loth to go. It is cool in the long shadow of
the trees, and once they have embarked they are in the empyrean and have left this world for ever. A young woman, in
carnation-pink, will be among the last to leave. She is still
listening to what her kneeling swain is whispering. Behind
them, a cavalier helps his lady, in black and yellow, to her feet.

He lifts her by both hands. Another couple are standing upon the highest point of the bank or mound. He is the pilgrim, the *pèlerin* of the piece, and we notice that, like three or four more of the chief actors, he wears a pilgrim's hat and cloak, and that a pilgrim's staff is in his hand. He has his back turned to us, and makes as though to lead his lady down. A little spaniel barks at their feet, but she turns to look back. She is reluctant to go. Or she would have us look at her once more and ever. Further down, another pair stroll happily arm-in-arm, by the stern of the barge where it is carved and gilt with the figure of Venus and her shell. The unfairness is that all the ladies and their cavaliers are of the theatre. Their attentions and sentiments are all make-belief, and the fiction is made doubly more poignant when we think of this.

Our theme is that of Watteau's *L'Embarquement pour Cythère*, but our version or replica takes place in modern clothes. Such is the case, too, in the original, for the men and women of Watteau's painting are wearing the clothes of their time, yet not entirely. We see no long periwigs. His men are wearing the short coats and breeches of contemporary actors ; and we remember that the subject of *L'Embarquement* was taken from a comedy, *Les Trois Cousins*, by Dancourt, a play which appeared in 1702, but the picture was not painted until 1717, proving that the project had been long maturing in the painter's mind.

Which of the two paintings of *L'Embarquement* do we prefer ? For one is in the Louvre and there was one at Potsdam. The first was sent in by Watteau as his presentation piece upon appointment to the Académie (he was the object of several reprimands between 1712 and 1717 for not having handed in the work required within a reasonable time) ; the other version was bought by de Julienne, his friend and patron, and sold by him to Frederick the Great. It is a larger picture painted a year or two later. The trees are fuller in shape, the statue of Venus has been developed from a garden term into a whole group of Venus and Cupid, and the waiting barge has been rebuilt and furnished with a gilded mast. The principal figures in both pictures are the same, but a flight of cupids has come to raise the sail and man the rigging. The galleon is departing, but as in the other painting the ladies and their gallants are loth to go, and a pair of cupids hovers in the air to warn them. The coppery-haired phantom of *L'Embarquement* has not come down to go on board. She waits in the wings, and will come on again.

Watteau had first arrived in Paris from his native Valenciennes in 1702, without friends and without money, when he was barely eighteen years old. It was through Claude Gillot, who painted from comedy, and made etchings of fauns and satyrs, that Watteau was introduced to the theatre and became stage-struck. There exists another painting in which we may think we can identify the moment that inspired him in *Les Trois Cousins*. It was when Mlle Desmares, with the full company gathered round her, came to the footlights and sang the following verse:

> Venez dans l'île de Cythère
> En pèlerinage avec nous,
> Jeune fille n'en revient guère
> Ou sans amant ou sans époux ;
> Et l'on y fait sa grande affaire
> Des amusements les plus doux,

and in the picture we are given this scene much as it must have appeared to a spectator in the theatre. Of Charlotte Desmares, whom he saw at this time, we know little more than that she was celebrated for her pretty voice and delightful way of laughing. An early work, Watteau being little more than twenty years old at the time he painted it, but under the immediate impact of the emotion which was to inspire him to paint *L'Embarquement* many years later (only four years before he died), and in a more imaginative or poetic setting.

During this long interval, it is probable that the painter thought as often of the words of the song as of his picture, for having been in love with the leading lady it is likely that he read into those lines some allusion to what himself had experienced or seen to happen. It may have become, as it were, his own view or comment upon the sentimental life until, unconsciously, after all that time he was ready and could paint the picture. Such is the process in the minds of so many artists in all the arts, and it is their opportunity. How wonderful an opportunity !

But we cannot allow the ladies and Mezzetins to depart as easily as that. We see them, as in others of his paintings, sitting upon the grass, grouped close to a shimmering fountain. It is, decidedly, a Mezzetin who stands in his cloak and cap, with his back to us, beside the falling water. And there is another, lying at his feet, leaning on an elbow, talking. The four young girls of *Les Champs-Élysées* (in the Wallace Collection) are as clearly of the theatre as if we had visited them in their dressing-rooms. As much is implied, too, in the manner of their conversation, which is that of persons who are continually in each other's company. But we know why it was that Watteau, nearly always, drew his inspiration from the theatre. We have already told the reason, and looking from one to another of the young women we notice that they are of small height, like dancers, and our glance rests on the one who looks at us out of the painting in her gown of rippling, yellow silk, so like the ' grain ' or ' touch ' of his chalk drawings.

Is it the same, or another young woman, in the beautiful little *Harlequin and Columbine* of the Wallace Collection? Her gown, which is nearly indescribable in colour, except to say that it is like *café au lait* mingled with *marron* or chestnut, resembles more than ever the ' watering ' or ' handling ' of his coloured chalk on paper. The material flows or ripples with his touch. In her sleeve and skirt it has, positively, a lateral and a downward run or current. But she looks away.

The exquisite drawings by Watteau provide further evidence of his obsession with the theatre. Some are working drawings done, that is to say, not as finished sketches, but in order to help him with his paintings. Often the drawings are of his friends, or of a young woman who appears to have been his housekeeper or servant, but in so many of them the hat or ruff of Mezzetin, or something in the attitude or in the hands, betrays his predilection. It would appear that Watteau, granted his obsession, would have none other than actors making love, or painted in company with his young women. Contemporary characters, in the form of living persons, he would not tolerate or allow to mingle with his world apart. If it is not the actors, themselves, it is his friends or servants, whom he could trust, dressed up as actors. They are working drawings, as we have said, but something exquisite in his temperament made his chalk or pencil give to them a silken finish, even to the hurdygurdy player or little Savoyard.

And so back to *L'Embarquement*.

Our meaning or purpose is that we have it in mind to embark, here and now, in the waiting galleon in company with a few persons, real or imaginary, and set sail for the isle of pleasure. Whither this will lead us we shall know later, and whether or not it will be in the direction of that rose-hung island. And whom do we invite to come on board? For there can be livelong companions who are imaginary, or nearly so, phantoms of flesh and blood for ever in our eyes, or walking by our side, persons who must take their places, certainly, among the invited though they have never spoken and we do not know their voices. Poetry, music, painting, are full of parallels, for in such matters the absolute truth does not exist, the fiction, ever, is a little further or a little nearer, and in this instance no more remote than the little foot which keeps the door ajar, but which in its white satin slipper with the blocked toe is as pointed, but impersonal, as the feeling of being looked at through the slant eyes in a mask when we do not know for certain who is the wearer.

Shall we say that the scene is the lake of my childhood, at my old home, below the hanging wood, for it is on those waters that I used to lie in a boat and dream, at a time, too, when I had read of *L'Embarquement*, when I was, perhaps, fourteen or fifteen years old ? Many young children have thus felt the breath of that other world upon their faces, and it can be the utmost fascination of which the life of flesh and blood is capable ; or it can come back, again and again, as though it had not died between. But the interest is less in the scene than in the persons. It is not even certain whether it takes place in life or in the theatre. But the confusion gives beauty, as in the paintings we have described where the young women are all dancers and the men are Mezzetins. Every one of them could be, or is, a musician or an actor, members of the profession, therefore, like the writer, and, as such, belonging to the world apart.

It is another golden sunset and we set sail. But only from left to right across the stage until the curtain falls. We look again for that undisguised and unhidden ankle thrust round the door, to keep the door ajar, but still concealing who is its owner. We are not to know her for the moment. And we follow with our eyes to where the golden line of her leg, beginning, draws us after her into the world that she inhabits. But, when we look again, the foot has lifted and the sparkling form has gone. Gone, without warning, and in that moment while we looked away.

BOOK I

EMBARCATION

I

Pierrots on the Sands

C'est Cythère,
Nous dit-on, un pays fameux dans les chansons,
Eldorado banal de tous les vieux garçons.
Regardez, après tout, c'est une pauvre terre.

Ch. Baudelaire

EVERYONE to his, or her, own isle of Venus. Mine, for better or worse, being not so much Fusina, " on the mainland opposite Venice, port of embarcation for the Queen of the Adriatic, and in the same breath, terminus of the tramline ", as one of those landscapes to be admired from the train window to both sides of the railway line between Rotherham and Sheffield, and in that vicinity (I speak of particular and native scenes), where there are black streams of sluggish water (the Rother and her tributaries), flowing slowly, the waters of a blacker Styx, with banks of slime, shallow precipices above the stinking mud, black savannah of the collieries and iron-works, with slag-heaps and hills of clinker for the halcyon and for Himalayan vale, and here and there a low-lying island, heavy with wild rhubarb and giant hemlock, where the Naiad in hiker's shorts giggles under the willow-herb, and her bicycle leans against the rowan tree.

Listen! Do not be afraid. That is the panting engine that draws the coal trucks. Where is the barge of Venus moored ? The silken sails will be marked with smuts where

19

they dragged below the branches. The ropes and rigging will leave black marks upon the hands. Cupid, at the prow, looks as though he has been playing down a coal-mine. Nectar and ambrosia. The mobile fish-and-chips van halts under the long wall below the railway, halfway from Eckington to Renishaw. For temple of the ' rose-hung island ' there is the L.M.S. signal-box, not two hundred yards, that is the fun of it, from where my father intended his lake pavilion. But in the garden upon the hill there are statues of Neptune and Venus, brought from Venice ; there are stone warriors guarding the walks into the faunal woods.

It was upon the lake, I have written, " that I used to lie in a boat and dream, at a time, too, when I had read of *L'Embarquement*, when I was, perhaps, fourteen or fifteen years old. Many young children ", I continued, " have thus felt the breath of that other world upon their faces ". Would " that other world " be much altered during all this time between ? It would not. No more than religion, the bonds of which grow stronger as one gets older. If one has religion ! It would even, so it seems to me, concern the same number of characters, real or imaginary, for the total of those does not diminish or increase. But no sooner is that written than I disagree with it. Then, as now, the statues stood in the garden and the Naiad, dressed more demurely, laughed under the willow-herb. But the Naiad has jumped the wall into the sacred park. Do not look at her. She is attractive, and warmer than the Venus of cold stone. She is making up her face, and has such pretty legs. She is a miner's daughter. So much has happened since I used to lie in a boat on the lake ; two world wars (four years, and again six years of it, ten years in all) and, I write as an individual, all the years of my life as a writer during the years between. The world of my choice, as I would have chosen it, has altered, but not changed in principle. The lines, or direction of that, were already laid down when I was a child. I then felt and knew the wind of that other world upon my face and forehead, and so it continues, now that I have a feather of the firebird in my hand. Even so, the shadow world, or that part of it which dances and does not speak, is but a portion of the whole. I was thinking of much else besides, when I used to lie there in a boat and dream. In a sense I boarded the barge of Venus during those far-off summers when I was a child. I hope that lake with its willow trees and bulrushes will be haunted by me and that someone, it matters not who, will walk the banks and think of me lying far out in the middle of the waters while my brother was at the war. Ah! so much has altered. Human beings change as they get older. The ghost of his father inhabits Hamlet and makes him a little forgetful, it seems to me. Listen, then, for that ghost, also! He is not at peace, and haunts his son. I have made an oath with myself never to see that long house or those tall trees again. They have brought ill fortune to me.

I remember coming up the steep wood, the hanging wood where there are so many dead husks of bluebells, where you look down and see the lake between the trees, and thinking of Mezzetin in his black mask. I must have been looking at books on Watteau. I cannot have been more than fourteen or fifteen years old. I mention this because I believe it to be unusual and peculiar, and because I wonder if there is a young boy anywhere in Europe or America to-day who dreams of such subjects and characters, or has even heard of them. I doubt that. I remember thinking of the trees in Fragonard's paintings (I only knew them from reproductions of engravings) and looking up at the light among the leaves.

I have had to be content in my life with knowledge. I have never (however much interested in architecture) been able to express myself in bricks and mortar. I have certainly no talent for decorating or arranging rooms. My expression has been, only and entirely, in poetry and prose; and I would have preferred, I must not deny it, to have been born a painter, or better still, most of all, a musician. That could not be. I have had to enlarge what talent I have from poetry into prose, for it is not possible to write poetry, and only poetry, the whole time. I have had to invent special and particular vehicles in which to proceed, and push forward into the interior, and traverse the great distances that I wished to cover. For I am not a novelist. I have seen my particular world more from the point of view that it is the perpetual grape harvest, and that I am treading the grapes and making and tasting wine. The consequent slight intoxication is my purpose, and the sign, or otherwise, of my success. For I am unsuccessful if I have not achieved that. I would like all, or any, of my images to be like a sip of wine, or like a sip of honey. Such is my interpretation of the purpose of poetry, and I do not like it to be a cold intellectual game. For sign and emblem of my Muse, if I have one, I would choose the humming-bird moth which, late in the season, and this is the autumn of our world, like some being, a little strange and formidable, hovers upon the flowers, darting from one to another with purpose and determination, returning, ever and again, as though his task is not completed, and away to the blue ceratostigma and up into the rose bells of the double hollyhocks, and over the stone wall out of sight, and back again high up in the crimson clematis, hovering and darting, so that no one can see him in detail, and many persons mistake him for a humming-bird and ignore that he is a moth. The work of the humming-bird is the nectar of the flowers. I am aware that some may be reminded of that by my excursions and changes of subject, if any read me in another age, and it is for this reason that I choose the moth as being more serious and diligent, and the creature, too, of night as well as day. For my chosen topics have not all been pleasant and sunlit, any more than the world of my youth which flowered between two wars. But I have lived to see what I was born to see. I cannot go down in unhappiness after that. It is not *une pauvre terre*, ' a poor earth ', after all. It has splendours as well as miseries to recommend it.

Many, indeed, most of those, I may have touched and seen. It is my pride, and I hope it is true, " that perhaps no other writer has ever covered a wider range in the arts that make life beautiful ". When I was eighteen years old and had begun writing, I thought that, by now, we would be living in a golden age of knowledge and creation. I saw no wrong in attacking the world from its far corners, as it was so small a world. There was nothing peculiar to me in meeting Mezzetin walking in a wood of bluebells. It was as natural to me as the distant sound of a cricket bat. And more poetical, and more interesting. I have chosen Mezzetin because I can never think of the light in the leaves, and at the tree foot, in those particular woods of my childhood and adolescence without being reminded of Watteau. But, in fact, the Derbyshire woods do not resemble the woods and parks in Watteau's paintings. Those are the woods of Belœil (in Belgium) so far as there can be a parallel. The Derbyshire woods are dark, dark, and have ' Alpine ' grass (I do not know the botanical name) growing upon banks and in dark corners, a straight, lank, dark green grass, like a Nereid's hair. If you find a stone or pebble on the ground it is, as likely as not, a piece of clinker from the mine, and a seam of coal may come to the surface upon the side of any hill. It is only where the woods have been half-tamed, shaped, brought into the scheme of things, had vistas cut through them, perhaps to show the curve of a cornfield, white in August, but too far for the sound of voices or the distant flail, and had walks laid through them with statues to guard the entrances, that they begin to resemble the woods of Watteau.

Now the poetry of Watteau's paintings, I do not speak of his exquisite handling, is because it gives a shock of surprise to meet his Italian comedians strolling, making love, playing their lutes or mandolines underneath the trees. He has removed them from the theatre, or the pierrots' booths, and this was something that had never been done before in either painting or poetry. It was a new race of inhabitants, at once more romantic and more lively than the classical gods or heroes of the statues. More unexpected still, to find comedians out of the theatre lying on the shores of the lake, or in wild, overgrown corners of the garden. It is the overlapping of the one life into the other that makes the fascination. But the theme of the theatre has altered since the early years of the eighteenth century. No consideration of theatrical lighting enters into any of Watteau's paintings. The lighting of his day was an affair of candles or pine torches. Yet more, in his instance, it was the open-air theatre of the Commedia dell' Arte, strolling actors who played at fairs or in the market place.[1] Even in *Les Trois Cousins*, the comedy in which he saw Mlle Desmares, and that inspired him to paint *L'Embarque-*

---

[1] It has been suggested (though I have read this subsequent to writing my description of *Le Grand Gilles* in this present book, where I arrived at the same conclusion) that the painting in question may have been done as a signboard for a troupe of strolling players. This, if true, would explain the curious, doltish, full-face pose of *Gilles* and, also, the flat, rustic technique of the painting.

ment, the lighting must have been so feeble that, compared with what we are used to in our time, you scarcely saw the actors' faces. And in any case Watteau did not set his comedians inside a theatre ; as we know, he grouped them always in a landscape he had "visualized or got ready". He depicts the comedians taken away from the theatre and put in a formal park, or beside a fountain. There is a lake below feathery, over-arching trees (*L'Assemblée dans un Parc*, Louvre) or a colonnade of pink and black marble (*Les Plaisirs du Bal*, Dulwich) ; but never the flickering candlelight upon their faces, and only the light of late afternoon or sunset. We are to imagine that the comedians are lodged in the attics of the château. But, soon, in their silks and satins, they become the guests themselves, and we begin to wonder if they have ever danced or acted. And, also, whether Watteau had personal experience, and more than an imaginary acquaintance with *la vie du château*, for his actors are not guests staying in a great country house of the time of Louis-Quatorze, and just as certainly, the guests do not make good actors. This other life, this intermediate set of appearances, as invented by Watteau, is poetically beautiful, but not real. It has sentiment, but not pathos. There is only Watteau's *Le Grand Gilles* to compare with Picasso's harlequins.

Not that it is his fault, entirely. For this is not all. There is another life, yet another, and this the true, 'intermediate set of appearances ', between the two, but not telling us of either. Nobody, meeting a dancer in the long passages of the theatre, in ignorance, could describe her to you, whether upon the stage, or as a living person. For this existence, in between, is only hieratic. It tells us nothing, and is but a painted idol, the puppet in the robing-room, not the goddess upon the altar. But that magical pencil should have been employed upon this chrysalis from which the moth emerges. For here is the mystery. The mystery, and the absorbing interest, so that one can imagine an artist of considerable powers devoting a lifetime to these metamorphoses which overplays Watteau and shows him, magical as he was, a mere amateur of the theatre, unable, or unwilling, to pursue these mysteries to their ends.

This subject, in all its endless ramifications and subdivisions, is what I mean by ' theatre ' ; and, poetry apart, it has been one of the passions and intoxications of my life, as much, or more so, as music or architecture, not as one directly concerned with the theatre, but as participant and spectator. I would like to have it said of me that " among much else, besides, he wrote of scenes and subjects taken from the theatre ", rather in the sense in which one looks up a name in the dictionary of painters to find that the painter in question, whoever he may have been, in addition to everything else he did showed in one phase of his work that he loved the theatre. I suppose my interest is mostly from the visual and emotional point of view, the proof of which is that I do not go to the theatre in order to hear words and speeches. My attendance is in order to look and use my eyes, and listen to the music. I am drawn in lesser degree to ' straight ' plays than to ballet, opera, and comedy. Where music is concerned (this is contingent), the musicians of whom I have written have been Mozart, Domenico Scarlatti, and Offenbach. And I have written of Bach's organ music, and of his 'Goldberg' Variations ; and have composed episodes to do with Couperin, with Glinka, and with Johann Strauss, and much, too, dealing with the ballet music of Tchaikowsky and of Delibes. That must be, in a sense, my gamut of the theatre.

I have been, ever since I was a child, a lover of Italian

scenic architecture, by which I intend Bernini's colonnade to St. Peter's, Piranesi's engravings, and the scenic drawings of the Bibiena family and their school. I would like to add to this that I knew, and greatly admired, the masquerade paintings of G. B. Tiepolo, carnival scenes from the fair of Bergamo (there are four of these easel pictures), and the drawings from the life of Pulcinella by his son, Domenico. Also, all sorts of other and lesser documents ; for an instance, the tapestries of Italian comedians which used to hang in the palace of the prince-bishop of Würzburg, in Bavaria, designed by a Swiss painter, Rudolph Byss (1660–1738).[1] One of the set depicts a company of Italian comedians at supper, and is curiously reminiscent of Picasso's great drop scene for the Russian Ballet, *Parade* ; another shows the company arriving in the Piazza of St. Mark's, complete with performing bear, only the buildings are wrongly placed and the square is empty of persons, except for the back view of a group of Venetian masqueraders in their hats and cloaks, a silhouette that for a century was one of the familiar sights of Europe but is gone for ever.

I admired, too, such books as that by the Venetian dancing master Gregorio Lambranzi, with its marvellously theatrical plates by Johann Georg Puschner of Nuremberg. This wonderful work of art has analogies to the dance movements in Bach's English and French Suites for clavichord, and his Partitas.[2] It is exactly contemporary to them. We know

[1] Two of this set of five tapestries are reproduced in plates 23 and 24 of my *German Baroque Art* : London, Duckworth & Co., 1927.

[2] *Neue und Curieuse Theatralische Tantz-Schul,* Nuremberg, 1716, in two volumes, each containing fifty plates. This book was reprinted by C. W. Beaumont, Charing Cross Road, London, in 1928. It contains examples of the Sarabande, Folies d'Espagne, Bourrée, Rigaudon, Romagnola, Bergamasca, Furlana, Corente, Lourre, Scaramuzza, Galiarda, Chicona, Bolognesa, and dances or hornpipes for English and Dutch sailors. The frontispiece to vol. 2 depicts the author in the rôle of Mezzetin. The connexion with Bach's dance movements is very near, and not only in his keyboard Suites. A Furlana (Venetian fishermen's dance) occurs in his Suite for orchestra

that Johann Sebastian Bach never visited Southern Germany, but are tempted to think that he may have seen this, or a similar troupe, in Dresden or in Leipzig. This was a work to set any kindred imagination upon fire, and that certainly had much influence upon me when I was young.

It was under such tutelage that, as a writer and poet, I approached the theatre, but, combined with this, there was the architectural, the Palladian scene, the prime instance of which was the false perspective of Palladio's Teatro Olimpico at Vicenza, a theatre begun in 1579, during Shakespeare's youth, and which one could wish that he had seen, for compared with it the Globe Theatre in Southwark was but a rustic bear-pit or a bull-ring. There was, also, the Teatro Farnese at Parma—by Aleotti, a pupil of Palladio — like a huge theatrical panorama by Jacques Callot come to life, and in which one could place his fantastic foreground figures in all their swagger leaning against the permanent built arch of the proscenium.

There were smaller, lesser known theatres, too ; the deserted, haunted theatre, little bigger than a barn, in Sabbioneta, one of the Gonzaga duchies, near Mantua, but by no less an architect than Scamozzi, the most famous of Palladio's pupils. I cannot forget the dusty, curious atmosphere of this early theatre when the high windows were unshuttered, for, in fact, it had the dimensions of a fair-sized room, but out of all proportion and in false perspective so that it was eloquent of painters' lay figures or dummies, phrenologists' heads, and the metaphysical paintings by Chirico, which is to say, dumb, with a heavy, pregnant silence, that is no more than an empty theatre without life and movement. And as though to give

No. 1 in C major. I remember well the excitement of Diaghilev upon being shown a copy of this work, and his remark that there is no such thing in this world as a new invention. Surely the influence of Italian comedy is audible, too, in Bach's 'Italian Concerto'.

this little town of Sabbioneta, with a few hundred inhabitants, in the valley of the Po, yet another tie to the theatre, one of its churches has presses or vestment cupboards in the sacristy which were designed by a member of the Bibiena family. Did I not, for that matter, know the Pantheon Estense, a church built by one of the Bibienas to hold the tombs of the d' Estes, in Modena, capital of their duchy, " one of the most fantastic flat-roofed creations of the Baroque style " Burckhardt calls it, but, in truth, it is dull and uninteresting and not at all theatrical (it does not compare in this respect with Guarini's circular domed chapel of the Santissimo Sudario, in Turin, that astonishing funereal piece of ' theatre ', in black or dark brown marble, which is one of the most dramatic effects in all architecture).

In pursuit of this order of sensations, I visited every old theatre that I knew of : the Opera House of San Carlo at Naples, connecting, so typically, with the Royal Palace, and Vanvitelli's theatre in the Palace of Caserta, with its twelve Corinthian columns of *giallo antico* taken from the Serapeum at Pozzuoli, the spoils of Ancient Rome ; and the theatres in various Italian towns ; [1] the lovely, green La Fenice of Venice, worthy of the Venetians and one of the beauties of the Rococo ; while I must mention too, the foyer, upstairs, in the Teatro Grande of Brescia, with its walls painted with masked carnival scenes, probably by Alessandro, son of the

[1] The Teatro Comunale of Bologna by Antonio Bibiena, dating from the middle of the eighteenth century, and the Teatro Filarmonico of Verona by Francesco Bibiena, are both disappointing and give no idea of this great family at their best. For that, their drawings apart (of which there is a good collection in the Print Room of the British Museum), and the great work in theatrical perspective, *Architettura e prospettiva*, Augsburg, 1740, by Ferdinando Galli Bibiena, it is necessary to see the Opera House of Bayreuth with its golden interior by Carlo Bibiena, its Court box for the Margraves and their retinue, " a miniature stage and counter-attraction to the stage proper, which it faces ", and little golden balconies for trumpeters.

more famous Pietro Longhi (just like his painted staircase in the Palazzo Grassi on the Grand Canal at Venice) ; and the beautiful little Teatro Regio built by the Empress Marie-Louise, when she was Duchess of Parma, in perfect Empire style, though belated (1821-29), in marble, stucco, and painted scagliola, one of the most complete interiors of the period, where Paganini often played. I own a copy of the Court Almanack of the Duchy of Parma, printed in Bodoni type, in which Baron Niccolò Paganini appears as *virtuoso de camera* to Marie-Louise. A curious macabre interest attaches to every place in which Paganini performed, and when I went to this theatre in Parma I could not but think of his gaunt shape entering the stage door.[1]

The Italian style of theatre interior or auditorium was thus established. It was as Italian as the technical language and the expression marks in music, and so it continued during the whole of the nineteenth century, as may still be seen in a few provincial theatres in England that, to those who remember it, are in the style of the interior of the old Café Royal in Regent Street. A pair of beautiful theatres, not to be bettered for their purposes of entertainment and amusement, are that of the Spa at Homburg and the little theatre in the Casino at Monte Carlo, all golden and glittering, both by Garnier, architect of the Opéra at Paris, and the ideal settings for operettas by Offenbach, Lecocq, and the school of French light music from Delibes to Planquette and to Messager. What

---

[1] I have been told, just when I write this, of the Bibiena theatre in Siena, of all places, on the ground floor of the Palazzo Pubblico, in what was the Sala del Gran Consiglio. It is the Teatro dei Rinnovati, " last rebuilt by Antonio Galli da Bibiena in 1735 ", described to me as an oval interior, painted in gold and various fresh colours, and that I have never heard of before to this day, although I have lived near to Siena for months on end (at Montegufoni), and although I thought I knew of every Bibiena theatre in Italy, or anywhere in Europe. Such is Italy, the wonders of which never end !

an evocation of ' period ' are the mere names of Homburg and of Monte Carlo, but the singing of that light music is a lost art ! It is only possible, on hearing the adroit and magical orchestral accompaniments, models of their sort, composed especially by Offenbach for particular singers of his little Théâtre des Variétés of the Champs-Élysées, altered and improvised, almost, during rehearsal to suit their individual mannerisms and tricks of style, to imagine for oneself a Zulma Bouffar or an Hortense Schneider while we listen to *La Vie parisienne* or *La Périchole*. Such arts are evanescent and die quickly. Now, only fifty years after they were written, it is no longer possible to hear Puccini's *La Bohème* and *Tosca* sung as was intended, for the voices of Caruso and his generation are no more.

This is the art of the theatre ; such is theatrical art. It dies, and is gone for ever. It can be over and finished when the performer is in his or her youth, which is a reason for going again and again to see this mortal and perishable thing that cannot last, that may be in bloom for a few weeks only, or a few days. A painter paints a picture, a writer writes a book ; and they do not change, they remain for good or bad. It is only taste that alters ; that goes away, but may come back again. But the art of the theatre dies, and is gone for ever.

Nevertheless, the theatre is likely to be for a long time to come the only palpable, living realization of what an ever-increasing public for works of art knows, now, to have been achieved in the past and to be possible of accomplishment. This is the importance of the theatre, that it takes the place of what is missing from life. It could be argued that our age, which is denied music, costume, architecture of our own time, can look nowhere else for living and breathing beauty but upon the stage. . . .

II

Embarcation

WHEN I was young, not long ago, and now, I have ever been able to recapture inspiration — however much exhausted in the labour of literary creation, or by circumstance — in thinking of two works of art which by force of fate were never accomplished or achieved. One of them is the grand symphony or suite for orchestra " with harps and piano " that the dipsomaniac and dying Moussorgsky mentions in the last year of his life as upon the point of completion, for this would have been, surely, one of the most original and extraordinary of all works in music ; the other, the set of grand classical or mythological pieces in prose that the nineteen years old Rimbaud intended, having written *Les Illuminations* (he had thought of the title *Photographies des temps passés*) but, instead, he renounced his genius, wrote no more, and took to an aimless life of wandering and trading.

Passing through Paris the other day, I saw again his portrait beside that of Verlaine in the group by Fantin-Latour now hanging in the Musée de l'Orangerie, a portrait done, presumably, from memory (I do not know the history of this painting), but I am unwilling to believe that Rimbaud accorded to Fantin anything so patiently acquiescent as a sitting, and it is probable that it was done after the poet had already vanished, leaving no address, and this most sudden and brilliant of all the meteors of poetry had flared up in

premature intensity and magnitude, and burned out of the
night air of Paris. But there he sits in the portrait group, his
head upon his hand, Verlaine beside him, and — do I only
imagine this ? — there is a curious disharmony in their corner
of the painting. It is a disharmony and a disproportion for
the reason that the two poets, despite their awkwardness and
poverty, are so much the most interesting and important
persons in the painting.

When I stayed in an hotel in Rome during the winter of
1926–27 I used to watch with amusement every night after
dinner an old man who would lie on a sofa in the salon of the
hotel, laughing at the painted ceiling. It was an allegorical
affair in full-fledged Italian nineteenth-century fashion, with
the Eternal City — shall we say ? — crowning Liberty and
Commerce with a wreath of laurel while Popes and tyrants
averted their gaze and cowered in a corner, and the person
who was so amused at this decadence of the art of fresco was
the French painter and caricaturist, Forain. Now Forain,
more than fifty years before, had been a friend of Rimbaud,
and I could have asked him about Rimbaud, but I do not
suppose he would have told me anything. Indeed, I believe
that Forain was anxious for the world to forget that he had
been a friend of Rimbaud, and his answer, had I asked him,
would probably have been that he was young, not much more
than twenty years old at the time, and remembered little. He
was, in fact, only twenty, but Rimbaud was nineteen and his
career was ending. It was the briefest and most extraordinary
career in the whole art of poetry, only made possible because
poetry, unlike the other arts, comes of instinct, and has not
to be learned.

Even so, by what miracle could a boy of eighteen — he
was only eighteen at the time — invent the imagery of *Les*

Illuminations which in their violent originality could be said to contain all the poetry of every tongue for the hundred years to come ? They were, I suppose, written without effort in railway refreshment rooms, in cafés, in bedrooms in cheap lodging-houses, wherever and whenever he was in the mood, often, we may be certain, when he had had a lot to drink. They are, in fact, automatic, not reasoned writings : there is no other explanation for them : as subconscious in their origin as the prophecies of Nostradamus which that astrologer composed, it is my theory, in the trance or twilight before you fall asleep, Sibylline moments when your mind forms sentences you cannot understand, and when, in paradox, you may think you can interpret music. In the little that is known of the later life of Rimbaud there is proof of how easily poetry came to him in the letters that he wrote home from Harar in Ethiopia demanding to be sent books upon any and every enterprise in which he was interested, evidently considering that difficult and extremely technical subjects could be mastered as easily as he had caught and tamed the Pegasus of poetry when he was eighteen. But it never came again to him ; neither that, nor any other Pegasus, and he was only thirty-seven when he died of blood-poisoning, tired out, still poor, at Marseilles in 1891.

It seems reasonable to conclude that Rimbaud could not explain his poetical powers, or account for them, did not wish to think of them, and could not understand why nothing else had come to him so easily in life. For the poems had been effortless. He did not have to cudgel his brains to bring them into action, and they had left him as suddenly, and with no warning. It was his adolescence and it fled from him when he was full grown. " Je ne m'occupe plus de cela " was his answer, with a faint smile, when his school friend, Delahaye, asked him many years later if he dreamt, still, of his poetry. But, of course, in reality, Rimbaud wrote no more poems because he did not wish to. His genius died in him when he was nineteen. It is the most extreme instance in all literature, and we are left to imagine for ourselves what might have been his set of grand classical or mythological pieces in prose. Now the present writer, in all humility, has in his youth felt the same wind of inspiration blowing upon him, he knew not from where. His first book of poems was published in 1918, when he was twenty years old, and the poems were written when he was eighteen and nineteen, largely during the few hours of leisure from Chelsea Barracks, where he finds himself at the end of an episode in this book.

Thereafter, when the first world war was over, I set to with prose, and my first prose work, *Southern Baroque Art*, was written, as my brother will testify, in a clean copy, that is to say, without corrections, before and after an attack of blood-poisoning which kept me ill in bed for ten weeks in January–March 1921. I had returned to Scarborough with my brother after an expedition to see D'Annunzio in his pirate state of Fiume, the project being to get his support for an edition of Rabelais with drawings by Picasso, whom we hoped, also, to persuade my father to employ to paint frescoes in one of the big rooms at Montegufoni. We had seen Picasso in this matter, the price was agreed, and there were to be painted balconies with musicians over the doors and two great scenes or landscapes with figures upon the walls composed, we were led to hope, in the Florentine manner, that is to say, under the influence of Botticelli, Benozzo Gozzoli, Alessio Baldovinetti. I can remember lying awake thinking of the drawings or cartoons for these paintings. It was rage and disappointment at this scheme falling through that brought on my poisoning and the mysterious nervous breakdown that followed (it was not quite so serious as that, but for a whole year I suffered from insomnia, which is worrying and terrifying when one is twenty-two). As an instance of my curious state of health during this time, I may say that I was measured for new suits of clothes while I was in bed, and when I first got up I had grown so tall that I could not come in through any door without stooping. I remember my mother shrieking when she saw me. I had become six-foot-six during my illness, but in a few days I had shrunk two and a quarter inches to my normal height and I was left with the sleeves of my new suits reaching down my wrists to the beginning of my fingers. It was, as I say, immediately before, and during the months after my illness, that I wrote *Southern Baroque Art*. I began it a few days only before I was taken ill, and I can find the place, now, where I stopped writing upon the morning of that day, though I had a premonition of illness at the Hôtel Lotti in Paris, where we stayed on our way home from Fiume in December. It took the form of an unknowing and unreasoning dread of what was to come. I remember, even, wishing that I could be in pain in order to have some tangible and definite reason for my nervous dreads.

Upon reaching home, I took up my pen immediately, and began to write. It was as simple as that. It is impossible for anyone who has not experienced this sensation to understand how quickly and easily it comes to him. I can remember dipping my pen into the inkpot and having no other wish than to describe the feeling of a hot early morning at Naples. But I had only a few days. I could only complete a few pages before the pains and temperature began. What are my memories of the weeks I was in bed ? I could not read, and I could hardly bear to talk. But my one determined ambition was to get to Lecce (Lecce, the little town in Apulia, right in the heel of Italy, which is famous for its seventeenth-century Baroque buildings), and I achieved my desire in April. It was an extraordinary town. Except for the railway station, for the electric light, and for a rickety motor-car or two, it was very much as it must have been in Murat's day. There were huge black berlins (four-wheelers) standing for hire in the streets that must have plied there in the era of the Bourbon Kings. There were drawings of Pulcinella upon the walls of the houses. What a journey it was to and from Lecce ! We travelled all the way down the Adriatic coast to get there, from Bologna. It is so long ago, now, that I do not remember the journey back (I have been to Lecce upon three separate occasions), but at this, or at another time, I made the long train journey along the Ionian Sea from the heel to the toe of Italy as far as Reggio, and so to Sicily, and I remember passing the lonely station of Metaponto, on the site of the Greek city, and reading in the guide book that there were a restaurant and bedrooms at the station, and looking out from the train and seeing no sign of antiquity but a single, broken column.

Soon I was home again and writing poetry, and during the summer in London writing prose. But the larger part of *Southern Baroque Art* I wrote during the following autumn and winter, while I was at Scarborough ; and in a sort of poetical delirium, generally during the hours between tea and dinner (always my best time for writing), I wrote my account of imaginary paintings by El Greco at the Escorial, and of Bacchus invading India, this latter one of the most inspiring of poetical themes. But I recall, particularly, the ease and speed with which I was able to invent the imagery of the Serenade at Caserta, that I conceived and executed in the style of Domenico Tiepolo's ceiling paintings for his own

37

villa at Zianigo (that I had seen in the Museo Correr at Venice), and of his drawings for the life of Pulcinella.

A source book for my inspiration that I cannot forget, or forbear to mention, lay in the two immense folio volumes of the Abbé de Saint-Non's *Voyage pittoresque dans le royaume des Deux Siciles* (1781–98), a work of serious antiquarian purpose, but it is enlivened with etchings by no less a hand than that of Fragonard. Like other Frenchmen of genius since his time, like Ingres, like Hector Berlioz, like Debussy, Fragonard was studying in Italy, being one of the winners of the Grand Prix de Rome. In company with Hubert Robert and Saint-Non he set forth upon a leisurely tour of Sicily and Southern Italy, for they stayed long enough in each place to make elaborate drawings of what pleased them. His contribution to the *Voyage pittoresque* consists of some lovely etchings of classical bas-reliefs, families of satyrs, and so forth ; but, as well, there are views of towns and villas which can only be described as being in the style of Callot, and it was in this manner that I would try to write of, for instance, the huge convent of San Benedetto at Catania. But Fragonard, at this time, was studying the works of Solimena, Pietro da Cortona, and, particularly, Tiepolo ; I was in that mood myself, and this is the reason for my enthusiasm for the ' picturesque ' of Naples ; for the now destroyed church and cloister of Santa Chiara (the church was like a ballroom and the cloister had vine trellises and walks lined with painted majolica) ; for the double geometrical staircases by the architect Ferdinando Sanfelice in some of the Neapolitan palaces ; and for the frescoes of Luca Giordano, Solimena, and their school. I was studying Tiepolo, too ; hence my description of his frescoes of the *Banquet of Antony and Cleopatra*[1] in the first pages

[1] In the Palazzo Labia at Venice.

of my book. But, in general, these works of art had to be remade. They had no breath left in them. And the book treating of them had to be a work of art in itself. Opening it again, after the passage of so many years, I find many of the descriptions to be more beautiful than the works of art themselves.

And now I arrive at the most interesting point of all this poetical experience, for I was twenty-two or twenty-three years old and I had now to write of places that I had never seen, and that there was no possibility that I should be able to go to for many years to come. But I did not find this negative prospect in the least disturbing. My poetical diet had fitted me for such expeditions, and preparing and intoxicating my imagination with my description of Farinelli singing, and steeping myself in the Spanish atmosphere upon the strength of a visit to Madrid and Toledo in March 1919, immediately the war had ended, I set sail in my imagination for far Mexico. I had discovered the huge mounted albums of photographs from Sylvester Baxter's *Spanish Colonial Architecture*, in the library of the Victoria and Albert Museum, published at Boston in 1901 (and, I am sure, looked at by no one till my arrival) and I was able upon this evidence to concoct my account of the glittering convents of Santa Clara and Santa Rosa di Viterbo at Querétaro in Mexico, the former of which housed as many as eight thousand nuns before the dissolution of the monasteries, and I described the nuns working at their embroidery, and in the convent sugar plantations, and among the cactuses ; the huge gilded metal grilles for the nuns, starting almost from the floor of the church and bursting like a golden spray upon the ceiling ; the confessionals gilded and painted with metallic lustre over a ground of gold leaf, in which way ruby and emerald green effects of great violence and brilliance

were procured ; and the balconies or boxes for the Mother
Superior, waited upon and guarded like a queen bee, with an
elaborate golden base supported by the carved *retablo* of an
altar in Santa Rosa, and like a bridge over a richly carved
doorway below in Santa Clara. I wrote of the gilded grotto
or *Camarín* in the Santuario de Ocotlan, the work of a pure-
blooded Zapotec Indian who spent twenty-five years of his
life upon it ; and of the still more glittering *Camarín* of the
Seminario de San Martín at Tepozotlan. And I concluded my
account of Mexico at Taxco, not then, as now, at the end of a
two-hour drive upon a motor speed road from the capital, but
three days' ride upon muleback from Mexico City over the
stony mountains of Guerrero, ending in appropriate Spanish
manner with a magnificent festa and bull-fight, ingredients and
directions for which I had procured from a book written by
the earliest American traveller to discover the ruined temples
and carved monoliths of the Mayas. And so I finished writing
Southern Baroque Art, and after many delays it was printed
when I had paid the publisher (Grant Richards) the sum of
fifty pounds.

It is a haunting experience to take up again a work one has
written such a time ago. It bears out what I say on a later
page of this present book, where I put that " it is an axiom in
all of the arts, and with all human beings, that their earliest
maturity is the pattern, in little, of what they will become ".
And I continue " the first summer day is, and remains ever,
the hottest there has been ", which, also, is of present application, for my purpose in writing *Southern Baroque Art* was to
paint a picture of life and architecture in great heat and light.
I believe that I achieved this from my first sentence, for the
book opens with a description of a hot morning in the old
part of Naples. Not that I had been to Naples in the heat. I

only knew it upon a rainy day in March, but one has imagination and one knows the signs of heat. What astonishes me on looking into the book again is how much I knew, and how little I left out. It does, indeed, seem to me " that I knew and had read everything that I know now ". It was, truly, in imagination, my first holiday away from home, my first prose work, written at the age of twenty-two, " fresh, strange, and lovely as the music of *Petrouchka* " (that is not my description, it is my brother's), but, certainly, as a prose work it has poetry in nearly every sentence. And poetry, it could be argued, that was infused into new forms, for I must repeat, in case I have not stated it in so many words, that I wanted to create a work of art, in literature, from this wealth of forgotten material and perhaps the originality of my project lay in attempting that by means of the dead architecture of these Southern lands. I had proved that it is not necessary to have been in person to a particular place, a church or palace, a town, even a whole country, in order to describe it ; or indeed, more than one lifetime would be required before the writer was equipped and ready to begin. But it could never have been written, never been undertaken at all, especially, as I have stated, in clean copy, composed straight ahead, without faltering, without alteration, had I not spent so many years of my life, from eighteen years old onward, in writing poems.

I knew Watteau's painting of *L'Embarquement pour Cythère* when I was a child, and its meaning was not lost upon me. But I intend better than that. This is my opportunity. It is what I have been longing for since I was fourteen or fifteen years old, when I first knew the picture. For Watteau painted his pairs of lovers in every attitude. They are bidding farewell to the world and embarking for the isle of Venus, but he leaves them at the moment when they board the galleon. He takes them no further. And his figures are in fancy dress. It is that which irritates one after a time. One grows weary of his silks and satins. I can take up the theme at the point where Watteau had to leave it off. How many plays, how many novels, how many persons in life, and in the theatre, come to their end just when they should begin, when we know them and do not want to be parted from them ! The career of a writer of my sort (I am neither novelist nor playwright) could be called a perpetual exploration of the rose-hung island. And, indeed, during three decades I have searched it through and through. But this particular journey is not like the others. For one thing its conventions will be, not those of life, but of the theatre, and its players are of the sort who do not speak upon the stage. It is this — what else is it ? — that is the poetry of Watteau's paintings ; not that I admire his pictures overmuch, there are masters whom I prefer to him, but his stage machinery is appropriate ; the theme is as tenuous, the branch as wide-spreading, and as heavy with ripe fruit.

My purpose, now, is to establish that I have instinct and not only knowledge. More than that, I would like to throw away all that I have learned and go back to my beginnings. For I wish to know no more. I only want to feel. Sometimes I think that I have it in me to write the masterpiece of which Flaubert dreamed, the matter of which should consist of nothing, no plot, no action at all, nothing ever happening. But my world of imagination has been too lively and I could not keep it still and quiet for long. Here and now I would have it in flower upon the old wood, where it first blossomed. Let me run into the midst of it and shake the boughs !

III

In Modo Napolitano

I DID not see Naples and the South until I was twenty-three
years old. It was 1920 or 1921 before I went to Naples and
Sicily, and it was an inspiration, a transmission almost, one
could say, a transfusion of poetical germs and ideas that no
one of my temperament is ever likely to forget. Rome, to me,
was never quite so inspiring as the South, in spite of her
fountains and her aqueducts. The South, it seemed to me,
began from the moment you passed in the train in front of
the palace of Caserta, built by the Spanish Bourbons, but now
the electric train takes you another way that is just as beautiful,
and you come into Naples through Posillipo, and see the
islands, the volcano, and the siren bay. The slums of Naples,
and its rainy days, are as much a part of Naples as the Neapolitan songs, the carnations, and the mandolines ; but, in those
days, I lost myself in the forgotten architecture and in a
forgotten school of painting. I suppose, if those could be
characterized in an adjective, it would be that they are ' theatrical ' ; theatrical, certainly, were those double geometrical
staircases of Ferdinando Sanfelice ; the church of Santa
Chiara (with its majolica-lined cloister that was at the same
time a vineyard), and the Certosa di San Martino with its
brilliant and flashing white cloister by Cosimo Fansaga. If
you could imagine yourself held up by some form of invisible
scaffolding so as to have the nearest possible view of the

golden detail of these churches you could only compare the sensation to that of being upon the painters' cradle while they regilded the proscenium arch of an opera house and you could look down through the scenery onto the empty stage and auditorium of some huge theatre. Churches like those I name were in the nature almost of a personal discovery, so long was it since any one had admired them. I believe it could be said without exaggeration that the last generation who had come, prepared to admire, and not forewarned to despise and denigrate, had been in the middle of the eighteenth century, at the time, I have just remarked, when Fragonard, winner of the Grand Prix de Rome, was studying the paintings of Pietro da Cortona, Baciccio, and Solimena. After that day they were ignored, forgotten for the greater part of two centuries, and so was the brilliant and theatrical architecture that was their setting.

For it *is* a theatrical architecture. What else are the arcades of St. Peter's ; or all the Roman colonnades and fountains ? What else are the waters of the Fontana di Trevi, a buffet or sideboard of falling waters ; the two fountains of the Piazza Navona ; the twin churches of the Piazza del Pópolo ; Bernini's baldacchino in St. Peter's, with its twisted columns ; or his cathedra Petri ? What else are the altars by Fratel Pozzo in the Gesù and in Sant' Ignazio, and his painted ceiling in the latter church which, if nothing more, is certainly a triumph of theatrical perspective ? It is the apparent shortcomings of this theatrical art, its glitter and illusion, that are its fascination. It is the school of brilliance. I am thinking at this moment of Rome because, there, it obtrudes itself ; it would be difficult for a person of intelligence of any kind to leave Rome without having heard of Bernini.

But at Naples it is another matter. You had to seek out

the seventeenth and eighteenth centuries for yourself. There was no book, no living person, who could help you. I will recapitulate some of those discoveries, if only for my own pleasure, for their names are like music to my ear. Let me think again, then, of the morning when, having with much difficulty found the slum where lived the sacristan, I first set foot inside San Gregorio Armeno and saw its marble walls and golden ceiling. There was a grille to the right-hand side of the high altar through which you could look into the convent and see the red and black robed nuns against the long white stuccoed corridors and tessellated floors. Let me behold again Vanvitelli's sunken courtyard of San Marcellino ; and the white horses of Solimena in the sacristy of San Paolo Maggiore ! How well I remember driving out to the villa of Solimena, somewhere, I think, between Torre del Greco and Torre Annunziata, upon the slopes of Vesuvius at any rate ; and, also, going through his birthplace, Nocera de' Pagani (how often !), upon the road to Amalfi ; but in neither place were there paintings by Solimena, *L' Abate Ciccio,* as he was called, nothing in his villa, nothing in his birthplace, though you could see good paintings by his hand in Vienna and, of all places, in Assisi, where he frescoed the refectory of the Franciscan convent. And I remember on a beautiful October day going up through the chestnut woods to the convent of Monte Vergine, finding nothing there of my period, and coming down the mountain, down the winding road, to the Badia de Loreto at its foot, " where the abbot and the older monks spend the winter " in a large octagonal building of the eighteenth century with fine ceilings and rooms hung with Flemish tapestries. I recall the old tortoise-like monk in his white robe opening the door with a huge key and letting us into that confined space where nothing had altered since the period of the Bourbon Kings ; Royal apartments still kept in order and, apparently, but waiting for them to drive up in their carriages ; portraits of Ferdinando I and Francesco I ; a complete and beautiful pharmacy of the eighteenth century in full Rococo ; nothing altered in the building, nothing out of place, since the Bourbons left Naples and it was no more a Kingdom.[1] Nothing theatrical here, nor brilliant, but a bucolic poetry nodding, nodding its head, finding it hard to keep awake, for what are all monarchies but things of false architecture, sham façades ? Yet they kept the arts alive ; with their going the arts have gone, everywhere, in all the continents.

And my thoughts went from Italy to Sicily, remembering the sculptures by Serpotta in the little Oratorios of Palermo, and thinking of what was in a particular sense my own personal discovery, for I believe I was the first person to write an account of it in any language, I refer to the golden town of Noto, its façades (that is all they are !) and balconies, a more beautiful town than Lecce, in Apulia, which it much resembles, and a creation of the Rococo, terrace upon terrace, church upon church, palace upon palace, as you come up towards it out of the orange groves, a city which is one of the beauties of all civilization since man left the damp, dark caverns or ceased to roam the shell-strewn shore. Yet, theatrically, there is nothing behind it. It is all façade. The grilles of the convents set into frontispieces of the soft golden stone which, yet, at their height are but screens or lattices with nothing behind them, they are but set scenes in architecture ; the balconies

---

[1] " An interesting sight is presented on Whit Monday " (I quote from an old book on Naples), " by the Return of the Pilgrims, often twenty thousand in number, from the shrine of the Madonna di Monte Vergine, near Avellino, which is welcomed by crowds taking up position about 5 P.M. in the streets along the harbour." The Badia de Loreto (see above) was designed by Giovanni Antonio Vaccaro.

supported upon consoles that are carved figures of mermen and merwomen, pierrots, Chinamen, even galloping, winged horses, but there is nothing inside the palaces, a rickety chair or two, an iron bedstead, a cracked mirror, a faded wallpaper, that is all, and there is the degree of comfort you would find in a stage drawing-room when the curtain has come down, or by pulling a cheap chair close to the scenery and pretending to yourself that this is luxury and splendour, but, all the time, the setting is lively and elegant beyond all experience and you would think, in Noto, that you had arrived at some city famed for conversation, music, the theatre, what you will, and it is nothing but a small provincial town no one has heard of, in the interior of Sicily. There is nothing behind the architecture: and there does not pretend to be. It is all for effect. The effect is everything, and the rest can take care of itself.

Zimbalo and his pupil Cino were the architects of Lecce ; the names of the architects of Noto are not yet determined. No portraits have come down to us of those worthies. This pastoral Baroque, this Rococo of vineyard and orange grove, blossomed again in the huge churches of Modica and Ragusa, twin towns lying beyond Noto, churches which stand upon terraces at the head of great flights of steps. When I wrote *Southern Baroque Art* I had been to Noto, but only knew Modica and Ragusa from hearsay and upon strength of imagination. I have been there since ; and now, twenty years later, I hear of three more Sicilian towns still further into the unknown ; Grammichele, a considerable place with streets laid out in the eighteenth century on " an ingenious and symmetrical hexagonal design built in the form of a spider's web " ; Vittoria, with a main square " than which few architectural designs could be more delightful . . . and with some of the finest wine of Sicily . . . and the towers and domes of Comiso ".

47

It is an architecture of which the first intimations are at Naples, and which I followed like a will-o'-the-wisp till I found it again in the huge open-air staircase, " with its great apertures open to the sun and air ", built by Vanvitelli, in the vast Certosa di San Lorenzo, at Padula in the Basilicata, down, almost, at the beginning of Calabria — an immense motor drive in those days from Amalfi along the impassable roads (I am speaking of 1920–21) — and coming, even then, at the far end of all the buildings when you have traversed three courts or cloisters and may think you have exhausted all its sights : a monastery that I can claim as my personal adventure and dis- covery, for no one had mentioned or written of it since the middle of the eighteenth century. But the new picturesque, for that is what it is, it is the new scenic or theatrical back- ground, it has displaced Gothic, which was never so suited for those purposes — and I take the credit in extolling it, for having to a little extent altered or diverted the stream of taste — this new picturesque begins, as I have said, at Naples. I sensed it in the double line of beggars drawn up in the court of the Carmine, down by the harbour of Naples, the church where was buried Conradin, last of the Hohenstaufen, and which has associations with the revolt of Masaniello, but it had become the beggars' church, nothing else, and they were to be seen collected together in their horrid ranks, wailing for alms, and exhibiting their sores and stumps. I saw it again in the ' Venetian ' blinds that two men hawked in the slums from door to door, blinds of green lattice painted with Mt. Vesuvius, or with a white-clad Pulcinella. It was present, or prophesied, in the copper statue of some Jesuit saint over an archway, a saint who wore a nimbus that was like the sun's rays, and his copper robe was green with verdigris. It spoke out aloud from those double geometrical staircases which I have men-

48

tioned more than once, but they are peculiar to Naples, no one except myself had observed them, and how am I to forget reading myself to sleep with poetry, hearing a little rain fall in the court of the Hotel Santa Lucia (we could not afford rooms looking out onto the Bay), waking next morning, and, after coffee and rolls and marmalade of fresh oranges or tangerines, rushing out into one more golden morning, under a blue sky, in search of churches, palaces, and double stairs !

And Amalfi ? And Ravello ? I used to hear the *zampognari* or *pifferari* every year before Christmas, during the years when I spent the winters writing poetry at Amalfi. I do not know if the shepherds still come up any longer from Calabria to play their bagpipes, but how well I remember those far-off winter days when I was at Amalfi with my brother, and with the composer of *Belshazzar's Feast* and of *Façade* ! We would be sent for to come down from our rooms, where we were working, to the cloister (the hotel had been a Capuchin monastery) where the shepherds would be waiting to play to us, and one knew their music instantly in Handel's pastoral symphony to *the Messiah* and from the *Siciliennes* in his *Concerti grossi*. So Handel, too, on cold days at Naples, had heard the *zampognari* or the *pifferari*,[1] and meanwhile, upstairs along the terrace, past the white columns, there would be frost upon the tangerines. There can be few sensual sensations in the world more beautiful than to pick the red gold tangerines out of their dark leaves and find them iced with frost. Always at the height of a hand, where the hand can reach to them, never too high or tall. That one thing, the music of the

---

[1] Cf. *Handel*, by Percy M. Young: J. M. Dent & Sons, 1947, p. 188. While at Naples in 1708, towards the end of the year, Handel wrote French canzonets in the style of Lully, and heard the Calabrian shepherds sing and play their Christmas songs. Cf. also footnote to p. 80. Handel would be twenty-three years old in 1708.

shepherds, had not changed in two hundred years, and in truth with its loud pipe and its discordant bagpipes it was harsh and ugly, it was goatlegg'd and hairy, but behind it there was the pastoral life coming down out of classical antiquity and pre-antiquity, twenty-five and more centuries ago. To this, I remember that I liked to think, oranges and tangerines had been added from China or Arabia, and prickly pears and cactuses from Mexico.

The blue screens of cactus and prickly pear are, indeed, essential to the fanciful or theatrical architecture of which I am thinking. Were it not contrary to the French genius it would have flowered in Provence, where all, sunlight, landscape, mountains, are in waiting for it. Instead, it begins again in Spain — at Valencia, continuing in the golden façades of Elche, Alicante, Murcia, into the deep South. A little town like Lorca, with its façades and domes, its belfries and balconies, famous for its processions, is a model of the style. So are Carmona and Écija ; the latter, the discovery of Théophile Gautier who saw its beauty more than a hundred years ago, but the poet of *La Péri*, the friend of Fanny Elssler and Carlotta Grisi, was used to the theatre and quickly recognized those china towers and belfries which he compared to Hindu temples, though, in truth, they are the ' pagodas ' of a scene painter, they burn in an unreal light (Écija has the hottest temperatures in Europe), and by and large, using the term ' Indian ' in its widest connotation, they bear no resemblance to any buildings whatever in Java, Cambodia, or Siam. . . .

Écija is one of the beauties of Spain. It was found by Gautier, who did not know what to do with it, for architecture, even stage architecture, was not quite in his province, but it was forgotten again for another hundred years. When I

first saw Écija and Carmona in 1925 I do not believe that the
beauty of these little Andalusian towns was known or appreciated. Carmona, as spotless as a Dutch town, has several red-
brick seventeenth-century houses which lend it a peculiar air
within its dazzling white alleys. It has a Moorish town gate ;
there are Mudéjar courts that are tiled with *azulejos* ; it stands
above a Roman necropolis ; there are golden Churrigueresque
altars in its churches. Écija, only twenty miles away, is quite
different ; three church towers faced with *azulejos*, and several
china monuments and fountains. Gautier was entirely correct
when he wrote that he had arrived in a new country of pagodas
and Hindu temples, with strange porcelain statues and monuments. But even Gautier does not mention the palace of the
Marqués de Peñaflor, a provincial noble, with its curving
façade, flowered window-boxes for carnations, Salomonic
door portal (of twisting columns), its interior courtyard,
and still more Salomonic staircase, like a staircase in an old
pantomime.

But such are discoveries to which there need never be an
end. Even while I write this, news comes to me from a
correspondent of little towns, Lucena, Cabra, Aguilar, Priego,
between Córdoba and Granada, in a never visited corner of
Andalusia. He has found the name of the architect of the
sacristy of the Cartuja at Granada, hitherto one of the minor
mysteries of architecture, and that this man, Francisco Hurtado
Izquierdo, was born at Lucena in 1669, and died in Priego in
1725. This sacristy of the Cartuja with its fretted pilasters and
fluttering cornices, all dazzling white, is an interior that
Gautier rightly describes as being in emulation of the filigree
courts of the Alhambra, but in fact it is, or was, unique
in architecture until, in 1949, Mr. R. C. Taylor identified
the other buildings that follow and this unknown school of

architects. Perhaps even more interesting than the discovery of Hurtado is the identification of a pupil of his, F. X. Pedraxas. In the town of Lucena, Pedraxas built the *Sagrario* of the parish church, a brilliantly polychromed affair of Mexican complexity, with no space free of vertiginous ornamentation which, indeed, in its units, resembles the broken up, inchoate cirrhus of a ' mackerel sky ', blown wildly into a confusion of its own shreds or wisps, and then floating, drifting, but held together in the calm of a golden sunset. If you look more closely, the stucco is carved into a multitude of angels' or cupids' heads and bodies, with a profusion of curling leaves like those of acanthus, kale, or parsley, and places where the *stuccador*, failing of other inspiration, has pulled out the wet, soft plaster towards himself, and given to it a twisting, spiral whorl or knob, like the bosses in a Jacobean ceiling. The *Sagrario* of Lucena, as its discoverer remarks, " represents the final stages in the development of the High Baroque in Andalusia ", a style which to my own taste is always a disappointment in Córdoba and Seville.

However, the masterpieces of Pedraxas are all in his native town Priego, a little place of which there is no mention in the guide books, but it contains the churches of La Aurora, Las Angustias, La Merced, and San Francisco, the *Camarín*, dome, and chapel of the Soledad in the church of San Pedro, all with work by Pedraxas, a pilgrimage church by him on a hill overlooking the town, and lastly, the *Sagrario* of the parish church. His style is changing and the Rococo makes its appearance. As this influence increases in his work, his cornices " begin to rock and undulate with an extraordinary rhythmic motion ". The *Sagrario* of the parish church consists of a small square ante-chamber, leading into an octagon of two storeys surmounted by a dome. The ante-chamber is domed also, and the walls are covered with stucco decorations in high relief. It is in these that the art of Pedraxas reaches to its zenith. Perhaps there has never been more graceful modelling in stucco. Over an archway there is a cupid caught or enmeshed in garlands, and above that a relief of indescribable delicacy and beauty, with a landscape background and many figures, while the spandrels of the dome rising above the cornice, that flutters and that has the form of an octagon within an octagon, are themselves beautifully in flower, with four great busts in niches in their angles, and a great floreated ornament or pendant in the middle. Mr. Taylor tells me that the treatment of the cornice in the octagon is the supreme achievement of Pedraxas. I have not been shown a photograph of this in detail, and only of the octagon as a whole, but I have seen enough to convince me that the claims made by Mr. Taylor are correct and that in discovering the works of Pedraxas in Priego he has made a major contribution to the history of late Renaissance architecture in all Europe. The late date of the *Sagrario* (1772–86) makes it the more interesting still. When he tells me that the little town of Priego has better things in it than are to be found in the whole of Valencia, the fantastic Palacio de Dos Aguas included, I am induced to think that Mr. Taylor has discovered the Andalusian equivalent to Lecce or to Noto. . . .

" A very unusual eighteenth century canvas of St. Francis Xavier, painted in the Chinese manner by a European. . . . A country palace with curious Chinese eaves, semicircular wings, arches over the road, and dependencies, all painted a delicate rose-pink. . . . A most beautiful and unique set of six large oblong *grisaille* canvases of the Passion, painted in the Chinese style with eighteenth century Chinese figures, and false frames of red velvet painted on the canvas. These astonishing objects are hung high on the walls, unglazed and unframed, above bright blue eighteenth century *azulejo* panels. No one in the church knew their origin. . . . Outside [another] church, a little fair is held with things laid out on the grass, such as rough pottery images of the Phœnician Ashtaroth, globe-breasted, narrow-waisted, snake-entwined. . . ." This is in a small village, significantly named Janus. . . . " A lane leads up behind the Misericordia through mounting country under three archways, one of which is pure Chinese with a kind of flat *pailou* on the top, to a seemingly lost and almost unknown village . . . where at Whitsun there still takes place a most unusual survival from Roman times. An ox is driven through the streets in procession and then killed. On Whit Sunday there is another great procession to the church, meat from the ox is given to all the poor, and the children get cakes. . . ."

There is a fishing village, Apulia, where the fishermen wear white woollen coats with broad leather belts, like those worn by the Roman legions. . . . What, then, is Peniche, a town of fishermen, with a name that tastes of Tyre and Sidon ? Or Amarante (listen to its syllables !), a country town, where upon the first Saturday and Sunday of June every bakery sells special cakes called *testículas de S. Gonçalo*, " which the young men and women are not embarrassed both to offer and to ask from one another. . . ." Or, to continue . . . " green, black, and gold choir stalls in the organ loft with painted panels behind, on which stand cherubs holding wreathed chains . . . a wooden painted ceiling of cherubs and flowers on a duck-egg blue ground . . . the deep green of the lemon trees by the fountain . . . twin organs in scarlet and gold supported by mermen and tritons . . . a sacristy ceiling in bronze green and dull Indian red ; boars, apes, and satyrs abound. . . ."

Boats like Venetian gondolas, but with huge red sails ;
others, like a sickle or a half-moon ; or with poops and
prows curved like a swan's neck, one and all, brightly painted
. . . shepherds wearing the coroça, a straw cloak, or in fact,
a coat of thatch, but it stands out, it rustles, it runs down with
rain, it is like the cloaks worn by Chinese peasants in the rice
fields ; and what does it matter if, instead, the shepherds
guard the 'tangerine-coloured lambs' of the Cova da
Beira ; or at Vila Franca de Xira, famous for its black bulls
which are fought on horseback, the Campino dancers in white
shirts, blue kneebreeches, and green stocking-caps, carrying
over their left shoulders a very dark, short jacket of Andalusian cut.

Here is the wine of Mateus from the Tras-os-Montes, a
vin rosé which is the colour of orangeade and comes in flagons
that bear a label with the palace of the Conde de Vila Real
and its balustrades and urns and statues, a central block set,
far back, with coats-of-arms and heroes, two lateral wings
projecting, with more stone figures and vases on the balustrade ; the finest country house in that country, and as
certainly the most refreshing and delicious of all wines upon
a hot evening. Further into the Tras-os-Montes, and particularly towards Bragança, and in the province of Beira Baixa,
many Jews fled during the persecution of the Inquisition four
and five hundred years ago, and their descendants have been
found of late years in remote towns and villages still practising
their half-forgotten rites ; Castelho-Branco, Guarda, Bragança,
have these crypto-Jews ; Pinhel, a Jewish scholar describes
as a " Jewish town ", and the narrow streets of Vilarinho, he
says, " seem full of them ". Idanha, Penamacor, Monsanto,
are three villages of indescribable remoteness in Beira Baixa,
near the Spanish frontier, with which there is no communica-

tion except by mule track, and it appears that the population of these three villages is largely Jewish in origin, which is the more curious because Monsanto has been called " the most Portuguese village in Portugal " ; it is a town or village built up and down a granite mountain, in and between boulders of granite, " the steep narrow alleys being steps cut in the granite, or slanting slabs of granite ", and no wheeled vehicle can come into the town. The inhabitants are " splendidly handsome and well built men and women, young and old alike, the women very heavily adorned with gold chains and earrings ".

As much could be said, too, of the goat-faced fishermen of Nazaré, in their check or tartan shirts, with their black-clad women, their long, narrow boats for sardine fishing, with square sterns and high, pointed prows, and the twenty-eight pairs of oxen sleeping on the sands to haul the nets ashore. They are a race apart from the rest of the population, that is evident, and it is almost too easy to believe they are Phœnician. Who, then, are the inhabitants of the Berlengas Islands, eight miles off the coast, opposite Peniche, who, a friend tells me, are excessively marked and curious in appearance, with sur-names, for the most part, of Samuel or Ishmael ? Whoever they may be, it would appear that their forebears must have been driven by violent force of circumstances into these islands, " considered the most perilous of any in the European seas. . . ."

Such is Portugal.[1]

In Mexico, now that I know Spanish architecture so well,

---

[1] ' Resumed ', to make new use of an old word, from *The Selective Traveller in Portugal*, by Susan Belloc Lowndes and Ann Bridge : London, Evans Bros., Ltd., 1949 ; and from my own observations during four visits to Portugal. The afore-mentioned book is the first in the English language to mention a great many of the architectural beauties of the North of Portugal, particularly in the provinces of Minho and Trasos-Montes.

I am able to tell the good from bad, and one of the golden visions of my youth glitters before me with some parts of its gilded surface dimmed and blurred. I do not want to weary the reader with Mexican names, musical as they may be, albeit the music is of a peculiar nature and intonation like that of a marimba band, but I am compelled to mention what seem to me to be the two or three outstanding buildings in all Mexico, for without them the picture of my world of the imagination is not complete. They are the church of Taxco, too well known, now, for it has become an ' artists' colony ', but at the time I wrote of it, in 1922, for the closing pages of *Southern Baroque Art*, staging a bull-fight in its chief square, Taxco was still a three days' ride on muleback over the mountains and was not yet connected with the capital by a motor-road. The façade of Taxco, with two pairs of Salomonic columns in its upper storey ; the twin towers, to either side, with all four faces of each two floors decorated with balconies supported on leering, sardonic masks ; the matchless display, in the interior, of no fewer than twelve gilded Churrigueresque altars or *retablos*, such an array as exists nowhere else in the world, these make Taxco unique and apart, not inferior to anything in Italy or Spain.

I still admire the convents of Santa Rosa and Santa Clara at Querétaro. Both convents are the work of Tresguerras, a Creole, or native Mexican of Spanish blood. In both convents Tresguerras has let his imagination be fired by the choir screens and the screened balconies for the Mother Superior and her nuns. In Santa Rosa di Viterbo a number of his own paintings are framed into the choir screen ; while, below, the grille of gilt ironwork is revealed by angels who pull aside a pair of golden curtains. The golden *retablo*, here, was destroyed by the troops of Bazaine during the wars of Maximilian ; but, in Santa Clara, there are six golden Churrigueresque *retablos*. I admire, too, the Seminario de San Martín at Tepozotlan, for this is something entirely new and original in architecture, unlike anything else in the world. It has a façade between two towers ; the façade and the two storeys of the towers being of a dazzling white, while the bases of the towers from the top of the façade downwards, so that they frame it, are of scarlet glazed bricks set in brilliant white mortar and shaped hexagonally, so that the outline of the mortar is like the meshes of a net. The effect is of scarlet shagreen.

So much for Mexican architecture. What of Mexico's lakes, its landscape, and its clouds ?

What could be lovelier in the imagination than the lake of Patzcuaro ? The little town with its narrow, cobbled streets and old churches and houses is the nearest equivalent in the American continent to an old town in Italy or Spain. But it is the lake, such a lake as D. H. Lawrence wrote of in *The Plumed Serpent*, that is unique and beautiful with the Tarascan villages upon its shores. The Tarascan Indians had the art of making tapestries or paintings out of the feathers of humming-birds, *picaflores*, or as the Indians called them, *huitzitzilin*, a word that suggests the fluttering and hovering of the humming-birds in the throat of the nectar-bearing flowers. What else of the Tarascans ? They flattened the heads of their infants by binding the skull so as to give an exaggerated, slanting forehead, and filed their teeth to the shape of swallow tails. They work, now, at indigo dyeing and many of them, in consequence, have blue fingernails.[1]

[1] The Tarascan *caciques*, or perhaps their priests, carried mirrors of obsidian which were velvety-black with pale-green veins, and in these they caught the reflection of their copper features. A favourite food of the Tarascan Indians is the *axolotl* or salamander (in Aztec, ' water-slave '), a term which well describes that slothful, white, slug-like reptile that never transforms into an adult, remains permanently in the larval

Tupataro, a little village a few miles from Patzcuaro, and only to be reached on horseback or afoot, has a church with a lacquered interior — as it might be, a Jesuit church of the seventeenth century in Java or Bali, decorated with the help of Hindu craftsmen, and one of the few links between the East and West Indies of early discoverers.

And leaving Lake Patzcuaro I would descend the isthmus, where Mexico narrows, to Tehuantepec—where the Tehuanas, who resemble Malay or Burmese women and smoke cigars, wear low-cut jackets, skirts wound round them after the manner of *sarongs*, a scarlet or yellow handkerchief folded into a turban, and the *huipil* upon Sundays and feast days, which is a frilled and starched headdress in the shape of an Elizabethan ruff as worn in portraits by Zuccaro or Marc Gheeraerts, the more dazzlingly white against their Indian or olive skins ; or it is worn hanging down the back, when it becomes the feminine counterpart to the trailing headdress of eagles' plumes of the Red Indian warriors — cross the Guatemalan border, and arrive at the Lake of Atitlan. Three extinct volcanoes overlook it, and in the fishing villages upon its shores are worn the brightest costumes in the whole of Indian America, each village different, long red skirts and white *huipiles* with purple stripes, in Santiago, and a headband which is formed from a red woollen ribbon, an inch and a half wide and ten yards long, wound round and round until it forms a halo.

And in other Guatemalan towns and villages : *huipiles* of red and brown stripes, widely spaced, and red *servilletes* or carrying cloths ; pink and purple blouses with many figures ;

condition, yet becomes sexually mature, and lurks on the muddy bottom of the lake. Another food of the Indians is the marsh fly, *axayacatl*, which lays its eggs on flags and rushes. The eggs are pounded into a paste with the insects themselves, and boiled in cornhusks. *Axayacatl* means ' water-face ' and was the name and symbol of the sixth Indian Emperor of Mexico.

red and yellow striped blouses with bright yellow or purple figures disposed at random ; magnificent blue *huipiles* (but, in Guatemala, they mean skirts, not headdresses) ; *huipiles* with diagonal, zigzag, and diamond patterns on a white ground ; pink and white, or with white figures on a lacy white ground ; a brown or white cotton background, with broad red stripes and rows of designs in magenta, purple, and green silk or wool ; brown, of brown cotton with red stripes and finer, thinner, yellow and blue stripes ; white ceremonial *huipiles* in another village ; red and white striped or cross-barred trousers (like the caricatures of ' Uncle Sam ') in the village of Todos Santos ; long white *huipiles* with deep flounces round the neck ; or of yellow, which is rare in other parts of Guatemala.

Let us see the Indian blankets of Momostenango, spread out along the streets, and wetted with water to prove the colours do not run, and the three hundred shamans, men and women, sorcerers and intermediaries between the people and the gods ; the dresses of twin villages, San Pedro and San Juan Sacatapequez, near the capital, with conventionalized patterns of double-headed eagles that recall the arms of Charles V ; the men of Santo Tomás Chichicastenango in dresses that are adapted from the clothes of sixteenth-century Spain, dark blue breeches and blouses, worked with crimson, and powdered with sunbursts and other symbols ; (it is in this village that the festival of the *voladores* is to be seen : a high pole is set up in front of the church, round which the players swing on ropes, in ever-widening circles, till they are flying as high up as the roofs of the houses or the church towers) ;[1] or the *caciques* of Momostenango, village headmen

[1] It was discovered, not long ago, that the *Juego de los voladores* is still practised by the Totonac and Otomi Indians in remote places in Mexico. There are drawings

in wide-brimmed 'ten-gallon' hats, always the 'Indian' in
Buffalo Bill's circus, dressed in sober black wool, with many
fringes, and worked with stylized bat symbols, for their
villages are haunted by the vampire bat !

I have described my 'Indies' of the imagination and will
not weary the reader with a further pursuit into Colombia,
Ecuador, Bolivia, and Peru ; the scarlet-lacquered churches
of Quito and its school of painters ; Cuzco with its
Renaissance churches and a *plaƶa* as fine as those of Salamanca
or Santiago, probably as fine as any square or *plaƶa* in the
world, with the cathedral, the church of La Compañía de
Jesus, the convent of La Merced : the wonderful costumes
and peasant arts of Peru, of which a collection may be made
merely from objects sold by Indians at the railway stations
(not even in Japan are there so many toys and small objects
of entirely local manufacture) ; the ruined mints and palaces of
Potosí, the relics of her silver mines ; there is no time for these.
But I have described, at least, how I came to the 'Indies',
never in person, through my love of Italy and of Spain.

of these 'flying games' in two Aztec codices, those of Porfirio Diaz and Fernández
Léal. It was seen by Bernal Diaz and Fray Juan de Torquemada. The flyers were
clothed as various birds. Cf. *Mexican Mosaic*, by Rodney Gallop: London, Faber &
Faber, 1939, and my *Sacred and Profane Love*, p. 310: London, Faber & Faber, 1940.
By a most extraordinary coincidence a pole trick of a like character is performed on
13 February, every year, at the foot of the Potala in Lhasa, as part of the New Year
ceremonies. Formerly, a yak-hair rope was stretched from the roof of the Potala to
a stone edict pillar at the foot of the southern staircase, hundreds of feet below, and
men, protected by leather saddles, slid down it at terrific speed. Now, a tall pole,
fifty feet high and covered in yak-hair cloth, is set up at foot of the Potala staircase,
and a man is hauled to the top of it, throws his boots down to the crowd, raises himself on the little platform in the strong wind, and fitting a piece of wood to his
stomach, spins round and round upon the iron cap of the pole, with arms and legs
outstretched. The ceremony is watched by a huge crowd, including monks in claret-
coloured robes, and by Tibetan ladies of fashion, some wearing the enormous tri-
angular Lhasa headdress, somewhat similar to the horned headdress of the Middle
Ages, and a few, the tall hooped headdress from Gyantse. This curious spectacle is
described, and illustrated, in *Lhasa, the Holy City*, by F. Spencer Chapman: London,
Chatto & Windus, 1938, pp. 313-16.

Bucknell's Wood

Autobiography of the Imagination during a Moonlight Walk

A NIGHT is announced that is loud with nightingales, but not " the white nightingale hidden in the branches and heavy leafage of the clouds ", for that was a nightingale of another order altogether, the nightingale of the electric comedies, of my first master when I was sixteen, the Futurist of Milan ; [1] but, instead, it is a spring evening and we are walking in the poplar wood far down in the valley, listening to the young birds who are practising their notes, trying them again and again to get them perfect, so that the poplar wood is like a school for opera, like an academy or conservatoire of singing, and we look up through the vines, blue-painted against the phylloxera, towards the distant castle standing on its hill among the cypresses, and slowly make our way back to it in the hot evening, up the steep cobbled path to the fountain where the laundry is spread out to dry under the fig trees, to the stone statues of lions, or rather, wolves and lionesses that guard the terraces, up the steps of green tufa, treading over the antcolumns, and into the high and empty rooms.

How noisy the night when you throw back the wooden shutters and look down upon the fireflies, and after a while hear the piercing sweetness of the nightingales ! The frogs

[1] F. T. Marinetti, Corso Venezia, 48.

are croaking wherever there is water, and now the owl starts
from the cypress tree. I would lie awake in the hot night
thinking of Florence, of its noisy streets and, probably, of the
frescoes of Benozzo Gozzoli which I loved, particularly, at
that time. Or, it may be, of Fra Angelico, whom I loved
equally. He was the first painter whom I heard mentioned
when I was a child. I remember, too, the paintings of Filippino Lippi from when I was seven or eight years old. I have
known them for as long as I have known the music of *Casse-
Noisette* or of *The Sleeping Princess*, and like that immortal
music they have not grown stale. So many generations of
Englishmen had lived in Florence that, what with that, and
with the Pre-Raphaelite pictures of Rossetti and Burne-Jones,
the school of Florence had become more English than Italian.
Botticelli was an English painter, nothing more nor less.
And it was not the fault, entirely, of the English dilettanti for
the models of Botticelli and of Filippino Lippi bore a most
curious physical resemblance to the youth of England.

Already I had seen everything that there was to be seen of
the Florentine masters, and during the years 1920–25, just after
the first world war, I went upon several separate occasions to
Pisa in order to study the frescoes by Benozzo Gozzoli in the
Campo Santo ; and I knew, as well, his frescoes at San
Gimignano and at Montefalco. I have written of *Noah's
Vintage*, the greatest of his Pisan frescoes, in *The Golden Reign
of Saturn*,[1] and described in the same book the *Triumph of
Death*, that most tremendous and terrifying masterpiece of
the mediaeval imagination, also in the Campo Santo ; and I
wrote, too, of the great mediaeval paintings in the Spanish
Chapel of Santa Maria Novella in Florence. In another work
I composed a fantasy upon Signorelli's frescoes at Monte

[1] In *Splendours and Miseries* : London, Faber & Faber, 1943.

Oliveto Maggiore, outside Siena, paintings in which the young
warriors wear the piebald costumes of the Pálio, and upon
Signorelli's painting of *Pan and Apollo*, destroyed during the
war, and formerly in the picture gallery in Berlin. This was
the most poetical and beautiful of all the pagan paintings of
the Renaissance, and, indeed, one of the loveliest paintings
in the world. I knew very well, from frequent visits, Pinturicchio's painted library in the cathedral at Siena. Where
the Venetian painters were concerned, I loved especially the
paintings of Carpaccio and of Cima da Conegliano ; and
knowing well the pictures by the former in the Scuola degli
Schiavoni, would go again and again to see Cima's *Baptism of
Christ* in San Giovanni in Bragora, and his painting over the
altar on the right hand of the door in the Madonna dell' Orto,
with the little strawberry plant in the foreground that Ruskin
loved to copy. Parma I had visited, on purpose, for the sake
of the small paintings of *Pan and Endymion* by Cima. Cosimo
Tura and Ercole de' Roberti I knew from Ferrara ; Crivelli
from his paintings in the Brera. I had seen, several times, the
frescoes of Piero della Francesca at Borgo San Sepolcro and
at Arezzo. I mention all this because I would not have it said
that I attached myself to the Baroque in ignorance of what
came before it. The opposite is the truth ; but it was
necessary for my career as a writer to discover some field of
exploration that had not been worked before.

Oh ! how much I loved Italy, if not Florence ; and now,
many years later, it is difficult for an Englishman to forgive
the Italians or forget what they have done. But this was not
the night I wanted, despite the nightingales. I would lie
awake, thinking of another climate of the mind. It was not
enough for someone of my temperament to live in Florence.
The fiery song of the nightingales was of another mood,

teaching one not to be contented. Now, not a year sooner,
not a year later, it was the climacteric ; now, and ever, the
moment for adventures and explorations of the spirit, for the
seizing and capture of the rare and curious.

The climacteric, I say, is now and ever, not a year later,
not a year sooner, and I move it forward twenty years from the
time I am thinking of to another night of the nightingales,
when, owing to the exigencies of the war, I had to walk at two
or three o'clock in the morning, in the white, chalky moonlight,
down the whole length of a great wood in this corner of
Northamptonshire, but parallel to its edge, about a hundred
yards away from it, and, in fact, across the fields. I have
never in my life had an experience more beautiful than the
singing of those nightingales. It was at the most exciting
and, in the same breath, most terrible moment of 1944, during
the weeks just before what I suppose will be called into
perpetuity D-Day, when the greater part of the known
world was in a state of hope and expectancy that something
was about to happen which would mean the war was ending.
The excitement had communicated itself even into this remote
part of the country, in the middle of England. A group of
Polish or Czech parachutists was hidden far down in the
wood, where they had lain for three days, sending out one of
their number in the evening to buy food in Wappenham —
the village name makes the narrative sound more real — but
not a sound was to be heard, not a footfall, nor the creaking
of a twig. We had passed the earlier part of the night in an
empty barn, not smoking or talking, and the point of the
exercise (so far as it had one) was to find the parachutists, as
much as it was to be *their* endeavour to lie low and hidden.
Two of our men who were woodsmen or foresters had gone
forward deep into the wood, but they had seen nothing, heard

nothing, only a noise " like the noise made by a rabbit ", near by, practically in their ears, but " it was not a noise made by any animal ", it was a human being, someone hidden only a few feet away from them, and they had not liked it, they returned a good deal quicker than they started. Nothing more happened, and an hour later the word came to go home.

There had been five years of death during which one could not remember or believe in anything. I could not believe that I had ever been in Venice, or seen Venetian painting. Yet I have never known stronger aesthetic emotions of any kind — even in listening to music — than in standing before Carpaccio's paintings during the years I was in love with Venice, and in searching him out and looking for him in unlikely places. Carpaccio goes back a long time in my memories. I had been told that he was a Dalmatian — that he was ' born in Istria ' — even when I went to Venice as a small boy long before the 1914 war.[1] I can remember looking out of a side window, high up in the Hotel Danieli, at sunset (it may have been in 1908–9), with my brother, and watching the weekly steamer, the *San Marco* (I can see it now), raising anchor and starting for Dalmatia. How I longed to go there ! It was many years later that I went, at last, to Ragusa and to Traù, and found in the latter town that there were little round hats and caps for sale in the shops which were the same round caps as worn by the young popinjays in Carpaccio's paintings. How thrilling it was upon Sundays and holidays to see the three flags flying from the great bronze pedestals in front of St. Mark's ! These had been, once, the flags of the Venetian Republic for her three territories, Cyprus, Crete, and Dalmatia. I remember finding the one Venetian wine shop where they still sold Comanderia, the wine of Cyprus. No wonder

---

[1] This is wrong. Carpaccio was born in Venice in 1455.

in those days I thought the Italians should have Dalmatia, and certainly it has done the 'democratic world' no good that it should now belong to Marshal Tito. What a pity the Venetian Republic was ever abolished, and that it was swallowed up into the vast hereditary dominions of the house of Austria ! It had a greater history than any other of the Italian states. I am in all things against a united Italy. This is directly contrary to the Italian genius. I should prefer Italy to consist of little independent states like Central American Republics. For the greatness of modern Italy, down to less than a century ago, was when her painters, poets, musicians, men of science, were citizens of states no bigger or more important than Tuscany, Lombardy, Modena, or Parma. Always excepting Venice, La Serenissima ! There is no need for me to set down my love for Venice and for the Venetian painters. It is not necessary for me to state again my admiration for Tiepolo, I have already given enough proof of that in my writings. I loved Tiepolo when he was himself ; I can still get the taste in my mouth of that early winter morning when I first went inside the church of Sant' Alvise (it was in November 1920),[1] or saw his frescoed ceilings in the Pietà, or in the Gesuati ; and I loved him when he painted in the grand manner of Veronese, as in his frescoes of the *Banquet of Antony and Cleopatra.* How can anyone, who has ever loved them, forget the Venetian painters !

It was like walking on air to be out there in the moonlight remembering all the wonders I had touched and seen ; only to think of the paintings in the Madonna dell' Orto, and particularly the huge *Adoration of the Golden Calf* by Tintoretto; or the 'sea staircase' — it is like a marble staircase leading out of the sea — and the great Tintoretto paintings upon both floors of the Scuola di San Rocco. As soon forget that most

[1] This church was closed after 7.30 A.M.

marvellous of all interiors, the interior of St. Mark's! Ruskin, in his madness, dreamed that he saw the Horses of St. Mark's saddling themselves with golden harness. St. Mark's was the building, and probably the object of all objects, alive or dead, that he loved most in the world, and it is tragic, but typical, that Ruskin should revert to some detail of it in his dreams during the wrecking and foundering of his intellect. What can have been the meaning or interpretation of his dream? That the Horses of St. Mark's — which had stood upon a triumphal arch outside the Golden House of Nero, drawing a quadriga; removed by Constantine to adorn his Imperial hippodrome at Constantinople; taken, thence, to Venice by the ninety-nine years old Doge Dandolo in 1204 when Constantinople was sacked by the Franks and the Venetians; set up by Napoleon upon the triumphal arch in the Place du Carrousel, at the entrance to the Tuileries, to witness the reviews of the Imperial Guard, probably the most thrilling military spectacles there have ever been; and returned to Venice after Waterloo by Francis II, last of the long line of Holy Roman Emperors — that the horses of gilded bronze were harnessing themselves in order to draw him, or his spirit, to some landscape, some state of being, that his eyes had seen, but that he had not attained. We know enough of Ruskin to be certain who he would have had to wait for him in the 'rose-hung island'. Or it may have been no more than the play of the horses and their golden harness. His brain and heart were broken, and his vision of the Horses of St. Mark's harnessing themselves with golden reins and bridles was but a little toy to keep him sleeping.

How beautiful to think of that dream, in either or both interpretations, out in this moonlight! Not that I had, then, been told of it. I only heard the story lately. But I am

writing, now, of an experience that was as tenuous as that
dream. I am painting a picture of the moonlight and I must
make it as much like moonlight as I can. It has to be the full
moon out in the pale fields, along the edge of a wood where
the nightingales are singing. How much more there was to
remember, in thinking of Venice ! The portrait of a man upon
a white horse, by Moretto, in the Palazzo Donà dalle Ro'se,
of the lovely name, and the little canvases by Pietro Longhi ;
the ceiling painting by Tiepolo of Apollo in a chariot drawn
by white horses among white clouds, in the Palazzo Rezzonico ;
the one painting by Tiepolo in the Doges' Palace, of Neptune
strewing the treasures of the deep at the feet of Venice (it was
painted in place of an earlier picture that had been injured by
a fire) ; the little gambling saloon, the Ridotto Venier, and
its small rooms with inlaid floors and coloured *stucchi* ; the
early Madonna by Fra Antonio da Negroponte in San Francesco della Vigna ; all the towns with the Lion of St. Mark
upon a column in the main square, or upon the sides of
buildings ; but, chiefly, Brescia with its churches and its
portraits by Moroni, perhaps the greatest portrait painter of
the Italian Renaissance, excelling in noblemen in armour, or
half-armour, with colder lights and more detailed than Veláz-
quez, but not inferior to him, the characters, entirely, of
Verdi's *Don Carlos* or *Otello* ; and the later Brescian portrait
painter, Fra Galgario, who is magnificent, at his best, in
characterization and bold handling, but, probably because he
was a Carmelite friar, painted men better than he did women ;
but, beyond and above all, Bergamo with its beautiful picture
by Lorenzo Lotto in a church upon the way to the Upper
Town, and a wonderful cloud background in the painting,[1]

[1] I believe I may have confused this painting by Lotto in San Bernardino in
Bergamo, with a painting by Lotto in the parish church of Asolo.

with the Guardis in the picture gallery, and the frescoes by Tiepolo in the Colleoni Chapel. Bergamo, the city which according to tradition was Pierrot's birthplace, and which one cannot think of without remembering the music of *Don Pasquale*, written by Donizetti who was also born here. So I wandered in my thoughts. But I would always come back in my mind to that most lovely of all Venetian buildings, the Villa Masèr, near Belluno : architecture by Palladio, painted decorations by Paolo Veronese. The coupling of their two names in that emphasis is not by accident, and it is not by mistake that I have written down their names as upon a theatre programme. How lovely the Villa Masèr must look in this moonlight, for the same moon shone upon its white columns and pediment and upon this wood of nightingales !

And walking across the fields at three o'clock in the morning in the moonlight I remembered motoring down the left bank of the Danube and seeing for the first time the huge monastery of Melk upon its hill above the river. How little and provincial Austria seemed, and how remarkable that it should have been the centre of a great Empire ! Its monuments and works of art were nearly all Baroque and Rococo. How lovely and typical was the little town of Dürnstein, where Richard Cœur de Lion was imprisoned, where Blondel played his harp, where there was an old inn upon the river with Austrians in their *dirndls* and *lederhosen* eating the eternal *forellen*, the music of zithers, and a church in bucolic or pastoral Baroque. I thought of Seitenstetten, an old Benedictine abbey in the lush sub-Alpine meadows, with its white staircase and abbot's room with paintings by Magnasco, a monastery I had looked for all over Italy and Austria, but found no other with paintings by that monkish master. And I remembered the gleaming white staircase of Göttweig, another huge monastery

upon a cliff above the river ; and this made me think of St.
Florian and the white stuccoes in the church, the magnificent
wrought-iron gates in the church, and upon the double open
stair, the Kaisersaal, and the rare painting by Altdorfer in the
picture gallery. All these monasteries were Baroque, not
Rococo, but a few miles away, near Linz, was Wilhering,
another monastery upon the river, and this was the Rococo
at its most graceful and fantastic. The doorways and picture
frames in this abbey had the elegance and freshness of a violin
sonata by Mozart. Never before, and never again, but here,
and in Bavaria, have such refinements and turns of phrase
found expression in building, qualities not generally associated
or brought into play with architecture, but, equally, it could
be argued that they did not appear in music until the time
of Mozart. I thought of Diessen, like a Rococo church in
snow, built near the green waters of the Ammer-See, where
the Augustinian canons had sent to Venice for altar paintings
by Tiepolo and by Piazzetta ; and of the pilgrimage church
of Wies, white as snow, again, as to its interior, but with
scagliola pillars painted pink-porphyry and lapis lazuli, and a
golden altar. There were the two extraordinary Benedictine
abbeys of Ottobeuren and Zwiefalten, not, like those others,
in view of the snowy mountains, but deep in the goose plain
of Suabia, and both built by J. M. Fischer, the architect of
Wies. There were monastic theatres in both monasteries.
The many altars of Ottobeuren were so many separate and
entire theatrical compositions, permanent ' built scenes ' of a
most complicated order of invention. The altars of Zwiefalten were more elaborate still, treated with stalactite and coral
motifs so that they resembled grottoes, and lacquered in
bright colours, which brought me to the brothers Egid Quirin
and Cosmas Damian Asam.

71

Why not think in this moonlight of Osterhofen, the convent of the Englische-Fräulein, a rare order of nuns ? The high altar was by Egid Quirin, the sculptor of the family, and I could see in my mind the statues of Duke Odo of Bavaria in black armour, with his wife carrying her prayer book and rosary, at one side of the altar, and at the other, Duke Heligo, the blue and white banner of Bavaria in one hand and the plan of the church in the other, while his wife beside him smiles across at Duke Odo from behind her fan. The painted ceiling (a very good one) was by Cosmas Damian Asam. How much I would like to know what would have been Baudelaire's opinion of this chapel ; Baudelaire who more than two generations in advance of his age saw the beauty in this ' decadent' architecture, and who was struck down with mortal illness in the Jesuit church of St. Loup at Namur that he had gone over to see from Brussels in company with Rops ! It seems to have been his intention to write some kind of description of the Jesuit style, so far as he had been able to study it during his last months in Belgium. Baudelaire would have delighted in the six side altars of the Englische-Fräulein at Osterhofen, each with the standing skeleton of a saint wearing the Spanish Court dress of the time. Their dresses had been embroidered by the nuns, and worked with pearls and semi-precious stones, and were complete down to the swords at their sides.

How bare and empty it is, now, in the moonlit fields ! And I remembered another of the Asam churches, Frauenzell, a Benedictine abbey lost in the forests of the Bayerischer Wald. The interior was a wide ellipse, an oval larger in scale than the other Asam churches, with white walls, all in white, but with accents of jade green in the decoration. There were balconies for the choir, one on either side of the high altar, and these had exceptionally rich *avant-scènes* or decorated surrounds securing them upon the chancel wall. How inappropriate the words, nave, chancel, narthex, when writing of the Rococo churches ! the terms used for Louis-Quinze furniture, *bergère à confessionnel, poudreuse, bonheur du jour,* would be more descriptive. Each opera box was reached by a separate staircase in the thickness of the wall, and the walls were painted with a beautiful freehand decoration upon the plaster in the style of the most lovely of Rococo wallpapers. What drama, what opera, what ballet, could be about to play at the high altar ? One could look out of the opera boxes into the church — but could it be a church ? — and see the huge painted ceiling of the Assumption from the hand of Cosmas Damian, his largest, and the most fanciful of all his paintings, and not content with opening the body of the church into the clouds Cosmas Damian had painted the ceiling of the chancel as well (again, how indescriptive and inappropriate that word !), so that the white, snowy surfaces of the cornices and the stucco decorations all played up to the wide-open heavens.

I think that the most graceful and loveliest of all the white Rococo churches was the old Cistercian abbey of Stams, not far from Innsbruck ; it was white, white, it had the white of *blanc de Chine*, or *biscuit*, enhanced with splendid wrought-iron gates and grilles. But Stams was in the Tyrol ; it was of a particular category in this sub-Alpine art (a little different from the Swiss of Einsiedeln, or St. Gallen) or from the Austrian, or Bavarian. This was the Rococo of the Tyrol. With their genius for the nuance and for what was pleasing to the eye, I had often wondered why the Rococo architects and craftsmen who were such masters of white that their white churches and monastery staircases are in a class or category to themselves had never made experiment with tones of rose-petal and *bois de rose* ; and I fell to thinking of these felicities, and to imagining villages under the mountains with houses that had painted fronts and window-boxes full of zinnias and petunias, and convents where the nuns were coryphées of that order extolled by Bernini in his *Ecstasy of St. Theresa,* or of the pair of nuns in Tiepolo's altar painting in the Gesuati, religious who were not far removed in spirit from the Vestal Virgins. The churches I was thinking of under the mountains were all in echo of Rome and Venice. The Asam brothers had been to Rome (where they studied under Pier Leone Ghezzi), and almost certainly to Venice, which in the eighteenth century in its decay was the most wonderful spectacle of the Western world after Byzantium.

This mountain or sub-Alpine Rococo was in emulation of Rome and Venice. At its best it was one of the beauties and graces of the civilized world. Certainly, those who had not seen it had missed one of the refinements of the hand of man ; and next morning, after recovering from this long walk in the moonlight, I intended to look up in my old guide-book and find some of these lovely Rococo churches which I had seen, and nearly forgotten, it was so long ago. And (I anticipate) I began turning over the pages, finding church after church, and remembering some detail in their decoration, and looking from the better known to the less known, and so, having read the short and curt descriptions of some that I remembered very well, I turned to a certain page, searching for a church with lovely details that I recalled seeing in the suburbs of Munich, or just outside the town, and this is what I found.

". . . Berg am Laim, built by J. M. Fischer in 1737–51, with plasterwork and painted ceilings by J. B. Zimmermann, and six large altars by J. B. Straub ", and lower down upon

the page I read, ". . . Dachau : two hotels, both with
verandahs affording a good view . . . the Hof-Garten, behind
the Schloss, commands a fine view of Dachau ". So Berg am
Laim was upon the road to Dachau ! It was a Court church
(whatever that may mean !) two miles outside Munich, and
Dachau was less than ten miles further on. I must have passed
it several times upon the road to Ingolstadt, where there was
another " masterpiece of Bavarian Rococo ", the sodality
chapel of Maria de Viktoria by the Asam brothers, with inlaid
doors, carved pews or benches with much gilding, and a flat
ceiling painted with the Four Continents by Cosmas Damian
. . . I could not think any more of the German Rococo, and
for some months I could not listen to music by Mozart.

So to the nightingales.

Up to that moment there had been no sound of them, out
in the moonlight, but now, as we had to come nearer to the
wood and began to move in front of it, along its side —
and it was more than a mile long — the nightingales sang with
utmost violence and brilliancy in every fresh part of the wood
we came in front of, down its entire length. The moon was full,
and very high in the heavens, and the open fields were steeped
in moonlight. It was as light as day, but a curious daylight, it
was so calm and milk-white. The long black edge of the wood
lay like another world, like the shore of another planet. There
must have been dozens, perhaps hundreds of the nightingales.
Why should they so particularly haunt this wood, I wondered !

Sometimes the slope of a field took us further away, but
we could still hear them singing, and then we would come up
the rise of a bank and be spilled down in the direction of that
dark wood, when the purity and violence of the singing would
become something extraordinary to listen to. But it was most
beautiful when keeping a proper distance, say, a hundred yards,

between ourselves and the nightingales. I would not have wanted to be out there in the moonlight, by myself, listening to them. It would be an experience that would be unbalancing because it was so unreal. Yet this was a wood famous for its nightingales. But who could ever think to find them in such number singing in the moonlight, as though the wood (as it certainly did) belonged to them ? You could lie still in that wood, listening, but not moving, and not catch sight of one single solitary individual of all those nightingales. Perhaps the beat of a wing, perhaps a gentle stirring of the leaves, that would be all, and nothing more. And you would not hear the singing of the whole body of them, but only of the nightingales in the near trees. But, out here, in the empty, bare fields, you heard the whole chorus singing, as well as the song of certain individual nightingales that you could recognize again and again ; now — or now — stopping still to listen, when the incredible song soared up in ecstasy, higher, higher, singing above the other nightingales ; and now — and now again — never flagging, but losing itself in fiery liquefaction ; and, at once, beginning to sing again out of the fire, which, for all that, was a cold fire, a mechanical fire, like the fire of emerald or diamond, something which glittered, but did not give heat.

If music has meaning, the song of the nightingales is in interpretation of the moonlight, and miraculously in mood with that. What a peculiar feeling in the height of the moonlight to be walking in the fields ! It is the dominion of another and different lot of pastoral gods, or of the one goddess only, but the degree and quality of the difference is as though another company of actors was performing in the same theatre, for they are the same woods and fields, but it is an old and alternate order, an old and another school of poetry and morals. Not an older school or an older order, but the light of a goddess, more infrequent than daylight, coming at rare but known intervals, as now, at full moon, a reign or order we know nothing of, for we are not there to see it.

To-night it is entire and omnipotent. No one could think there is the alternative of day, which is like another religion, another hierarchy ' taking over ' ; and it was extraordinary in the middle of this moonlight walk to pass where there was a pair of thatched cottages, the only sign of human habitation during all this long time, and to look down on the woodsmen's or gamekeepers' houses (that is why they were built so near the wood) imagining the tall spires of the hollyhocks that would come later, nearer to the harvest moon, at the time of the lilies, in the season of the blue clematis, when the hayricks are like shadow houses, but all we see, now, in the moonlight is the simple shape or outline of the cottages and their tall roofs of thatch, and the ladder of the thatcher at one cottage, by a window, which must throw a shadow on the ground, a haunted shadow, for it is easy in imagination to put a figure on the ladder, or, for that matter, to call the thatcher by the name of the goat god, or call him Midas in the pear blossom, or any name we choose. There is a pear tree in blossom upon the wall (there is always a pear tree upon old houses in this part of England), and now I heard the nightingales singing out louder than ever in the moonlight, and the cottages had dropped out of sight as though we had never seen them. I would not think of the families living in those moonlit houses, for it was the transcendental hour, the hour of the climacteric ; it had lifted even my companions out of themselves for, perhaps, the only few moments in the four years I passed with them ; they were not companions of choice, the war hysteria threw us together, and I knew the woodsmen or foresters would be just as these others ; I loved them not, and they

loved not me, but this exceptional experience of our moonlight walk, so long past midnight, so deep into the shadow
dominion, but so brilliantly light, and so serene and calm, had
made us momentary companions while it lasted, during that
night — or it could have been the night before, or the night
following, and perhaps once again in a lifetime, and no more.

The nightingales sang out loud, and louder still, in the
moonlight along Bucknell's Wood. When the other war
ended I was young, and went to Spain, and then to Italy, and
again and again to Italy, as poets, musicians, painters, of many
nationalities had done before me. Turner had to go to Italy.
Constable never left the shores of England. It is a division
of temperament, or two kinds of minds, and as regards achievement, little or nothing to choose between them. Some
painters, Watteau or Toulouse-Lautrec, ' travel ' in the ambience of a mile or two around them, painting from the theatre
or from night life, and get the exigencies of travel from their
nervous or irritable sensibility which makes them perpetually
change to new addresses. Another painter may live and die
in the house where he was born. Degas was content with
Paris : Gauguin had to go to Tahiti.

It is a division of temperaments that has existed all over
the world where there were artists. To the classical world of
the ancients it was the air, not of Italy, but of Greece, of the
Hellenes, that breathed of poetry. Was that not the reason
why Virgil, who was born in Mantua upon the river Po, had
his body or his ashes buried, looking down upon the bay of
Naples ? " *Mantua me genuit, Calabri rapuere, tenet nunc
Parthenope* " (" Mantua gave birth to me, Calabria carried me
away ; and now Parthenope has me in her keeping ") ran the
inscription upon his tomb — Parthenope, one of the sirens,
whose body according to tradition was found on the seashore

of the bay of Naples, but it is another way of saying that
Naples, or Neapolis, was a city of Greek foundation (Dorians
from Rhodes, Chalcidian immigrants from Euboea : Naples
" retained the use of the Greek language, and Greek customs,
until well on in the Imperial age of Rome ".) Virgil had come
down from Rome to live at Posillipo (Pausilypon) in order to
breathe the Hellenic air ; call it Greek, or Italian, what you
will, according to the age, but it is a drug, a honey in the air,
that some artists crave for and that others feel no need for,
or find it close to home. The poets and painters of Japan in
their great period knew this emanation coming from China ;
the Chinamen of the classical age felt it in India. They wrote
of the holy places of Buddhism in the valleys under the
Himalayas in just the spirit of a traveller seeing the classical
beauties of Greece or Italy for the first time. But other sages
were happy in the hermitages in their own mountains, and never
left China. India — Greece, Italy — meant nothing to them.

The poet of all poets never left this island — from which
it can be argued that there is no need to — but in the following
generation, Milton went to Italy, saw Rome, and went down
to Naples. Milton knew well the Latin poets and wrote, himself, in Latin. He was one of the last of the Latin poets. But
this is not enough ; there is the direct evidence of Italy in his
imagery. Shelley lived in Italy. Keats went to Rome, too
late. Blake kept to Lambeth, near to the bubble-dome of
Bedlam. His Italy was Felpham, in Sussex. That was the
capital of his pastoral kingdom. But, among musicians, there
was Handel. As to one side of his talent Handel is to be counted
as Italian. He is one of the prime instances of invention in
emergency, of sudden blossoming when there comes the
opportunity. This is not the prerogative, entirely, of the
lighter sorts of minds, for it is to be found, by contrary, in

someone so ponderously nimble and sure-footed in his genius, we say, as Handel, if there be evidence, as Romain Rolland suggests, that each one of his twelve *Concerti grossi* was composed and written in a day. But then Handel, like Mozart, was a theatrical or improvisatory composer, an inventor for the emergency. Both musicians had experience of Italy. This is to be felt in the adagio of any sonata or any piano concerto of Mozart. He had heard Italian singing and known Italian singers. His slow movements must be played as those of a composer used to the air and climate of the opera house.[1]

Now, in contrast, neither Bach nor Beethoven ever set foot in Italy. They are the two giants of music. Yet, if there be anything approximating to a deficiency in this pair of Titans, it is that they are lacking in just that experience of Italy. Perhaps we do not feel the need of it in Bach. He could be ' Italian ' by instinct, when it suited him (in the Italian Concerto, in the little harpsichord Fantasia in F minor with crossed hands in the manner of Domenico Scarlatti, whose harpsichord sonatas Bach had never seen), though we may think of Bach

---

[1] Handel had met Gian-Gastone, ' last of the Medici ', at Hamburg, then the great centre of opera in Germany. This prince who, later, was to collapse in hopeless, sordid dissipation, in early days still loved to play the flute. The bust of this strange, bloated individual, a Caligula or Commodus in a periwig, used to stand at the top of the stairs at the Uffizi among the others of his family, and I have written, elsewhere, of the impression they made upon me as a child. With the advice and encouragement of Gian-Gastone, Handel set forth for Italy. He appeared in Florence in 1706, and stayed for a while with Ferdinando de' Medici, the prince's brother, at Pratolino, where he worked at his opera *Almira*, meanwhile enjoying the fountains and the ilex woods. He went to Venice, where he made friends with Domenico Scarlatti, who is said to have identified him at a masquerade by his playing of the harpsichord. The two friends, it is probable, journeyed together from Venice to Rome. At Naples, Handel heard the Calabrian shepherds (*vide* p. 49), and at the same time he was commissioned by Cardinal Grimani, the Austrian Viceroy of Naples, and a member of the famous Venetian family who owned the principal opera house in Venice, to compose an opera *Agrippina*, to be played during the carnival in Venice, which opera ran for twenty-seven nights, and shortly afterwards Handel left for his first visit to London, in order to bring Italian opera to England.

in Venice or Bologna trying out the organs in the churches, visiting the musical grammarians, listening to the singing; but the landscape and air of Italy would certainly have taken effect upon Beethoven, who was 'Italian' in the adagio of the Eighth Symphony, in the tremendous Bacchanale that ends the Seventh, in certain movements of the last Quartets. It would appear, then, that Bach and Beethoven, the two greatest of the composers of music, as, likewise, Shakespeare and Blake, the two greatest of the English poets (the latter, prophet and seer more than major poet), went not to Italy. But is Italy such a touchstone to the Italians themselves? Probably it is just as necessary for certain Italians to get out of Italy in order to fulfil themselves.

For myself, I loved Venice so much, and its churches and palaces and paintings, that I cannot but believe that some small fragment of my admiration, perhaps no more than a line or two that I have written, may attach itself and be, in little part, a gloss or mildew to the stones of Venice. Did I not see with my own eyes, when a child, and describe later, the legendary Don Carlos embarking in his gondola from the waterstair of the Palazzo Loredan? I wrote a fantasy upon the names of the Venetian families, Loredan, Grimani, Foscari, Dandolo, Mocenigo, Bragadin; and wrote *The Shoal of Pearls*, my best writing in prose, dedicated to Venice, but inspired, 'supplied', as it would be printed in a theatre programme, from studying the works of Rumphius and Regenfuss, periwigged and learned conchologists (as their names suggest) of the early eighteenth century, of the age of the contrapuntists and the art of fugue, the former, merchant and Dutch senator for Amboyna in the Moluccas, and it is probable, coiner of the names of many of the seashells which came pouring in from the East and West Indies to adorn the cabinets of collectors, names that are not less beautiful in imagery than those given to the tulips, hyacinths, ranunculuses of the old Dutch and French florists. Yet it seems to me that the import of *The Shoal of Pearls* has been lost upon most, if not all, who read it, though it was followed by *The Different Sounds of Thunder*, a description of a thunderstorm, by night, in Venice, all over Venice, in the different quarters and parishes, so loud a storm of thunder that no one could sleep that August night in Venice, but had to lie awake, listening and wondering, for it boomed and rattled in one part of the town after another, an hour or three-quarters of an hour away in either direction on foot across the little bridges, ending with the peal of thunder on the Zattere outside a certain window, a lodging close above the masts and sails of the *trabaccoli,* where, in imagery, were heaped the pearls and seashells, were strewn the treasures of the deep at the feet of whom ? Ah ! That was the Cinderella who is dead, the ghost of whom I met, or thought I saw, under the white syringa tree. I wrote of this poor dead thing, then young and beautiful, as the second of the masks or travestissements of Gavarni in my *Dance of the Quick and the Dead,* connecting her with the Écossaise danced by Swanilda in the second act of *Coppélia* ; and also as the Fée Dragée ; and as the Columbine of Florestan and his two sisters, for this dance from the last act of *The Sleeping Princess,* one of the supreme moments of classical dancing, was then performed, as many persons will remember, by a columbine and a pair of harlequins. I wrote of her as the *Dormeuse de Naples,* the last picture painted by Ingres for Murat when King of Naples ; and in the ballet of the Elysian Fields ; and then, again, under the white pallor of the gingko as a T'ang dancer ; and described dreaming of her in *Three Visions,* as the ghost of the well-head, the Xantippa of Peele's poem coming up as a ghost out of the well ; as a circus acrobat upon a white horse ; and the bayadère with blue eyelids ; as Isabella or Franceschina, too, among the Italian comedians, sweeping with her goose wing, Cinderella once again. It was farewell to her ; my last sight of her was " in the light of all the lamps like a goddess in a nimbus, but smiling, as though we were to meet upon the morrow ". Never again. We never met again ; though I wrote of her later, in *The Miming of the Golden Cornstalks*, as Swanilda, the peasant ballerina, " in a square in a little town on the borders of Galicia " ; or in the cornfield, in a corner of the golden harvest, in her short ballet skirt, walking bird-like, in the convention of the ballerina, in her satin shoes. But, horror of horrors, all those years ago I wrote of her as a dead thing ! I did not know, then, what would happen : I never thought I would know another Swanilda, Cinderella. For the first was the beauty of the small or intimate theatre ; the mermaid coming out of the wave to dance upon the margin of the sands ; the Lady of Shalott in the misty sedges, by the lake below the castle, long before the barley ripened ; while this other takes the lights upon the great stage, and fills the theatre. There were Russian dancers in my youth, but these are of our nation. But I return to Venice and to the *Vision of the Bucintoro* running for safety against a livid sky, moving as slowly as a huge tent drawn by horses, passing us, throwing out gold upon the surges.

Another war was ending. You knew it in this moonlight, and in the singing of the nightingales. But when it was over I had no desire to go to Italy. There was a year more of war, and hundreds of thousands still to die in the gas chambers, and of starvation. No one could wish to go to Italy where there had been fighting from end to end of the peninsula, up and down the land, owing to the treachery of the Italians.

Nor to go to Paris, as after the other war, in order to see the modern paintings, for that was an age of painting over and done with, it was dying, already, in 1939. There was nothing more to come out of Paris. Perhaps we had better painters, even now, in London. And having written as well as I could of the architecture of England, during the war, at the very time when every single building was in imminent and perpetual danger of destruction, I determined not to go to Italy again but to choose some other subject that had been neglected, that lay in obscurity, or of which but one half was seen, and the other hidden, and when the moment came for this to be possible, went to Holland. It is probably the flat façades of the Dutch town houses, so akin to the street architecture of London or of Dublin, that have kept secret their exuberant interiors with painted rooms and rich stucco decorations. There are old houses at The Hague by the Huguenot Daniel Marot, that the Dutch themselves have ignored or forgotten, but which are ornate and splendid specimens of the Régence, the transition from Louis-Quatorze into Louis-Quinze, high, stately, white interiors with great halls and stairways in a manner of pomp loved by the Dutchmen. There are the houses upon the canal at Leyden, a sort of Grand Canal, it could be, ' ordered ' by a Doctor Faustus or a Doctor Coppelius when he had returned home from his travels and was getting old. There was Friesland, a ' far ' Holland at the end of the causeway across the Zuyder Zee, with a language of its own and flaxen-haired inhabitants (of whom Rembrandt's Saskia is typical), an Arcadia of the rich peasants, with bucolic and pastoral beauties unique and apart, the like of which are to be found nowhere else in Europe.

I am thinking of the extraordinary costumes and headdresses that the Frisians evolved ; golden skull-caps of solid metal, close fitting to the head, like a symbol or image for their own flaxen hair. It is a curious sensation to behold the golden helms of the Frisian women ; and since writing *The Netherlands* I have had correspondence with an Englishman who had to proceed to Friesland upon dairy business, some years ago, and wrote to me of his experience in the little town where he was working, when he looked out of the window the morning after his arrival and saw what he took to be, for a moment, a fireman in a polished brass helmet stooping in a garden at the far side of the canal. It was a Frisian woman in her golden skull-cap, but he had not been warned, or told of this, and it was a long time before he could look at the Frisians in their golden helms without astonishment, or recover from his surprise. Now, the wearing of the golden skull-caps is dying out, and I saw no more than six or eight during my stay in Friesland, all worn by old women.

But, formerly, they had headdresses which were more peculiar still, the cart-wheel *Deutsches muts*, like a great tambour, with long ribbons like the streamers of a bird-of-paradise, worn with a bodice and hooped skirt of chintz bearing a pattern of flowers and birds and urns on pedestals ; or, in another district of Friesland, the young unmarried girls wore top-hats of beaver or of plaited straw, so that they were top-hatted milkmaids, and the country fairs and markets had a flavour of the Fourth of June at Eton. There were the town halls of Friesland ; the red-brick Dokkum, like the harbour master's office in an Elysian inland port, with a painted room by an unknown artist ; and Sneek, among the lakes and meers and white sails of the summer yachts, a square stone building of improbable fantasy, with a Court Room which must be the only magistrate's court in the world to be decorated in green *chinoiserie*. The little port of Hindeloopen, on the

Zuyder Zee, had a population of a few hundreds in surcoats and gowns of printed chintz in imitation of the *batiks* of Java and the Indies, so gorgeously apparelled that they were the cotton or linen counterpart to the nobles and court officials of Byzantium in their silken gowns. A dress or two in a museum, and the descriptions of travellers, are all that is left to us of this heyday of the painted chintz. In so many parts of Holland, and not only in Friesland, the straw hats of the women, " of glittering white straw, lined with glaring East-India chintz ", were in warning of what was to be seen in Zuid-Beveland, and other low dairy islands lying out into the North Sea, where, in the words of an old author : " We meet with peasants and country women of whom it may properly be said, these people are entirely of gold and silver ". And the coloured plate in Maaskamp shows them, indeed, glittering with precious metals. That was in 1808 ; but still to-day there are the milkmaids and fishergirls of Spakenburg with shoulder ornaments of glazed chintz ; and the Sunday parade of Staphorst, where may be seen several hundred women coming from church in column of three, all walking in step and dressed alike, and all carrying in their right hands a Bible in silver clasps secured to their waists upon a silver chain.

It was in July 1946 that I visited Holland, and having written my book by January or February of the following year, I went to Seville in time for the Feria of 1947, and in the spring of that, and of the next year, travelled from end to end of Spain, seeing again what I had known before, but also going to the smaller towns in an endeavour to miss no building of importance or work of art in the entire land. It is a hundred years since Ford wrote his Handbook, and since then no considerable work on Spain has been written in our language. Owing to special facilities, I was able to cover in a couple of months what took Ford several years of travelling on horseback to accomplish. Ford had, in any event, compared with Borrow, the limitations of the amateur. He could compose a handbook, but not a *Bible in Spain*. My intention was a work of literature and not a guide-book. But Spain is gigantic and bewildering as a theme. It is not compact like Holland. I could bring to it, at least, a knowledge of Italy. But the Spanish cathedrals are a world to themselves. I found myself thinking of perhaps fifteen or twenty of them, separately, as so many entities in the elaboration of their bare shells or vessels ; wrought-iron screens or *rejas* of Seville, Toledo, Burgos, Cuenca ; *retablos, coros, sillerías* ; Spanish organs ; tapestries of Zamora and Zaragoza. Even now, with travelling made easy, it is not possible to see everything in Spain. Long before, I had spent a month in Toledo, a month in Seville and Granada, and had been three or four separate times to Burgos, León, and to Santiago. The Escorial I knew of old and, also, the paintings of the Prado. But the project I had in mind entailed journeying to much more distant places. And, in the end, it must be no mere catalogue. I believe that I went everywhere in Spain where there is architecture, excepting Pamplona, Huesca, Soria, Morella, Tarazona, Teruel.[1]

---

[1] And excepting small towns, or even villages, like Santo Domingo de la Calzada, near Logroño. I went there, and to Pamplona, Soria, Tarazona, and Morella, in September 1951. Santo Domingo de la Calzada is named after a local twelfth-century saint. His tomb has a canopy surmounted by figures of white cocks and hens. These occur also in paintings of his miracles ; and opposite the tomb, descendants of the saint's chickens, of a breed apart, live in a wrought-iron cage of the fifteenth century, high on the wall of the choir. There are figures of white cocks and hens upon the shutters. During the daytime the birds fly about the church. When I saw them they were roosting, and looked to me like white Leghorns. The cock is immolated every year upon the saint's feast day, another of the brood succeeds him — and there is a grand *corrida de toros* in the evening. Ford has no mention of this odd survival in his Handbook ; and this may be the only description of it in our language. It must be exceedingly curious at cockcrow, when *cock-a-doodle-doo* echoes from the cathedral, and the challenge is answered from every quarter of the little town.

The huge open landscape of Spain had to be assimilated, which in its ' monotony ' is one of the ever-changing wonders of the world. There were villages, Villahermoso, Lagartera, La Alberca, where costume was still worn, but it was utterly different from the ' Spanish costume ' of convention. A painter or a writer could spend his lifetime in the Paralelo of Barcelona, among living characters out of the ' blue period ' of Picasso. This is not the place to write of their floured faces, like those of geishas or Japanese actors, their terrible cheap shoes, matador shirts, and that extraordinary moment when all are dancing in a quadrille, turning, stamping, snapping fingers (Ah ! how could one forget that !) ; or later, at three or four o'clock in the morning, taking their coats, ' leaving ', walking ' home ', past the bar where the stunted Gitano boy dances upon the counter, down the narrow, terrible street, up the noisy stair. I put all, excepting that, into my book on Spain, for that is another subject, it requires another treatment. I began with the Feria of Seville, which is incomparable as a spectacle and for the excitement of the music and the Andalusian dresses, whence the book opened in ever-widening circles until it covered nearly the whole of Spain, ending at the Gypsy caves of Guadix, a work which took much longer to write than my book on Holland, and indeed, first and last, it occupied two years.

That accomplished, it was time to pause and consider another subject. For, in fact, no more books upon that scale, and of that nature, could be attempted. The hour was too late. Being divided, through all my life as a writer, between the interpretative and the creative, between works that are factual and that depend upon marshalling and presentation, and those that are of the imagination, there was one more book of the former sort that I would wish to have attempted.

But the hour has struck. I have had to abandon it. The principal theme was to be Hungary, which I would have tried to present as excitingly as possible, for it is, in fact, like the Spanish landscape, another of those ' monotonous ' subjects which by the constant variation of its own limited material is one of the wonders of the world. I would have begun (I have long ago written the beginning) with an account of the playing of the Gypsy orchestra of small children in the Café Ostend at Budapest. They were little boys of eight or nine or twelve years old, who could not read a note of music, as dark as Indians, and I have never had a musical experience in my life to match the fire and frenzy of their playing. They had been brought to Budapest from villages and small towns all over Hungary, given new suits, of which some, you could tell immediately, were careless and oblivious, others inordinately proud, and they played every evening in the Café Ostend. One child after another would lead the orchestra in turn, playing on his violin. Some would know the tune from the first notes, others would listen until it had been played through. They had discovered music, and were of an age when it meant everything to them. Their playing made one's hair stand on end. I have never known more convincing proof of the Indian in the Gypsy. One could understand why it was that the Mongol hordes of Batu Khan invading the Danubian provinces in the twelfth century brought ' Indian ', that is to say, Gypsy musicians with them out of Central Asia to fire their blood to battle. These Gypsy children of the Café Ostend in their blue suits had already the long hair of the fire-eater or the snake-charmer. An extended description of this extraordinary musical experience was to open the book. Music may have a hundred qualities ; but if wild excitement and fieriness be one, then the god of music, under whatever name — and I would have him in the train of Bacchus invading India, teaching music to the Indians — was, nightly, in the Café Ostend. I have heard other Gypsy orchestras, but none to equal this.

There is no architecture in Hungary to make the hard bones of the book. It would have, therefore, to be of a different construction from a book on Spain. And there is little or no history. It would be all actuality, and the living figures that move before our eyes. But the excitement need never drop in violence and intensity from that moment when we come in through the doors of the Café Ostend and hear the Tzigane band playing. None the less, it would have been a work of much difficulty to prepare and write. There are no palaces, churches, picture galleries, but, instead, museums of folklore and ethnology. It would be, above all, music, costume, landscape. Probably two summers would have to be spent in travelling in Hungary. But I believe it to be possible to produce an effect of greater brilliance in a work of this nature than can be attained in any drawing or painting, or in any art but that of music, and I know myself to be perfectly capable of achieving it. But that time is gone for ever and will never come again. In one respect alone it would have been keyed up seven times in strength and brilliance from the original, for the costumes are only worn on Sundays and feast days, but this is no more exaggerated a picture of the truth than it is to write of Italy as though it consisted of nothing else than works of art, or begin a book on Spain with an account of the Feria of Seville, which lasts for three days only, and does not come again until next year. The subject of the book I had in mind was, in part, the wonderful costumes worn by the country people ; and these, with the music and the landscape, would need preparing and treating in order to become a literary work of art.

They are villages not known or mentioned in the guide-books ; and we will begin at a village where the women wear a contrivance of little metal plates upon the heels of their red top-boots to make a clinking noise as they walk or dance.[1] This device, which is almost too good to be true for a village where they dance the csárdás upon summer evenings, is found nowhere else in the world except upon the stage. Only a few miles to the north we are in the land of the peasant ballerinas, though not at the apogee of that, which we shall come to in a moment, but already at Kalocsa they wear seven or eight starched skirts, one above another, and all of different colours. Probably the peasant ballerinas of the Mátra mountains are the supreme invention of the Magyars. When the population of certain villages comes out of church upon a Sunday morning it is as though the doors of the opera house are opened and the corps de ballet, in costume, is walking through the streets. They are wearing ballet skirts, to knee length, the skirts being round as a bell and tightly pleated. The top skirt may be bright scarlet, as red as a geranium, or gentian blue. If it be red, the border will be green or white or blue. If blue, the red geranium will edge the gentian. Bright silk ribbons woven with flowers, and made at one time in Lyon especially for these villages, to the point that ' Lyon ' is their synonym for silk, are fastened round their waists so that the long ends hang down, close together, over the backs of their ballet skirts, and down to the parti-coloured rims. Their fronts are white frills or aprons, white bodices ; or black, as the case may be. No headdresses, but hair worn in long plaits or ringlets. In this particular village no two dresses are alike. In another village the colours are uniform, as though to the orders of a stage manager, and the difference is in the detail.

[1] Erzekcsanád.

G

This is at Kazár, near the Slovakian border. Here they wear white-frilled sleeves, white aprons of heavy open lace, like a bedspread or counterpane worked with colours, and crowns of embroidery and gold and silver paste, with the same flowered silk ribbons hanging from them. Probably the silk ribbons are the secret to the mystery. It seems unlikely that travellers with samples of silk from Lyon can have reached to these villages (though they are less than two hundred miles from Vienna) until the building of the railways. Peasant costumes, in general, are of later origin than would be suspected. It is not impossible that the peasant ballerinas of Kazár and Buják owe their invention directly to the seasons of Taglioni, Elssler, and Cerito in the opera house at Vienna. At Buják the stage illusion is complete and entire. The ballet skirt may be rose pink, closely ribbed, and with concentric rings of white ; with a band of green near the brim, then rose pink again, then white, then black with blue divisions and flowers in red and green ; more white, and then a rose pink edging. The bodice is of elaborate fantasy as in a costume portrait by Marc Gheeraerts or Cornelius Janssen, as fanciful as that, with arched and frilled shoulders, the frills continuing to the waist where they are gathered so that the ends spread out upon the bustle, so stiff and starched that they keep in position, and look from the back like a ruff, bent into the form of a figure eight, with the lower end left open. Two long flowered Lyon silk ribbons from her waist trail down upon this. And the ballerina has a broader, red-flowered ribbon tied at the back of her headdress and trailing down upon her neck.

But the theme enlarges upon itself and leaves the confines and frontiers. Hungary is but a part of it. Having seen the Romanian Gypsies, I can conceive of a painter or a writer content to spend his life in watching them. They are the negation of the peacock peasants. All they require is the round felt hat of the Romanians, and the long shirt worn outside the trousers. That, and a heavy belt of brass and leather. They need no more. They have their long hair that reaches to their shoulders. I saw the Laetzi at the horse fairs, walking in wonderful insolence ; better still, galloping upon their shaggy ponies. And the Calderarii (tinkers) ; some of them, who are stolen children, with blond hair to their shoulders. All actors, improvisers, masters of opportunity ; liars and thieves, who have the look of Old Testament prophets fallen from grace, or shepherd kings who have been spirited away from their Kingdom, and come back 'changed'. Their walk, only, could inspire a race of actors ; or the deep guttural voice that they affect. The blond ones were probably kidnapped from the Saxons, who have been here, in Transylvania, since the twelfth century, two hundred years longer than the Gypsies. In the villages round Sibiu (Hermannstadt) the Saxons may be seen upon Sundays ; the men in high fur hats and long embroidered coats, the unmarried girls in wide aprons and wearing tall round stovepipe hats of black. It is curious to think that the fairhaired Saxons for hundreds of years were vassals of the Turks, for they are as fair as Danes or Frisians ; but the black stovepipe hats may be of very early origin indeed, for they look like a belated echo of the hats worn by Court ladies of Constantinople under the Comneni Emperors who were reigning at the time (1141–61) that the Saxon settlers were invited into the Siebenbürgen by the Transylvanian princes. Thus may Byzantine court ladies have appeared as they walked at the foot of the Porphyra, a tower built in the form of a pyramid, in the gardens along the Bosphorus.

The huge, never-ending land of Cockaigne lies in every direction along the plain and into the mountains. I saw it at Rucar, upon the Wallachian side of the mountains, famous for its costumes, none alike, all worked with gold thread so that there is the glitter of tinsel in the bold patterns of the flowers, but the men in their long white shirts worn outside their trousers, and wide belts, are the counterpart of the Wallachians winding their way as captives around Trajan's Column. I met it again in Moldavia and in the Bucovina, where we passed a solitary village inhabited, no one knew why, by Hungarians, many miles away from any other Magyar population, and came, next, to a village of Ukrainians or Ruthenians, into another world altogether, for the men wore feathered hats, white breeches, and high black boots, while the women's dresses were embroidered with flower designs in glass beads and sequins. The old farmers, with their round black hats, great moustaches, and long hair reaching to their shoulders, were Poles in type and feature.

I saw it again at Łowicz, in the Polish plain, where the women walk to church from the neighbouring villages, barefoot, carrying their boots, and dressed in skirts of rainbow colours and necklaces of amber from the Baltic. The skirts are striped like the Swiss Guard, but in more violent colours, rose pink, much pink and yellow, and various blues and greens, of different colours according to their villages, but the stripes are vertical, and run from top to bottom, the women wear flowered ribbons, and, in fact, their costumes are said to be inspired by the uniforms of the Papal Guard. I have seen the mountaineers of Zakopane, in white, with eagles' feathers ; but not the Huculs, a race of Ruthenian farmers, usually upon horseback, living in the far corner of Poland and in Czechoslovakia (Sub-Carpathian Russia, now Russian territory), aquiline in type, unlike the flat-faced Slavs, who wear embroidered sheepskin jackets, while the women's aprons are horizontally striped in red and orange yellow. Red is predominant in the Hucul costume.

We come to cabins with roofs of thin slats of wood and may meet in the mountain pastures, in that thin, clear air, persons who belong to the century of tapestries ; farmers, walking stick in hand, with short fur-trimmed coats embroidered, back and front, like a herald's tabard ; hats, with the eagle's feather ; white sleeves, and the nobleman's white breeches. This is in the High Tatra, coming down from Poland into Slovakia, and it is Polish dress, to be known immediately by all who have seen the Polish dresses in the tapestries in the Uffizi. So is that of the boatmen in homespun white wool breeches, blue waistcoats, much embroidered, and black felt hats, among the floating logs along the river. At Čičmany, a mountain village, where the wooden cabins are painted, almost as if tattooed, with white designs, we shall find the inhabitants in white accordeon-pleated skirts, white aprons, and white folded headdresses like winged turbans, all worked with red. This is among the pine woods. But lower down, in the high tableland ringed with mountains, in Moravia, the country is cultivated in mediaeval fashion in long thin strips, like a striped quilt, and it is here that we enter another Arcadia of the farmer and rich peasant. It is the equal in this respect of Hungary and of Transylvania, a land of Cockaigne which would need several summers to explore, starting from the field of Austerlitz (Slavkov) and continuing for three hundred miles and more through Moravia, Slovakia, Sub-Carpathian Russia to the Romanian frontier, and I would have made this the other leaf of a huge triptych for which I have been making notes for many years.[1]

Scarlet handkerchiefs folded in so many manners for women's headdresses that a local painter (Úprka) devoted a whole volume to the different ways of wearing them ; this is round Uherský Brod in Moravia ; but among the scarlet handkerchiefs we must be content with green flowered dresses, flowered in white upon green, a pair of dyed red ostrich plumes, worn behind the shoulders like embryonic wings, and the extraordinary concertina sleeves of a particular locality ; lace cuffs, with a band of embroidery around the elbow, and then pleated in a hundred pleats nearly to the shoulder, where they reach to their greatest circumference, are wired like a crinoline, and pleat back again to join the bodice. These sleeves (of Blatnice, of Ostrožská Nová Ves), worn in some villages with a scarlet skirt and always with the scarlet handkerchief, are of an elaboration comparable to that in Elizabethan or early Jacobean portraits. And we end at Šardice, a few miles away, among another race of peasant ballerinas ; a dazzling chorus, in flower-embroidered stockings, pierced boots, puffed sleeves, and cherry-coloured handkerchiefs. It is nearly impossible to put into words the effect of four or five of these women talking together, in their black short ballet skirts, the backs of their flowered handkerchiefs falling down upon their necks, their bright ribbons, pleated sleeves, and the indescribable brilliance of their bodices and aprons ; cherry-coloured with yellow ribbons ; crimson with thin vertical strips of yellow flowers ; or bright scarlet with a

[1] Portions of, or studies for, this work are to be found in *Primitive Scenes and Festivals, Splendours and Miseries, The Hunters and the Hunted*, and others of my books, and I have attempted in this last essay of it (for it cannot, now, be written) to avoid repetition of what has already been printed by writing of other villages and localities than those already mentioned by me.

pattern of white flowers upon the scarlet. Ballerinas in cherry, crimson, scarlet ballet skirts; but, with that, the land of Cockaigne must fade away. In a few years more the Arcadia of the peasants, their dresses, their music and their folklore, will be gone for ever. The vast and lovely theme goes down and dies away.

V

Fantasia upon Things Remembered

I

I T is written, somewhere, of Johann Sebastian Bach that when he sat down to his instrument (the clavichord) he would begin by playing the music of some other composer, as though it was necessary for him to inhabit the thoughts of someone else before he could move, freely and at large, in the world of his own creation, and with so awe-inspiring and fearful a figure to cast his giant shadow before me I am less nervous than I would otherwise have been in adopting this same method for my own preluding. So I sit down at my table, and take up my pen to write, and there is the terrible sensation that between this moment and the days when I was young there has been time enough for a great artist, a Keats, a Schubert, a Mozart, to be born, and live, and die. A long period, more than a third of a century, and it is borne in upon me, in horror, how little I have accomplished. I was young then, and I am not old yet ; but it is a new world again after just another war, and I am old enough to have lived and written books in the new world after the war before.

And now the disintegration, the dissolving of the spectrum, the bursting of the rainbow, only to reassemble in newer, brighter colours, in the light of a new life, a reconsecration resolved and determined in the same year of age, and the appropriateness of which, with concern both to the abiding interests and passions of that life and to the purpose and purport of the present pages, will be apparent, in all humility, when we know that the overture, *Die Weihe des Hauses* (*Dedication of the House*) Op. 124, was intended by Beethoven as homage to Handel, and so, with " beautiful perception ", it was written for the theatre, while Beethoven, at the same time (1822), planned a companion overture on the name of Bach, which he sketched, but never completed. The overture for Handel was written for the theatre, the one for Bach designed for the concert room.

So the figure, or term, of music is of double and multiple appearances. There are musicians trained to the air and climate of the opera house, and the contrapuntists of the organ loft. But the scales are not evenly balanced ; and, for an instance, the most famous of all piano virtuosi suffered all through his career, and even took the extreme step of retiring from the public platform and never again playing for money, but by no stratagem could he live down his early notoriety as a performer, and to the end of a long life the public tried to hear him play but would not listen to his own music. And the public was right, within the strict limits of its understanding, because many of his compositions were those merely of a virtuoso, and at the same time wrong, because the extraordinary, dual aspects of Liszt's nature made it that he wrote, also, music that was far in advance of his time and that, even now, is neither known nor appreciated. By the same token, Mozart never recovered in public estimation from having been a prodigy. The little boy who played to the French Court of Versailles was buried in a pauper's grave in Vienna.[1] These are truths that apply, not to music only, but to all the arts,

---

[1] Mozart and his sister were invited to attend the supper of Louis XV at Versailles on 1 January 1764, and play to the French Court. Mozart was not yet eight years old.

and to all living persons. What deeper contrast could there be than between the life of a writer, day after day, year after year, at his desk, and the careers of artists of another sort, who thrive and prosper on applause ? There is no physical reaction in the life of a writer ; there is mental, not physical fatigue, and no tiring of the muscles. It is a sedentary life, with few of the excitements of success and all the drags of failure. It is a life of solitude ; how different from a career in the theatre or in the concert room ! The book he is working upon, all the books he has written, or can ever write, roll back upon him like the stone of Sisyphus. The theatre or the concert room is, in comparison, an Aladdin's cave. Yet you have only to read the lives or letters of virtuosi to know how much they suffer from the monotony of public performance ; and there have been such who would have given up every success they had in their lives to be able to write music.

There are writers (and I am of the sort) to whom their writing-rooms become something after the nature of the study or alchemist's den of Doctor Faustus. It is not at all surprising to me to read that Busoni, that greatest of pianists whom I have heard in my lifetime, when composing his opera *Die Brautwahl* after the story by Hoffmann, should have wanted Leonhardt, " a mysterious character who had apparently lived for several centuries and was possessed of magical powers ", to " look like Liszt at the age of fifty ". I was there, at the Queen's Hall, in June 1920, when Busoni conducted his *Brautwahl* suite and Liszt's *Faust Symphony* ; and I remember how badly Busoni, perhaps hardly inferior to Liszt as a pianist and his superior in musical intelligence, conducted the *Faust Symphony*, one of the greatest works of the entire Romantic movement in all the arts, and how disappointed I was, at twenty-two years old, with Busoni's *Brautwahl* suite. On the other hand, what a marvellous performer of Liszt's B minor sonata, and what an executant even of Liszt's arrangement of the *Flower Waltz* from Gounod's *Faust* ! Another contradiction ! His concerts at the Wigmore Hall were sold out, but when Busoni gave a recital for two pianofortes with his pupil Egon Petri there were many empty seats. It is well known that the inclusion of a single unfamiliar work in a concert programme, even if it be another of Tchaikowsky's four pianoforte concerti and not the eternal B flat minor, may mean a half-empty hall. Such contradictions are a commonplace in the career of every musician, every artist, every writer. When I was young, and published a book of short poems, I was told by the critics of the two leading literary papers that I must write long poems. I took the advice, and spent most of two years in writing longer poems, only to be told by the same critics, on publication, that I must write short poems and not long ones.

The long, long periods of inaction — a whole winter, two whole winters, may be but part of it — during which a book is written are very trying to the nerves. The growth is so gradual. A book can be an agony to begin, hard to sustain, and difficult to finish. Not so a poem. A poem exists in a mood of its own, and needs no more than two or three days in execution. You have not to remain in the same mood or frame of mind for a month on end. Poetry is a more plastic art than prose ; an art which more easily takes shape and kindles fire. Allowing for my time of childhood, it is my calculation that I have spent a sixth part of my life at my writing-table. This is equivalent to some five years of days and nights, a short time, according to some measurements of years, and yet a long one. However old I live to be I cannot hope to pass another five years in this manner. Long before that, I would have reached senility ! I have imprisoned myself in my cell for an aeon, and for no time at all. I feel like one of the lamas of Tibet who suffer themselves to be ' buried alive ' in the darkness ; and in the same breath, I have passed but a moment or two in a blinding light which is as eternal as the light of the sun. I have been held up and delayed for months, unable to proceed ; and I have found it as easy as getting the right number on the telephone. But, whether it is difficult, or whether it is easy, it is only by hours of work that it is possible to accomplish anything at all ; and for myself, unless I have spent my usual hours working in the morning it is very doubtful whether I can achieve anything at all in the afternoon or evening. I think you have to live and sleep with your work ; and that, I suppose, is the reason why it is necessary, in my case, to spend those hours in my room, whether I manage to work or not, in order to be able to accomplish something later in the day. I often lie down and sleep for a few moments ; and go on. I find that Tchaikowsky says in one of his letters that it is necessary to live with your work like a cobbler who spends his whole day in his workshop. " Inspiration ", he says, " is a guest who does not care to visit the indolent . . . those who imagine that a creative artist can — through the medium of his art — express his feelings at the moment when he is *moved*, make the greatest mistake. Without any special reason for rejoicing, I may be moved by the most cheerful creative mood, and vice versa, a work composed under the happiest surroundings may be touched with dark and gloomy colours. In a word, an artist lives a double life : an everyday human life, and an artistic life, and the two do not always go hand in hand." [1]

[1] *Tchaikowsky*, by Mrs. Rosa Newmarch : London, 1908, pp. 341-2.

I have found, for my part, that often two or three years have to elapse after some incident or experience has happened to one before it is possible to write of it. As against this, a personality can fix itself in the memory in a moment, so long as one has but an objective interest in the person. I am able, for instance, to remember every character in the fullest detail from a revue *Der schwarze Diamant* that I saw at Würzburg in 1932, because the personalities were of so haunting a nature, in themselves, and in whom they portrayed, being attempts on the part of a provincial German touring company to reproduce what they conceived to be refinement and elegance of a worldly or *mondain* sort, as of persons who spent their lives in international café society, played heavy-handed, being Germans, and in the knowledge that they could barely pay their expenses and must be half-starving. After the performance was over, which took place on a stage in a large café and dance hall, the company came down and joined the audience, and we could watch them sitting at tables, talking, or on the dance floor. I can lie awake in the middle of the night, now, eighteen years after I saw them for that one performance, and count ten or twelve of the characters and recall the fantasies I built around them. The Germans, particularly the Southern Germans and Austrians, have a long tradition in acting comedy; their ' intelligence ' in comedy is not inferior to that of the Paris or the London stage. You had the dregs, the relics of that, in this revue ; while, at the moment in history of which I am speaking, before the Nazi persecutions had begun, German-Jewish popular composers were writing tunes that had an imprint and a character of their own, but were in the American idiom. No one who has heard them could forget the sound of those German jazz-tunes, and the inclination of the line of the music and the sound of the words to pretend to

themselves that they were Parisian (Paris is always a mania
with the Germans, and although, for the purposes of a revue
of this sort, they may have to make out that they are American,
they would always, really, sooner be Parisian). I do not
suppose one single individual of that company is alive to-day.
They were doomed, when I saw them. They bore that mark
upon them ; though it seemed, then, that they must perish of
themselves. They had the look of the waiters in the hotel in
Würzburg when I first went there in 1922, at the time when
the mark was sliding, when it was beginning to collapse.
Those waiters wore old field-grey tunics from the first world
war, and I have never known anything to equal the grey, food-
less depression of the hotel. When, at last, we could stand it
no longer and had our luggage piled onto a cab and drove off
to the light and warmth of the Russischer Hof, they stood
round, but did not show resentment or surprise. They knew
what was coming to them. And the next morning our letters
were forwarded though we left no address. It is in the same
spirit that a scorpion on the wall stands still and waits for you
to kill it. It does not try to run away.

I remember that crowd of doomed persons, and can still
think of them and go from one another while I lie awake, and
I have the faculty of being able to remember almost every
piece of music I have ever heard, in the middle of the night,
tunes I have heard played once only in the theatre or the concert hall. Sometimes I can get the shape and the meaning of
them, but not the exact notes, so that it is like the ghost of a
tune, and then, or a little later, the real tune comes back. It
is in the middle of the night that you think you can interpret
music ; and it is in the middle of the night, in the trance before
you fall asleep, while you are yet lingering on its borders,
that, as I say in the beginning of this book, your mind

forms sentences you cannot understand, and that I believe the astrologer Nostradamus composed his prophecies. Trivialities very distant from him, though some of them of tremendous import. How else is it possible to explain how Nostradamus can have ' got ', there is no other word for it, not only the unlikely name of the village, near Varennes, which never before, or since, has come into history, where Louis XVI was arrested on his attempted escape, but even the name of the man, Drouet, postmaster of St.-Menehould, who recognized and gave him up, the whole quatrain with its mysterious refrain of a king escaping through a wood, at night, ending with the word ' chop ', which can only refer to the blade of the guillotine dropping in its groove ?

I think that the prophecies of Nostradamus came easily and were written without effort, being for the most part meaningless or with a meaning that only applies to the dream state and that has no application to the world of common sense, but occasionally, just now and then, of a devastating directness, as it were, hitting straight between the eyes. At other times, his subconscious seems to have been wandering in a world or demi-world that is not yet mapped or understood. Those who have read the writings of J. W. Dunne on the subject of prophetic dreams will find the origin of the prophecies of Nostradamus no longer so mysterious if we accept that he was a person of much intelligence, and predisposed in an occult direction, who set out, deliberately, to cultivate his gift. Nostradamus had the advantage, too, more difficult of achievement in our time, that he could surround himself with all the appurtenance and abracadabra of magical association, and this without drawing ridicule to himself. The semi-trance was not his occasional and inexplicable visitant, but a habit of mind of constant and continual invitation, nightly expected, and waited and attended upon hand and foot ; after long habit probably as swift and easy of inducement as the eye exercises done by shortsighted persons to improve their vision, which consist of no more than the mere lighting of a candle, and the change of focus from the candle flame to the index finger held in front of it, and back again, by which time his subconscious would be beginning to spout forth its rhymes, Sibylline utterances, for the most part, of little or no importance, but then, as Mr. Dunne points out, that is their way. Even so, the most trivial of truths, the merest details that identify, can be more convincing than the larger evidence that might fit two or more cases and confuse the lot.

If the working life of an actor, a musician, a painter, be the elaboration of a fantasy, the sustaining of a fiction, this is no less true of a writer during the long months and years spent in his working-room. His interior life is more fully peopled than the world of every day, and with scenes and persons that may have a deeper reality. It is not without considerable personal experience of its glories and vicissitudes that I have compared it to the laboratory or alchemist's den of Doctor Faustus. This is the more convincingly true where a writer has worked year after year in the same room. The study of Flaubert must be haunted by him ; or else his ghost has fled. But the bedrooms in cheap hotels where Baudelaire lived in order to escape his creditors ; the workman's flat tenanted by Madame Verlaine where Rimbaud was unwelcome visitor, and wonder child ; or the cheap lodgings off Tottenham Court Road where Rimbaud and Verlaine lived in London and where Rimbaud must have written many of *Les Illuminations* ; the taverns and thieves' kitchens of Villon ; these are the travelling caravans of genius. They are fierer of associa-

tion than the anchorite's cell of Croisset. The dread persist-
ence of Flaubert in searching for *le mot juste* ; his disgust and
disillusionment with nineteenth-century life ; the compilation
of his *sottisier* or anthology of human stupidity and misunder-
standing, leading to the composition of *Bouvard et Pécuchet*,
where his two bourgeois heroes embark upon every branch
of scientific knowledge, one subject after another, only to be
dazed and confused by too much reading, and too many
conflicting opinions ; the fact that all that vast accumulation
of authority, for Flaubert formed a scientific library for the
purpose, is itself, by now, completely obsolete and out of
date, an anticipation which may have delighted Flaubert's
sardonic sense of humour, and even been the culmination and
end of the book which he never lived to finish ; so many
considerations, we may like to think, have worked themselves
in and out of the walls of his study until there is nothing of
his personality left, and his ghost has gone. Out of it all, in
spite of *Salammbô*, in spite of *Madame Bovary*, there came no
work of art to equal the poems written by Baudelaire in dingy
hotel bedrooms beyond numbering, where he installed himself with a heap of books, a few clothes, and his fresh linen —
relic of his days of dandyism.

What doest his mean, in *Mon Cœur mis à nu*, under date
23 janvier 1862 : " Aujourd'hui, j'ai subi un singulier avertisse-
ment, j'ai senti passer sur mon front le vent de l'aile de
l'imbécilité " ? By what ghosts must Baudelaire not have been
visited in his room at Brussels, whither he had fled from
Paris, and it was growing late for him to write ? Last night,
and two nights before that, I have had dreams that were so
horrible, and haunting, that it is better not to think of them,
though it is certain that they must have a meaning. All day
long, and still this evening, I can hear the iron footsteps ;

but it went on four feet, not two, it was four-footed when it walked. The horror of the dream, that clanking apart, which was like some kind of engine lifting its feet and putting them down, was that it was a human being, mutilated and degraded, not only that, but a being of intelligence, and in the comic vein which comes into all nightmares, a baronet (!), brought to me by a friend who is dead, and whom I knew to be dead even in my dream, but the *magister*, the grand master of all evil. The dread creature leaned on a bed to talk to me, throwing himself on the bed so that I thought he must have hurt his stumps of legs, and slipping off the bed nearly to the floor, only saved in time ; about sixty years old, having led a life, I knew that, of ferocious dissipation ;[1] and the next thing I remember is the sound of his iron feet and hands, walking on all fours, up Berkeley Street, on the left-hand side, going towards Piccadilly, nearly outside the restaurant or night club, The Gay Nineties, and the dream ended. Now, the next morning as I begin to write, and this is my first sentence looking out onto an iron frost of January, the memory fades and I have nearly forgotten it. But I am a person of a singular imagination, and why should it come to me when there are so many other things I would sooner think of ?

> Par instants brille, et s'allonge et s'étale,
> Un spectre fait de grâce et de splendeur.
>
> Quand il atteint sa totale grandeur,
> Je reconnais ma belle visiteuse,

as in the Musée Carnavalet, upon that rainy afternoon, though the vision was nearly spoilt for me by the horrible little painting in another room of the severed head of Fieschi, who attempted the life of Louis-Philippe with an infernal machine, a head

---

[1] This dread individual in my dream bore a marked facial resemblance to the figure in Beardsley's drawing called *Et in Arcadia Ego*.

with the blood drained completely out of it by the knife of the guillotine, but still bloodstained, with some kind of a dent or old wound — from the wars of Napoleon ? — in its forehead, and the inscription below it : " La Tête de Fieschi, le lendemain de son supplice ".[1] Could this experience of the head of Fieschi have no ghostly or spiritual connexion with the dream I had, a long time ago, where I cut off the head of someone I loved, and held up her head by its golden hair, and while I looked at it in horror it turned into the head of a ' coloured ' American actress and singer of a generation ago, the forerunner of Florence Mills and Josephine Baker ? Only long afterwards did I discover that this ' coloured ' woman had, in the end, married the great-uncle of the person in my dream. This is a coincidence of so extraordinary an improbability that it is nearly impossible not to believe there must be some purpose behind the ' turning up ' of so contingent and appropriate a pair of numbers. Do the same ghosts, I speak but of daydreams, come to visit one as in youth ? That I will not know till I am older, for they are not yet old enough of their substance for me to note the change. I only see a little alteration of fashion, a little difference in manners. Could there be anything sadder than the pictures in the newspapers of a dinner party of old stage favourites ? How can they bear to be seen together ; the gayer and sillier, once, the more tragic, now ? It is the sadness of the schoolboy going back to school, who cannot stand the parting with his mother upon the last night at home, and if his miserable feeling be probed down to its depths it is that what he really fears is to find his mother looking older when he returns, which is what must happen, inevitably, one day, though that may lie so long a

---

[1] I have since discovered that Fieschi was injured by explosion of his own infernal machine.

way ahead that it is, in itself, frightening to think of. I speak for myself. Those were my feelings. And by the time it happens you are not the same person ; and neither is the person whom you loved. You are both changed. You are grown up and become a man, no more a child ; while an old woman, in comparison with the young woman whom you remember, is like the seashell with its lovely inhabitant that moved on the sea bed, that like the nautilus put up a little sail, or lay uncovered on the golden sands, compared with the same seashell in a cupboard, or upon a window ledge. Its lovely inhabitant has gone : its youth is fled.

I have described how, often, a considerable period of time has to elapse after some experience or incident, and that it is not possible to write of it immediately. This seems to be in degree or ratio to the interest. An objective interest, I have said, can leave an instantaneous memory, and in tremendous detail. I have spent much of my life writing of works of art, and I have seldom had to make a single note. I travelled in Romania and in Morocco for the particular purpose of writing books upon those countries, and I never kept a diary, or wrote down anything at all to help my memory. Those were books, for neither country concerned has much in the way of works of art, dealing more especially with landscape, and personalities and incidents of travel. I was only in Romania for three weeks, and had to make the best use of the opportunity. There were the Saxon towns of Transylvania to describe (*vide* p. 93), and the goose plain, and the Gypsies. Those, above all. Indeed, the picturesque interest of Romania is the Gypsies. I wrote, as well as I could, of the long-haired Laetzi at the horse fairs. In Bucharest, I wanted to write of the popular music in the cafés, and of the Skapetz (eunuch) cabmen. In old houses there were the portraits of Boyar ancestors in their Turkish and Byzantine headdresses, and there were the El Grecos belonging to King Carol. I described the tea party at Galatz in the house of Pedracchi, the giant cabman, in the street of the Skoptzi, giving as much as I could ascertain of the history of the peculiar Russian sect to which he belonged ; and I wrote of the monks of Petropavlovsk at Vâlcov in the Danube Delta, among the Lippovans, the most extreme specimens of the monastic life that can exist anywhere in the modern world to-day. I wrote of the convents of Hurez and Cozia, and the painted churches of the Bucovina, unique of their kind, for the exteriors are frescoed, and in the case of Voroneţ an inordinate amount of powdered lapis lazuli was employed upon the painting of the Tree of Jesse.

In Morocco it was another matter. To open, there was the Djemaa el Fna, the market-place of Marrakesh, and its sights and sounds ; the long-haired snake-charmers and fire-eaters who have come up from the Sous ; the Chleuh dancing-boys, with painted eyelids and downcast looks through their long eyelashes, wearing sashes and long surplices ; the blind beggars coming towards you, like the beggars of Hieronymus Bosch and Brueghel, in the traditional manner, with a hand upon each other's shoulder ; and the women bakers or breadsellers sitting in a row on the ground, with veiled faces, the ' merry wives ' of Baghdad and of Arabian legend. I wrote of the Sheikhat dancers, Berbers from Tiznit or Goulimine, down in the South, in long black, stiff gowns, many silver bangles, and white coifs, with the air of snake goddesses and priestesses, votaries of Astarte, and sacred prostitutes of the Phœnicians ; one of them, named Barakha, of another type altogether, for she resembled a Liotard pastel, and recalled the ' capresses ' of Martinique in the French West Indies, being among the most beautiful women I have ever seen. In her silken robe and white turban, standing, lute or guitar in hand, or sitting crosslegged on a divan, this dancer with her beauty and subtlety of movement would be a sensation among dancers in any land.

I wrote of the Kasbahs of Atlas and Anti-Atlas, mud castles and fortresses of the Berbers, identical with those of the Hadhramaut in Southern Arabia. I tried to depict the melancholy of Fez, and its *medersas* ; their cedar beams, *zellijes* or *azulejos*, and arches of stalactite and filigree. I wrote of the watersellers of Marrakesh, a ferocious crew, carrying their goatskins or pigskins, and clashing together their brightly polished brass cups and bells ; and of the Jewess laundresses of Sefrou, a scene like a witches' Sabbath taking place in a gully of mist and spray, with the Jewesses in little round hats or *tambours*, as though in parody of the fashions of the Second Empire. I crossed the Sahara from Casablanca to Tripoli and wrote of the negro towns of Adrar and Timimoun, outposts of the great Sudan, built in Sudanese style of red mud, and stuck or garnished with wooden ribs for decoration. The fascination of these negro towns was in the combing and plaiting of the young negresses' hair, stiffened after a variety of styles until it became as formal of shape as the wig of Pharaoh's wife ; and in their cotton dresses, long, full gowns down to the silver bracelets on their ankles, and of the brightest colours, white with round red spots, green or blue, or yellow with a design of red, cheap cottons from Japan, all of them, in place of those they had woven for themselves until five or six years before, but of startling and bewildering beauty. It was on the sand track between Adrar and Timimoun that a crowded omnibus came by, heading South, and with its destination in big letters, Timbuktu. After the lively negro towns the Algerian oases were dull and quiet with their white-clad inhabitants, until you come to the Ouled Naïl, sitting in the sunlight on the doorsteps of their houses, dressed in the brightest colours, and wearing necklaces of golden coins. They pour out of their dens at sight of a stranger, and walk like Gypsies and have tawny skins. Soon we reach the ruins of Roman cities, Timgad and Tebessa, and cross into Tunisia. Not many days' journey further on we are in Libya and come to a great theatre by the blue Mediterranean. It is the Greek amphitheatre of Sabratha, rising out of the rocks of the sea-shore, only a foot or two above the waves, a prelude to the ruins of Leptis Magna which had drawn us across the sands of the Sahara, all the way from Casablanca.

It had not been necessary to make notes upon any of these subjects, and they wrote up, easily, on my return. Books upon The Netherlands and upon Spain were no more difficult, and I even felt more at home with them because they dealt specifically with architecture and the attendant arts, painting and sculpture, and because I found the absence of landscape in the one country, and its eternal presence in the other, so great a stimulus to writing, and sought to enliven the monotony of the one with its costumes which are the most distinctive and peculiar in Europe, while the bare bones of the other clothe themselves naturally, the yellow plain is a cornland, the red soil is a vineyard, and the writer upon Spain has to tone down his colours, or they will be too strong for him. All through my life as a writer I have tried continually to go to Mexico and to South America, but have not succeeded, although I believe that the essay on Mexican landscape and architecture in *Southern Baroque Art* is the best description and interpretation of Mexico that has appeared in our language. I have also written of the modern buildings of Río de Janeiro designed by Viennese and Brazilian architects of the school of Le Corbusier, and making use of a particular invention, the *brise-soleil* or *quebrasol*, that filters the tropical light and cools the air, while the hard, uncompromising lines of modern building, which chill and repel in England, are relaxed and softened in the climate of Brazil. For their interiors, they are able to make use of the tropical woods for which Brazil is famous, many of which have never been employed before upon such a scale, and the Brazilians have also gardens bedded out with cannas, caladiums, and many other tropical plants, chiefly known in Europe in the stovehouse. One of their architects has begun hybridization upon a great scale, and keeps a card index of hundreds of varieties that he has raised. Anybody who has seen a blue jacaranda tree in flower will want to know of what the flora of Brazil is capable when cross-fertilized by human hands. I wrote, at the same time, of the old mining towns of Minas Geraes, and of El Aleijadinho, the crippled mulatto worn down with leprosy and syphilis, who carved the statues and built the churches of Ouro Preto. The tawdry churches of Bahia, with ornaments like gilt and coloured paper, and the music and dancing of its negro fishing quarter are part also of the Brazilian theme.[1] But it is not likely, alas ! that I will go to Brazil ; though many is the time that I have examined, in anticipation, the coloured lithographs of Debret, a pupil of David who was summoned to Rio by the Emperor Dom Pedro I, and in whose pages you may see the *hidalgos* of Portugal carried through the streets in litters and sedan-chairs, scenes in the market, and all the stir and bustle of the negro town. Other books, too : the travels of Prince Maximilian Wied ; and two volumes giving coloured plates

[1] Cf. *The Brazilian Style*, by the present writer, in the special *Brazil* number of *The Architectural Review*, for March 1944, where the baroque and modern styles of Brazil are fully discussed.

of every variety of Brazilian palm tree (I have lost the name of the author), a work of exactitude as complete and extraordinary of ramification as the fringed and tasselled fir bracts of Lambert's *Pinetum Woburnensis*.

But yet another Spanish-American project presented itself with a deeper degree of probability, for it was suggested in 1947–48 that I should write a book, at official invitation, upon Peru. I would have seen Lima, the most beautiful Spanish city of Latin America, with its churches, the palace of Torre Tagle with its ' pantomime ' doorway and huge wooden-covered balconies or window-boxes of Mudéjar workmanship, as Oriental as the pierced balconies of Damascus and Grand Cairo, and the villa and garden belonging to the actress La Périchole (La Perricholi), who was mistress of the Spanish Viceroy. I was shown drawings of the *tapadas*, veiled ladies of Lima, half-caste women wrapped from head to foot in long cloaks or mantles that left only one eye visible ; but their cloaks instead of being black like nuns', or white like those worn by the women in Morocco, were of the brightest colours and gave life and animation to the streets of Lima. I would have written of the Inca and Pre-Inca textiles and golden objects in the museum. This is the most interesting collection of antiquities in the American continent ; excavation in Peru has hardly begun but the treasures are, already, of incalculable aesthetic interest and value. The churches of Cuzco put that city on a par with Salamanca or Santiago de Compostela. Their style is ' delayed ' High Renaissance ; for the extreme fantasies of the Churrigueresque, carried to its furthest limits in Mexico, and which form the Mexican idiom in architecture, do not occur in Peru. The Spanish background is that of late sixteenth- and early seventeenth-century Spain protracted through another century, and continuing into the present.

To this are added the Andean landscape and the Indian costumes. The Mexicans wear huge hats with rolled brims and the white clothes of Pulcinella among the cactuses and prickly pears, against the towering and massing clouds of the Mexican empyrean. It is only in Guatemala that the Indians wear *huipiles* woven in bright colours (*vide* pp. 59, 60). In this respect Guatemala is an unspoilt Mexico, without the architecture, for the Mexican fantasy and golden vulgarity are lacking. The ruined churches of Antigua had never the glitter of those of Mexico. But Peru has a landscape less smiling than that of Mexico, more dramatic and threatening, churches of a more austere taste, and in comparison with the Guatemalan, Indian costumes that are yet more fanciful and beautiful. The Peruvians have an innate invention and originality in colour, whether it be in their blue-painted chairs and tables of a light 'Colonial' Rococo, 'à la Périchole', or in the coloured cloaks of the *tapadas*. It must not be forgotten that Gauguin was partly Peruvian, with Indian blood, and that his colour invention was part of his patrimony. He was a painter, not of Mediterranean but of Pacific origin, and his daring genius came to him from Peru.[1] There is a huge repertory of colour discords and harmonies to be learnt from the Peruvian Indians, even if it only begins in the knowledge that the 'shocking pink' of Schiaparelli, one of the 'colour breaks' of contemporary fashion, was taken from their dresses.

A whole arcana of curious facts and details concerning Peru can be collected and compiled ; the race of donkeys with four nostrils (instead of two !) which is to be found in a particular district, a peculiarity upon a par with that village

---

[1] The maternal grandmother of Gauguin was the famous Flora Tristan, a 'bluestocking' of Socialist leanings. Her uncle was President of Peru. Gauguin was taken to Lima as a child.

in White Russia where all the population have six fingers
and six toes, being all descended from a single individual
thus gifted ; and that has its counterpart in Spain in the village
of Cervera de Buitrago (prov. Madrid), where all the inhabitants boast a multiplicity of fingers and toes, sixteen or eighteen
fingers, it may be, between a pair of hands.   There is a definite
and understandable horror attaching to this swarming of the
digits, and one is led on to imagine the sensation of being
stranded without warning in this odd community, perhaps
through a motor-car breaking down, and the sight of first one
and then another individual with so many fingers on his hands.
I have been shown photographs of this extraordinary village,
the men wearing berets, and holding out their digits in rows
and bunches, immature shapes like parsnips, carrots, turnips,
and resembling the vegetable beings of Arcimboldo.[1] If forced
to spend a night there, what horror would attach to food
cooked by them, and even to simple everyday gestures, the
turning of a tap, the switching on of a light ; and one can
see oneself sitting in a room, the cynosure and unwilling centre
of attention of the whole village, all with fingers and thumbs
supernumerary and redundant, an experience that could be
as much of a nightmare, awake, as anything which could
happen to one lying alone in the darkness of the night, and that,
were it not so far-fetched and profitless a divergence from the

---

[1] Giuseppe Arcimboldo (*b.* 1533, Milan; *d.* 1593) painted "grotesque figures
and drolleries formed of flowers and fruits ", and worked during the greater part of
his life for the Habsburg Emperors Maximilian II and Rudolph II, and particularly for
the cabinet of curiosities of the latter in the Hradchin at Prague. This Emperor's
collections of natural history, his astrological studies, and the rare cups and vases
and Baroque jewels made for him by his particular craftsmen, were in keeping with
Arcimboldo's pictures. But a new interest has been revived in this rare painter by
those seeking precursors and analogies for paintings by Picasso and Salvador Dali.
Ann Boleyn, we add in parenthesis, had six fingers on each hand, and was a member
of a family who were noted for this peculiarity, but it did not descend to her daughter
Queen Elizabeth.

ordinary, would deserve fuller and more extended literary treatment.

In Peru, as in Bolivia, there are certainly human peculiarities among the Indians as curious as this, as witness the instance, which many readers will remember, of childbirth from an Indian girl who was only six years old, and before long mother and child were at school together. But, particularly, it must be the appalling mountain landscapes of Bolivia and the Peruvian highlands that I would wish to describe, villages of a horrible altitude, in itself affecting the mind, and of a chilly, iron bleakness noticed by every traveller who has seen them. There can be nothing in the world comparable, unless it be in Tibet. From photographs and written descriptions one can assimilate the landscape of Lake Titicaca, and the cyclopaean Pre-Inca ruins of Tihuanaco, all nearly at the height of the snowy summits of the Alps, but there must be lonely villages of Indians, more remote, seemingly, than any igloos of the Eskimos ; and towns, too, not only hamlets or villages. I am drawn in particular to Uyuni, in Bolivia, " lying bitterly cold and unprotected on the plain near some salt marshes ", a town with steep, stony streets lit with the " harsh and brilliant colours of the Indian and Cholo costumes ", which has a market thronged with herds of llamas and is the centre of the trade in vicuña wool.

II

I know well the French illustrated books of the eighteenth century, their engravings after Gravelot, Moreau le Jeune, and Eisen, and their *culs-de-lampe* by Choffard. I believe I have seen nearly every French, German, Dutch, or Italian book of engraved architectural and garden scenes,[1] and in particular, because of the years during which I was working upon German Baroque Art, the works of Paulus Decker the Elder and Salomon Kleiner. The first of these, in his *Fürstlicher Baumeister oder Architectura Civilis* (Augsburg, 1711–16), is the master of fugal palaces and gardens. There are triumphal archways, huge colonnades, Caesarean doorways, interiors of inexplicable fantasy and richness, state bedsteads and canopies of state, and in the last part, which is rare and not always found, fountains and clipped hedges, garden temples, green trellises, and theatre wings of lime and hornbeam.

Salomon Kleiner is different altogether. His engravings are views of Vienna. It is in his immense folios that you must look for the palaces built by Fischer von Erlach and Lukas von Hildebrandt, the two Baroque architects of Vienna. Here you may see the houses of the Kinsky, Harrach, Auersperg, Schönborn, Schwarzenberg families ; the town palace and summer palace of Prince Liechtenstein ; the town palace of Prince Eugène of Savoy and the Upper and Lower Belvederes, which were his summer palace ; and the palace of the Hungarian Life Guard. You will find the flashing white stairway of the Upper Belvedere and Prince Eugène's no less magnificent stairway in his winter palace, guarded by figures of Atlantes. They are still there. They have not been damaged in the war. Fischer von Erlach's own great folio of engravings, of which an English translation appeared in 1737, gives you the Imperial Hofburg, the great library or Hofbibliothek, and the Winter or Spanish Riding School where the white Lippizaners performed. But the Habsburgs are gone ; and no longer will you

---

[1] As far as, and inclusive of, Laurids de Thurah's *Den Dansk Vitruvius*, 1746–49, with its engravings of Danish Royal palaces and ' lay convents' (*vide* pp. 4, 5) ; and a large work of similar character upon the châteaux of Sweden, cf. Dahlberg, *Suecia Hodierna.*

see the Hungarian Life Guard in their scarlet hussar uniform enriched with silver lace, tiger skin pelisse, high yellow boots, and tall fur cap enriched with a heron's plume, on guard in the doorway of their palace, which was built originally by Fischer von Erlach for Prince Trautson, and given to them by Maria-Theresa ; or hear in the distance a light flourish of trumpets, and then the high-pitched tones of a mounted band playing the bloodstirring Rákóczy march, and watch the Hungarian Life Guard riding to duty on their grey horses with green housings and silver bridles. But they are to be admired in another and later book of coloured views of Vienna, by Carl Schütz (1779), a book which is contemporary with Mozart's *Die Entführung* and with the *Nozze di Figaro*, wherein you may walk among hooped crinolines by the clipped hornbeams of Schönbrunn.

It is a pity that there is no book of engravings of the great Austrian monasteries along the Danube, for Melk with its colonnades and blue and gold library, Göttweig with its great stairway, St. Florian's with its wrought-iron gates upon the landings and its marble Kaisersaal, are among the wonders of their age. A book which will never be written, for it is too late (I once collected the photographs for this purpose but had to abandon the project), could be devoted to the châteaux and country houses of the Austrian nobles ; or, if you prefer it, the nobles of the Holy Roman Empire. I would mention, from personal knowledge, these few of them : St. Julian's, between Linz and Salzburg, and therefore in Austria proper, a small country house by Fischer von Erlach, or, in fact, a one-storeyed Rococo pavilion with a domed centre and wings, belonging to a family who were falconers to the Habsburg Emperors ; Krumau, on a rock above the Moldau, in Bohemia, where, when I saw it, some of Prince Schwarzenberg's private regiment of grenadiers were still on guard, with an old theatre of the middle of the eighteenth century and the walls of its auditorium frescoed with figures of pierrots, harlequins, and, not incongruously, moustachio'd hussars ; Nikolsburg, the castle of Prince Dietrichstein, just inside Moravia, with fine Rococo rooms, and an irregularly shaped hall painted with Apeloosas and other tigered and spotted horses with flowing manes and tails by one of the Counts Hamilton, a family of painters of Jacobite origin ; or Schloss Pommersfelden, in Franconia, the property of Count Schönborn, a country house upon the scale of Blenheim or Castle Howard, designed by the brothers Dientzenhofer, the Prague equivalents to Fischer von Erlach or Lukas von Hildebrandt in Vienna. The three-storey ceremonial staircase of Pommersfelden is one of the outstanding achievements of the Baroque style and the painted ceiling is by J. R. Byss, who designed the ' Venetian ' theatrical tapestries at Würzburg (*vide* p. 27). Near by is the Cistercian monastery of Ebrach, with magnificent wrought-iron gateways in the church, and a ceremonial stairway by Leonhardt Dientzenhofer, not inferior to that at Pommersfelden. These châteaux of the counts and princes of the Holy Roman Empire dispersed through the former dominions of the House of Austria, their beauties of architecture, their treasures in the way of paintings, furniture, and German porcelain, and their curious traditions, form a subject that it would now be impossible to assemble within the pages of a single volume. It could have been done until 1939. But now it is too late ; and I regret this the more because I was given photographs by friends related to some of these families, of so many houses in remote parts of Bohemia, Moravia, Bavaria, Franconia, Hungary, the work of great Baroque architects and decorators, forming a corpus of domestic archi-

tecture and ornament which is quite unknown to the world
at large, the products of an Empire that has vanished, and the
proofs of existence of the only rivals to the English country
house. Neither must I forget, while thinking of this school
of architects, other books that I studied, such as M. D.
Poeppelmann's huge folio on the Zwinger, at Dresden (1729),
his plates enlivened by many splendid figures wearing Polish
dress.

III

Over a period of many years, beginning with a time when I
was ill in the summer of 1917 while at Chelsea Barracks and
had to obtain special permission as I was under age, I have
made it an almost daily practice while in London to work in
the mornings in the Reading Room of the British Museum.
In this manner I have accumulated many notes upon different
subjects and have before me, as I write this, notebooks filled
with information upon many and diverse topics. I have spent
many days in the British Museum looking at illuminated manuscripts and have notebooks dealing with them ; and as well I
have studied the Persian illuminated manuscripts. I admired
the borders of fruits and flowers on a gold background in the
Huth *Horae* and the calendar with medallions showing the
occupations of the months ; a man in a blue robe sitting by a
fireside, with a border of daisies and white violets ; two
peasants felling trees for firewood with a castle in the background ; training vines, this time, with a pair of castles rising
in the distance ; hoeing, with a gilded wattle fence, and the
inevitable castle ; and a man and a woman reaping, with blue
cornflowers and red poppies in the corn, a hot August harvest,
and the gold lightning breaking out of a cloud. I took note,

in Froissart's *Chronicles*, of the entry of Queen Isabel to Paris, with a satyr or wild man in the border like those I noted in the portals of the churches at Valladolid ; the masked dance tragedy (frontispiece to vol. ii), when the masquers dressed in leaves and rags were burned to death ; John of Gaunt, always shown in black armour ; a pig in a white steeple veil, walking on stilts, and playing a harp ; green-tiled floors, ermine and silver, and steeple hats. These notes that I had accumulated upon illuminated manuscripts helped me to write my descriptions of the Crusaders' castles in Syria and Palestine for *The Gothick North* ; Mirabel, Beauvoir, Belfort, Blanchgarde or Specula Alba, named from its conspicuous white chalk rocks, Nigraguarda, Toron, and Scandalion. Many years later I wrote descriptions of the castles in the *Très Riches Heures du Duc de Berri*,[1] one of the most lovely of all illuminated manuscripts of the Middle Ages, with miniatures by Pol de Limbourg, now in the Musée Condé at Chantilly, which once again takes the form of a calendar of the twelve months, with the castles belonging to the Duc de Berri (*d.* 1416) in the background.

I have collected for my own purposes of pleasure and information the auriculas, tulips, pinks, and carnations, from the ' florists ' magazines of the 1830's and '40's. The hand-coloured plates of auriculas are a delight in themselves. Already, in *The Florist* for 1850, a correspondent is lamenting that there is no book of coloured plates of the florist's tulip, and much more as this is to be regretted in the case of the auricula we may agree with his anonymous complaint after seeing the hand-coloured drawings in other contemporary publications of the tulips Dutch Catafalque, Solon, and Esther, informing ourselves again (if we did not know it before) that

[1] In *The Hunters and the Hunted* : London, Macmillan & Co., 1947, pp. 51-4.

tulips are divided into bybloemens which have white bottoms
to their cups marked with various colours — prime Baguets,
Rigauts, incomparable Verports — whatever that may mean !
— roses, and bizarres which have yellow grounds ; or looking
at the violet and white bybloemen Chellaston Beauty, typical
of the one hundred and more varieties of purple bybloemens
raised by one grower, Mr. Gibbons, for which the town of
Chellaston in Derbyshire was famous. The pinks and carnations are not less astonishing in their perfection scattered here
and there through the horticultural and florists' magazines,
and I have often thought what an anthology could be formed
of flakes, bizarres, and picotees. It is carnations like the old
Admiral Curzon, or another called Black Diamond, which had
dark maroon purple — so dark that it was black like a bumble-
bee's black velvet body — entering into their markings, that
are the most beautiful in form and regularity of even repetition ;
and some of the more meticulously perfect of the piquettes or
picotees. Of the latter, those spotted upon a yellow ground
which were particularly admired during the twenties of the
last century were of German origin, and no doubt that is why
Queen Adelaide had the best collection of them in her garden
at Frogmore.

Occasionally, but only at rare intervals in these magazines,
there are traces of the craze for hyacinths which succeeded to
the tulip mania in Holland. I have noted Bouquet Pourpre, a
hyacinth with green edges or " wedge-shaped dashes of
brilliant green " to its purple florets ; and there is a fine plate
of hyacinths in Dr. Thornton's *Temple of Flora* (1807), which
being nearer to the eighteenth century may give some idea of
what the French and Dutch florists aimed at and achieved,
thick florets piled and grown together like the modern hyacinth, and you inhale the spiced scent in just thinking of it,

differentiated, separated into clusters that droop a little from heaviness on their green stalks ; or with the individual flower shaped and developed into another character so that it is less like a hyacinth and resembles the curled and frilled bell of a snowbell or *Leucojum*.

I have notebooks filled with notes on books of birds. I have made a particular study of Gould's *Trochilidæ or Humming Birds* and Bowdler Sharpe's *Birds of Paradise*. From Gould's six volumes and supplement, and his four hundred and eighteen plates, I find I have chosen forty-four as being the most beautiful, and sixteen *Birds of Paradise* out of the eighty plates in Bowdler Sharpe. There are some fifty or sixty parrots in Gould's *Birds of Australia*, and nearly as many in his *Birds of New Guinea*, say, an array of more than one hundred of them, altogether ; and I never cease to compare them in my imagination with the one hundred porcelain figures of Italian comedians designed by the great modeller Johann-Joachim Kändler for the Meissen factory, of which the owner of a famous collection has all but one figure in her possession. It is a comparison that is inevitable ; so many of the lories and lorikeets have ' whiskery ' blue masks of powdery blue ; sometimes, feathery yellow masks with a broadening band of powder blue running through it ; or red skull-caps and blue feather headpieces . . . " the filaments of the mask are combed and fluttering, as though stuck on ; they are as though sewn or gummed onto the cloth or skin below . . ." features which I have been at pains to describe and demonstrate in the chapter called " The Kingdom of the Birds " in my book *The Hunters and the Hunted*, and which bring the parrots and lories akin to the comedians. And in the same work I examined the trogons, pittas or ant thrushes, toucans, hornbills, mergansers, pheasants, fruit-eating pigeons, Cordons bleus or fancy finches, halcyons, woodpeckers, and sun birds, upon the same principles, grouping them aesthetically as though, as is the fact, they were under criticism as works of art, further elaborating my views in the prefaces to Audubon's *Birds of America* and to Gould's *Tropical Birds*,[1] trying to write of them in the spirit in which I have studied Redouté's *Les Roses*, and costume books and books of costume plates.

IV

I have the notebooks by me in which I made a study of the entire run of the Japanese art publication *The Kokka*, with its superb plates in chromoxylography, an ugly word, but a system of illustration which could only exist in Japan and that there could never be time or patience for in Europe, noting for instance in *Kokka*, pl. 226 (for 1892), a splendid horse picture in colours by Kasuga Nobuhara (sixteenth century) with green hills, tree trunks spotted with lichen, and seven spotted horses, all different ; and a hillside and a whole nation of monkeys balanced upon rocks and branches by Mori Sosen, the monkey painter, but in loose, impressionist manner, making play with their long black arms and tails, not in his close technique when he rendered every hair. Also, two screens by Sotatsu in the Imperial collection, one of them a war scene which was the enlargement of one fan, only, from two eight-leaved screens covered with painted fans.

It was Japanese screen paintings particularly that I was studying ; and I find my notes made from *The Kokka* and other sources including, of course, Fenollosa's glorious *Epochs of Chinese and Japanese Art*, which should be one of the

[1] In Batsford's Colour Series, 1948–49.

formative influences for every poet, every painter or sculptor, I would add, every musician. I noted a three-fold screen of morning glories by Sotatsu ; magnificent screens by Kano Eitoku ; and a pair of screens depicting the temple cars or decorated waggons used in sacred processions, gorgeously painted, with musical ('nightingale') wheels, and bearing superb flower arrangements by the hands of great flower masters. In particular, the celebrated screen of clothes-horses by Sotatsu, a painting which I have written of, elsewhere, as being as " unpromising in subject as the opening donkey bray of Stravinsky's *Symphony for Wind Instruments*, and of the same order, but developing into a most subtle arrangement of the cloths and stuffs that are disposed at varying angles, and in their patterns and colours, upon the towel horses ". It was the school of Kano Eitoku and his successors, Koyetsu and Sotatsu, not excluding the more vulgar Korin, that interested me, probably the greatest school of decorative painters there has ever been ; and from my notes upon their painted screens I contrived to write " The Corn Screens " in *The Hunters and the Hunted*. Earlier, I had made a study of the woven textiles of Japan from which I wrote the description of dresses in " The Age of Genroku " for my book *Splendours and Miseries*.

How much I would have liked to see the great screen painters at work, and to have been able to enter into intelligent conversation with painters as gifted in ideas of decoration as those mentioned, or many others ; the painters of pine trees and flowering plums ; of barnyard fowls and hydrangeas (the only hydrangeas or hortensias in all painting, if we except Fragonard in his *Grande Foire de St.-Cloud*) ; and another screen of hydrangeas and long-tailed magpies — not forgetting the painter Kenzan, the brother of Korin, the originality of whose mind and touch is to be seen in the simplest pottery

bowl or lacquer box to which he put his hand ; an earthenware
cake box, perhaps, but it may have a pine tree and waves upon
it, suggested with an entire economy of means, and there are
more waves inside it in black and white and gold ; or another
box painted with mushrooms and funguses, so rich and choco-
laty, like chocolate truffles in texture ; two tea-cups with
flowers and plum blossoms by this rare lacquerer and potter ;
or another pair of cake boxes with aquatic plants !

How much I was thinking of the wonderful screen paintings of sixteenth- and seventeenth-century Japan, early last
summer (May 1949), when I was in Portugal and was shown
the Quinta da Bacalhoa, across the Tagus from Lisbon on the
road to Setubal, belonging to an American lady who has
restored this old country house of the son of Albuquerque,
conqueror of Ormuz, of Goa, of Malacca, and Viceroy of the
Indies, for this old château with its echoes of the early Renaissance villas of Florence — did not Sansovino (1460–1529)
leave Italy for three years of his life and come to Portugal,
where no known buildings can be ascribed to him ; were
there not, once, medallions by della Robbia set in the walls ?
— with its gardens of clipped box planted with orange and
lemon trees, pavilions with melon domes, great water tank
(like an echo of the Indian lotus tanks) and garden house with
three pyramided towers and tiled rooms, within, for summer
coolness and dalliance with coffee-coloured shades and waists
of amber — it must have been ! — this old garden which
reminded me of the water tanks of the Aguedal at Marrakesh,
and made me think of Portuguese forts and water cisterns
that I had seen at Mogador and conjectured at Ormuz, had
nesting in its trees a pair of blue magpies that are only found
in the Algarve, this part of Portugal lying south of the Tagus,
and nowhere else in the world nearer than China ! It is to be

assumed that the original blue magpies were brought to Portugal from China by the early voyagers and I could think of no subject more suited to the brush of one of those decorative painters, or more in the spirit of their great painted screens. There are Japanese paintings in the Musée Guimet at Paris in which the early Portuguese voyagers appear with their pointed beards, their doublets and trunk hose ; and I lay down my pen after writing this episode in thinking of the pair of blue magpies from China floating through the orange and lemon groves of the Quinta da Bacalhoa, making of its scented beauty an Orient of their own.[1]

[1] A pair of these azure-winged magpies *Cyanopica cyanus* from the Algarve has been given to the London Zoo by the Duke of Palmela. But I cannot close, while in the mood of these Japanese screen paintings, without thinking of another theme, the little isle of Corvo, smallest of the Azores, an extinct volcano eight miles in circumference, with a thousand inhabitants " living in Elysian peace and amity, with unlocked doors ", a single village of white cottages, and a lake inside the crater with a number of islets disposed like the whole archipelago of the Azores, in miniature. Corvo has a special breed of fairy cattle not more than ninety centimetres in height, the colour of *café au lait*, fairy Jerseys, in fact, yielding abundant milk and cream; and a landscape which is one great bank of blue and white hydrangeas. Allowing myself poetical licence, I have added iron filings to the soil to turn the pink hydrangeas into blue ; but the hydrangeas would be prettier still, were they the species *H. villosa* with porcelain blue umbels starred with lavender ; or others, like *H. strigosa* (both of these are from China), that have corymbs of small white fertile flowers and sterile pale blue bracts. The wild hydrangeas are of sensational beauty.

Envoi

HAVING now written something of what I have to write of the visual world of facts and places — which, even then, is only a portion, and a small one, of the greater world of objects, music, persons — I address myself to the more tenuous world of shades that move, and speak not, but have substance. What follows is within its limits a fragment or some part of a spiritual, not factual, autobiography. What has come before is concerned mainly with architecture and countries, even if it diverges sometimes into a discussion of flowers or of illuminated manuscripts. I have given sketches of many books I wished to write — with some account of those accomplished — but I have not mentioned poetry or persons. It is because I still have hopes in those directions. Of the rest enough has been written and it is finished. I come to a world that is poetical and personal. I move the shuttle, first forwards, and then backwards. I write only of things I love to write of. And all the time it is myself. For I have not altered : I am the same person. I have tried to enlarge the world, since I was young, with some new discoveries and into particular directions, in which respect I must not be confused with my sister and my brother, with whom I share certain affinities of temperament but not all topics of taste or kinds of talent. My own spiritual and physical entity makes it that, were I not living now, I would choose the sixteenth century when I hope I would have been a poet, and not necessarily a minor one. As it is, I have written poetry, and some of that in prose. I

end with a poem which I will quote once more, a madrigal by
Roberto Greene that I loved before I was twenty years old,
for it is of immediate contingency to what follows, it is the
picture of a mood, now as before, and I can express myself
out of it in my own personal philosophy, almost as if the poem
were my own.   This is how the madrigal runs :

> The swans, whose pens more white than ivory,
> Eclipsing fair Endymion's silver love,
> Floating like snow,
> Down by the banks of Po,
> Ne'er tuned their notes, like Leda once forlorn,
> With more despairing sorts of madrigals,
> Than I,
> Whom wanton Love hath with his goad
> Pricked to the court of deep and restless thoughts.

Read on !

end with a poem which I will quote once more, a madrigal by
Roberto Greene that I loved before I was twenty years old,
for it is of immediate contingency to what follows; it is the
picture of a mood, now as before; and I can express myself
out of it in my own personal philosophy, almost as if the poem
were my own. This is how the madrigal runs:

> The swans, whose pens more white than ivory,
> Eclipsing fair Endymion's silver love,
> Floating like snow,
> Down by the banks of Po,
> Ne'er tuned their notes, like Leda once so fond,
> With more despairing sense of madrigals,
> Than I,
> Whom wanton Love hath with his wand
> Pricked to the court of deep and restless thoughts.

Read on!

BOOK II
SPELL : VISION : AWAKENING

I

Inistioge (August 1947)

FIRST, we saw a field, green as a lawn, with great trees casting shade, and coming down into the little town, Inistioge,[1] planted with lime trees, climbed up, behind the church, and found ourselves in front of the ruined, burnt-out house. A man appeared, who talked, at first, about new motor-cars, about the Hillman 'Minx', but as though he had been a chauffeur in another existence, until I asked him if there were ghosts in the old house, when he replied that " We were serious people, who made him remember things that he had forgotten long ago, he having had many troubles and disasters in his life ", and he began telling us of the great voice, " loud enough to lift the roof of a motor-car ", that he heard coming out of the windows, every night, for a fortnight on end ; or it might not be there, he could not exactly tell, it might be in the high trees ; and another time, three years ago, up in the wood outside the forester's cottage, when the woodman's wife lay dying. At which point, another and still more peculiar-looking man came up, bareheaded and barefooted, a cowherd, for he drove away the cows and horses that came rubbing themselves in the heat against our motor-car, a man who looked madder than the other, and when we asked him, " Had he heard anything ? " at first, he did not understand, until his companion explained it to him, and then he answered, at

---

[1] Pronounced ' Inisteeg ' ; the ruined house is Woodstock, Co. Kilkenny.

once, " he thought he had heard some sort of a loud rumbling ". Our friend who said that we were " serious people " refused two shillings. " No ! No ! he was not that sort of person " ; and we turned and drove away, looking up at the burnt-out windows, the blackened front, and the rusty iron staircase leading into a conservatory. We passed some black chickens, a black billygoat, and got out to open a couple of gates, down the steep hill into the little town, never seeing the haunted house again, for it was hidden in the woods, and so away. And it was coming down that hill into the little square planted with lime trees, in the heat of the August afternoon, that I remembered and thought again of the road through the hanging wood, and thinking from one to the other, of a beginning for this present book.

II

August 1915

MY opening page is the hot August of 1915 when I spent the
afternoons of nearly a week wandering on the high banks and
under the hanging woods along the Thames. I had escaped
from home for the first time in my life at the end of the
summer ' half ' at Eton and was staying in the wooden annexe
of 'The Compleat Angler' at Marlow. My brother and two of
our greatest friends, both cousins, one to be killed within two
months, and the other within the year, both before they were
nineteen, were encamped, near by, with their battalion of the
Grenadiers.

The mornings I spent alone, but we met in the evenings.
It seems to me after all these years that, apart from one night
when I dined by myself in the hotel and sat for a long while
listening to the music of the weir, we dined together every night.
Once or twice we went to London. 'The Eiffel Tower', then
emerging into bohemian fame, was our resort for dinner. I remember the late train back to Maidenhead, and an afternoon
train from London during a thunderstorm. But the mornings
I spent with notebook and sharpened pencil, hoping to write
poems. I knew that Shelley had stayed in Marlow and that he
composed *The Revolt of Islam*, " partly in his boat on the
Thames, and partly during walks in the neighbouring woods ".
I waited and waited, but nothing happened. I walked instead,
not being very old, close to the river's edge and along the

weir. How well I remember the noise of the waters, and the electric flashing of the waterfall ! And the long mornings, and the salmon and raspberry luncheons, and the longer afternoons !

Some of the old red-brick houses in the town made me think of Randolph Caldecott's coloured drawings for *John Gilpin* ; and even as I write this, across the years, I hear my own footsteps on the wooden stairs of the annexe, I smell the resin in the walls, see the joints in the boards, and hear the falling waters. It could be, now, this moment, and not all that time ago, that I am coming down to breakfast upon another sultry August day. And the eternal morning passed in a moment, and it was the afternoon.

In the afternoons, as I have said, I walked upon the hills. In any August but during a war, there would have been young men in flannels and young women in print dresses on the river,[1] but now it was deserted and there were no other sounds but those of harvesting. And I seem to see myself walking in a high sloping meadow with the river down below to the left, thinking of the poems that I wished to write. Marlow, Henley, Maidenhead, all the towns on the river had this further enchantment that they were out of bounds from Eton, so that the summer winds were wanton and brought with them a breath of dissipation. My father had already begun telegraphing for me to come home immediately, which, of course, added an urgency to every moment. It was a paradise that could not last longer than for a day or two more. How lovely it was in the middle of the afternoon to look forward to the evening !

Now it is an axiom in all of the arts, and with all human beings, that their earliest maturity is the pattern, in little, of

[1] Before the era of sunbathing.

what they will become. The art of printing, to take an instance, was never clearer or more beautiful than in the first years of its invention. The same holds true of early painting, music, poetry; and, as we say, of living persons. It could even be said that they never improve beyond that, and that every further step is retrograde and a declension. And it is the same with human experiences and impressions. The first summer day is, and remains ever, the hottest there has been. This was my first summer holiday away from home. But it was more important than that. For the first time I felt it within me to create something. I knew not what, but I knew I had the power to do it. I was seventeen years old and very silent. But it seems to me that I knew and had read everything that I know now.

Perhaps later knowledge only confirms what one knew before by instinct. Certainly this is the time when soul and memory are at their most immortal. And in just the way one would expect, that they are not retentive of unnecessary detail. I do not clearly remember the trees and fields where I walked; but I recall, or so it seems to me, the flight and sequence of my trains of thought. There are certain single events or episodes in our lives that we put on one side for as long as half a lifetime, just as though they are unwrapped and untied parcels, the point being that they are memories reserved for further and later consideration. There is the afternoon walk that I and two other of my friends had planned for a ' whole holiday ' in the same ' half ' at Eton in order to visit some church — can it have been Stoke Poges ? this seems more than likely — our idea being to spend the day talking and discussing, a project that never matured, for some reason or other, but it has become connected in my mind, or private mythology, with Beardsley's poem and drawing of *The Three Musicians*.

I mention these things because my ghost of those August days at Marlow is that of a youth, callow and awkward in conversation and behaviour, but not in reading. I was at the age when one reads all the poetry one can lay hands upon, and marks one's favourite passages with a pencil. I had read the poets in the Mermaid series in their orange bindings; Marlowe and Peele were my favourites; I was reading D' Annunzio's *Il Fuoco* and *Il Piacere*, in French translation, and was an enthusiast for Marinetti, the Italian Futurist, with whom I was in correspondence. *Madame Bovary* and *Salammbô*, then, as now (where the first of these novels is concerned), I thought to be the supreme masterpieces of their age and time. *La Tentation de St. Antoine* I knew; the *Trois Contes*, also, but not *L'Éducation sentimentale*; and I had read Gautier's *Mlle de Maupin*, and much of Zola. I mention this because no amount of subsequent reading, making an exception for Marinetti as a phantom of his day, could much improve upon this foundation. I have always accounted it a miracle in my favour that I found an English translation of *Salammbô* (in the Lotus Library) in our village post office at Eckington two summers before this (in 1913), a discovery which has probably had more effect upon my life of the imagination than any other single fact except those accidents of birth which gave me my sister and my brother.

And I must have turned back in my walk and started to come down the fields to Marlow. We were all to meet in the evening, as soon as they could get away, some time between tea and dinner. On this occasion they arrived in Bimbo's car (I think that living in the country, as we did, and with only a pony cart to take us for drives or to the station, I had not got used to the idea of young men having motors of their own) and I remember the excitement when I heard their voices and saw them getting out of the motor underneath the trees. We seem to have driven across the bridge into Marlow, and as far as Henley, for I remember the red-brick inns of Henley, and the figure of a bear or a red lion over the porch of one of them ; and then we must have come back again through Marlow, across the river, passing 'The Compleat Angler', and into those woods between Marlow and Maidenhead past the old farm buildings, on the left, built of blackened weatherboards, a road with a hanging wood at the end of it, and a landscape which is ever to my mind one of the most beautiful in England. If there be another as lovely it can only be the road from Bloxham to Chipping Norton, with the red plough of Oxon and the old stone buildings, and Great Tew out of sight down in the valley with its steep thatch and mullioned windows, its foxgloves and hollyhocks and purple clematis. That is the end of a world ; the road in this hanging wood is, by contrast, but a corridor or place of passage.

I remember coming down the hill in the other direction on the same evening, but a good deal later, for it was almost dark. And we came back again much later still, for it was moonlight ; and on those rare occasions since, when I have been along that road, I have been overwhelmed with nostalgia, for I know that it was in those few days while I was at Marlow that my career was decided for me, and my fate was cast. In November of the following year I was in the regiment, and both our friends were dead. And within a month or two I was writing poems, despite Chelsea Barracks.

III

Prince of Denmark

MANY years later, it has not happened yet, we find ourselves buying flowers at a little flowerstall and the young flower-seller has her hair tied up in a silk handkerchief so that we scarcely see her face. We enquire for a carnation called *Prince of Denmark*, with white fringed petals, striped and spotted scarlet ; and *Jenny Lynch*, an Irish scarlet-flake carnation, pink and white, with slightly jagged edges, named in honour of a young lady who took Dublin by storm in the year 1768 by her beauty, called after her by an admirer Walter Deverel ; the clove scent, beautiful and very strong ; the scarlet in the form of stripes, flakes, and spots on a pink and white ground ; stalk, very slender ; all in a letter to-day, and as beautiful to write, or print, and as good a subject as the apples of Cézanne, or the asparagus stalk that Manet painted.

Or we can ask for others ; the flame-carnation *Old Man's Head*, a lovely shade of red striped with black ; or the old ' *Beverley* ' pink, in cream and red and yellow, a rather dark red, flaked in white and yellow. Of the stage auriculas I will not atttempt to write here, beyond remarking that their stippled powdered beauty is of the sort that we would expect to be native to the isle of Venus. Of what else could the incredible powdering of the leaves, and the white face of the auricula remind us, except of the bayadère, the ballerina of the sacred island ? And with heart beating, and blood rushing into our ears, we see the swan castle rising in the lakes and beech woods. . . .

IV

Florinda

THIS episode, or chain of images, is no more than a flourish or a flight of fancy upon a phrase or a part of a sentence that comes later. And it has a masqued or false beginning. It finds us with the dancer Florinda in the black cabin of a gondola.

Now there is nothing in the world quite like the cabin of a gondola. More poetical than the cockpit of an aeroplane. It may have a glass vase with flowers in it, but no mirror, and no ashtray. You can see the hoods of gondolas stacked, side by side, along the Molo. The gondoliers generally put them out to pawn during the summer. They look like the hoods of hearses, and fit on like the lids of coffins. And the gondola glides silently. It could be a hearse with secret police hidden in it. Funereal black, but black like the robe of confessor or inquisitor.

What ghosts inhabit the body of this dark moth of the waters ! As, now, its ghostly inhabitant, my companion, who is not there at all, but could be here in two persons. In her double personality, like a ghost seen in the eyes of a living person ; a haunting which is effected with no more difficulty than by carrying her practice clothes, or tights and ballet shoes, in her satchel or her handbag.

And we are conveyed, with no more ado, out of the mouth of one of the side canals, across the lagoon to Murano, bound for a supper party in a vineyard. When we step out of the gondola half of the Venetian courtesans are there already. They are the women who bleach their hair, and walk upon high pattens. They are to be seen bleaching their hair upon their balconies, and are the friends and companions of painters and poets, being the most highly educated and wittiest women of *La Serenissima*.

How much more do I remember of that evening, for it was like a feverish dream or an hallucination ?

It never happened at all, and is but idle imagining ; an entr'acte or mere interval during the shifting of the scenery, a device commoner in music than in writing, more often encountered in the theatre than in turning the pages of a book in hand.

And now the whole company turns towards us, for they see her in the golden mirror on the landing, coming up the stair. It is in this manner that we enter their century, which was four hundred years ago, and the experience cannot last for longer than a few moments. Florinda who has come out of the cabin of the gondola as though it was her dressing-room, still herself, and not in travesty.

A young girl of nineteen, whom I know now to have been the daughter of a Venetian nobleman, to be notorious one day, and who should not have kept such company, laughing in a corner. Her deep Italian voice, for calling down from her window into the cortile, and her bleached hair, bleached after the fashion of the courtesans. How dressed ? Ah ! I could not describe it, except to say that she wore a gown of yellow velvet or brocade to match her hair. Darker or lighter ? But you could not tell. It changed under the light of the torches, and later in the moonlight.

Her name ' Bianca ', indeed, the whole ' Bianca Capello ', hinting at her fair colouring and white skin, but ' altered ', made fairer, paler, upon the flowering balcony.

And the Venetian courtesans ! And the water chopping, chopping, down below, and a long wave of the tide striking like a whiplash on the landing stage !

They are the auburn women of Venice, Titian-haired, but the red has faded in his paintings. You may see one or two of them, black-shawled, dressed in black, walking across a campo, or climbing the steps of one of the arched bridges. It is like a little stage or platform, and they step down again. But the famous Venetian courtesans, born to the gondola, never walk more than a few paces " in their pattens or chopines, which are worn with a skirt divided in front to show their breeches, cut like a man's, and gold-clocked stockings. And in that manner " (I quote from my own writings) " walking as though upon stilts, for the pattens are as much as a foot and a half high, they clatter slowly and noisily up and down the bridges." But, indoors, they wear something more like a sandal or a Turkish slipper. It is with slippered feet that they descend the stair to sit at supper under the vine trellis.

But now comes the contradiction, for at this supper party in the vineyard at Murano we keep the assembled company waiting in the big room, the ' gran sala ' upstairs, waiting for someone to arrive, to enter in to them from another century. Florinda has come down to them in an aeroplane out of the clouds for this special performance only, and has changed in the gondola into her ballet dress. One half of this story is possible ; why not the other ?

Her metamorphosis achieves itself under our eyes upon the stair, at the foot, coming in from the watersteps. Time has altered everything, she has arrived with her partner in an aeroplane, carrying a small suitcase. She has changed in her hotel into evening dress, an ' off the shoulder ' dress invisibly held up, of apple blossom colour, made in that new fashion of the film star's first night, worn only for the foyer of the cinema and for the supper afterwards — and wearing this long dress, which shows her in her spring-like beauty, walking with the tread that only dancers and Gypsies have in common, we climb with her half-way up the staircase to the landing, where it turns, where you see the assembled company, first in the mirror as reflections, then as living persons, and she changes before our eyes into her other incarnation.

The stage direction reads " a splendid ballroom prepared for a festival " and it is, of course, the gran sala or riddersaal where, after the hunting parties, the prince dines together with his brother-huntsmen. Wherever you look there are swans, singly, or in groups of three, for symbols in the architecture. There is a pagoda on the right of the stage with swan capitals, and opposite, a pair of thrones, side by side, under a swan canopy. A great stairway, curving, sweeps up into the angle of the fan-vaulted roof, for it has pendant ornaments like stalactites. For backcloth there is a double colonnade of arches. Upon occasion the arches are hung with tapestries, but not to-night, for it would deaden the music of the dance.

The curtain rises to a blustering, enchanted fairground march, a quickstep or pasodoble, to which the prince and his mother enter and take their places on the pair of thrones. They are followed by pages and courtiers, by the guests from foreign lands, and by a group of débutantes or young princesses carrying feathered fans. A fanfare of trumpets announces a waltz by the young princesses. Towards the end the prince steps down, dances with each débutante in turn, bows to her, and goes back to his throne. But he comes down again in order to look out through the empty arches of the colonnade.

The swan princess has not come to the ball, and the hour grows late.

The identical fanfare rings out once more, and the wizard Rothbart enters with Odile, his daughter, whom he has transformed into the likeness of the swan princess. She wears a black and gold short dress or ballet skirt, cut low off her shoulders, and a golden headdress or diadem upon her coppery-gold hair. There follow the dances of the emissaries of foreign countries and in them we pursue our own fantasy, for we will have the Spanish guests in costumes more splendid, far, than the banal music which is the weakest part of the whole score. They shall be stage-Castilians, true inhabitants of castles in Spain, come here to compare the fretted Gothic battlements of their palace fortress, and its many turrets above the river gorge, with this swan castle rising in the lakes and beech woods. The music improves ; we have ringing in our ears the trumpets of the csárdás. The Hungarians wear high red boots and the Magyar cloak or szür with long loose sleeves that sway and dangle in the dance. They turn in their sheep-skin coats like shaggy bears but step like peacocks in the csárdás. The Poles, like mountaineers of High Tatra, wear white and red and have the eagle feather in their wide-brimmed hats ; we hear the counter tune and return of the mazurka.

And now it is the turn of Odile — Florinda. Her waltz — what can any dance be but a waltz ? — begins, and unfolds its flowers, takes them away, and offers them again, becomes more full-petalled, and more elaborate of step, repeats the phrase, again, once more, and another time, and expands and blossoms to the magic of the dance. The prince has come down from the throne to take her hand ; her father Rothbart lends her his arm for a difficult figure, but puts his other hand to his lips and whispers to her to do his bidding. This is underlined and made sinister in the music, which for its tender passages has the mocking viola instead of the violin. Each time she listens to what her father is whispering, and with dazzling vermilion smile turns to the prince who is her support or partner in the dance. He takes her hand and kisses it, at which moment one of the empty arches, behind them, burns with a strange light and we see Odette, the swan princess, beating with her wings against the window. Odile turns to look at her ; runs back and waves to her to go away. The prince sees nothing, but asks the wizard for his daughter's hand. He takes the ring and puts it on her finger ; then knows he has been duped, and starts back in horror. There comes a flash of lightning and a peal of thunder, and the ballroom is plunged in darkness. The magician takes Odile by the hand and, together, they run out through the wings. The prince stumbles a few steps and collapses ; his mother swoons upon her throne. The curtain falls. . . .

V

Firebird

EVEN while I write this I have a longing to be in some Spanish cathedral, it matters not where : Plasencia, Palencia, Sigüenza, or Huesca ; Teruel, Tortosa, or Tarazona ; choose where you will ! But there must be a Turk's or Moor's head, with turban and false beard, below the organ case (this is a Catalan custom), and there must be a row or two of pipes coming out at you like a salvo of artillery. Perhaps there could be two organ cases ; one upon either side of the *coro*. Nowhere does a Bach fugue sound so magnificent as upon the organ in a Spanish cathedral, even if it is not well played ! But in more than one church I have heard magnificent and splendid organ playing ; particularly in Córdoba, which is the last place in the world where you would expect to listen to Johann Sebastian Bach. It is one of those contradictions in nature, the law which makes a beauty of the fair Sicilian, or the dark Phœnician from Land's End. The Lutheran Bach is best heard, by the same token, not in a swept and whitewashed church, but in some treasure-house of all the centuries, with its sacristy wherein the shovel hat of the snuff-taking Don Basilio has not long been absent.

I have written, elsewhere, of hearing the organ of Buxtehude played in the Marienkirche of Lübeck. That is an experience that can happen nevermore. For it is all gone. But the old mosque of Córdoba has a court of orange trees.

Some are in blossom. The red-gold oranges have been heaped into a pyramid under one of the arches, and the cloister wafts and drowses in that scent of Araby. You may look up at the tower and its huge bells of bronze, in this sunset hour, and now, or later in the year, see the snapdragons nodding, nodding, upon that precipice. But the doors are open ; and it is like walking into a wood that has turned to stone, an orchard, but a barren orchard, for the over-arching branches have grown solid into cusp and leaf. It is as though they had been dipped for long ages in some petrifying well. But it is their age only, for they have stood here for a thousand years. It is easy to lose oneself entirely in the stony forest and not know which way to turn.

Let it be at this moment that we hear the organ playing and direct our steps towards the distant sound, for it loses itself, in intricacy, between the horseshoe arches. We may find ourselves deep down among the columns, where the wood ends, at the *mihráb*, but it could be the heart, the inner-most middle of the sacred forest, for nowhere is such arabesque and filigree. This holy place of the old Orient, the haunt of the turban, has the *media naranja*, ' half-orange ' dome of stalactite, and pineapple cupola, so that it is as though here, at last, marble stem and bough of stone had fruited. And we walk out of the wood into a clearing, which is to say, deeper, deeper into the forest of columns, but they end abruptly, they have been torn down. The *coro*, the Christian temple, rises in the midst, enclosed within itself, as though it would look inwards and not back to the pagan, turbaned past. It has wooden walls, as high as a ship's sides, which are nothing else than the *silleria*, the Baroque choir stalls in three decks or storeys, carved up all their height, with huge lecterns or book-stands upon the matted floor and great painted choir books.

The organ cases rise to each side of the *coro* like pavilions or superstructures, brightly painted, built upon the wooden walls, like the poop or cabin of a mediaeval ship, but, also, the painted organ cases are the kiosques or pavilions of a Bibiena theatre drawing. How strange and extravagant are the huge pulpits, one of them resting upon the kneeling figure of a bull, the animal of the Evangelist ! There are splendid railings of brass, as in so many Spanish cathedrals, leading from the *coro* to the *capilla mayor* (chapel of the High Altar), like the processional way in the Temple of Solomon, down which the priests pass in their mitres, as upon a time the mitred priests of Isis and Osiris.

I would love to hear Handel's organ concertos performed in this setting. They are so theatrical, they are pure theatre music ; or the minuet or hornpipe from his *Water Music* ; but, with Handel, the orange trees have been carried out from the orangery and put into their green tubs or ' *caisses* ', the walls have apricots or mirabelles trained upon them, the green pyramids have been lifted from the garden statues, by which I mean, metaphorically, that the end wall of the opera house has been taken down and the proscenium enlarged into the open air, or in fact, into the summer gardens, which are full of promenaders listening to the music. If hornpipe there be, it is danced upon a barge and the dancers are the King's bargemasters or watermen, who walk in state processions, and at the time of year, catch the swans, and pinion them, and let them go. As to Handel's minuets, they burgeon, they are in flower. The dancers are Flora or Pomona, when ripe cherries have been picked, or sunburnt Ceres resting from the harvest and pillowed on the hay. Handel had lived so long in England that his dances are English. His dancers have the limbs of English girls. His minuets are upon green lawns or in public gardens, at Hampton Court or Vauxhall, where the trees are lit with lanterns.

How is it possible to think of Bach or Handel, here in Córdoba, and not to babble of green fields ? Here is all of the Orient, except the smell of cedar beams. There is only that missing, planks cut from cedars of Atlas, those only, and the turban's shade. The citizens have grave Roman features, and tread like Romans. Some of the older priests wear their gowns like Roman togas. Manolete, the dead matador, had the face and manners of a Roman. He was Roman, not Moorish, nor Castilian. He was a Roman of Córdoba. Córdoba has the light and colour of a Roman city, golden as Tarragona, the ' aprica litora ' of the poet Martial, words which translate themselves ; but Córdoba has no shore, the blue Mediterranean is wanting, and the landscape is more tawny or ochre-coloured.

It must be darkening. There is no one left in the cathedral ; only the man who brought the key, and the unseen musician sitting at the organ. For we are in the middle of the Bach fugue. And Bach now comes in his turn and conquers Handel. They were rivals in life, except that Handel knew little more than the name of Bach and would not go out of his way to meet him. The genius of Bach is at once more cosmic and more closeted than that of Handel. But this is one of the ' domestic ' fugues of Bach. It is Bach in a little mood. How enchanted, yet busy, his music sounds in this cathedral shut in with orange trees, for the cloister, we know, is a drowsy orange grove ! And the fugue ends, but the musician begins to play another piece by Bach which I recognize immediately. It is the chorale prelude.

It is like a little window that opens. It could be as though a little window opened, high up on the wall of nave or transept, and a young maiden, a princess and virgin of ' blue blood ', of the Gothic race, lived and moved within that little room. It is the sensation of being present at the opening of a tomb, except that the occupant is living, and not dead, and has, perhaps, but been sleeping through the centuries. Have they not opened the Royal tombs, lately, at Las Huelgas [1] and at Toledo, and found dresses of silk and brocade, combs and ornaments, rings, pieces of *opus Anglicanum* (English needle-work done by the nuns), this in the tomb of a princess who was born a Plantagenet, and even long tresses of fair hair ? Such things could not be more poetically beautiful than in the dark land of Spain.

Or it is as though the walls are hung with tapestries, which can happen in cathedrals in Spain during certain festivals and feasts of the Church. The music — perhaps I should say the melody — may be more ancient than the time of Bach, may be his meditation upon a chorale written two hundred years before his day. This is something that you never get with Handel, who was in the forefront of his time. But Bach looks in two directions : he prophesies, and harks back to the distant past. Bach was considered old-fashioned in his day. The chorale is of so long ago that it is ageless. And un-contaminated. And I had it in mind to say that this chorale reminded me of the matchless tapestries of Zamora or Zaragoza, tapestries which are among the glories of Spain, wherein you may find for yourself, rising out of the flowering meadows, for it is perpetual spring or early summer in the tapestry, some small room in the corner of a tower which is crowded with young persons, knights in furs and velvets, and young ladies in horned or steeple headdresses (there could be a chapter written on their headdresses !), and feel that you

[1] The convent near Burgos.

have discovered this thing for yourself and that no one else has found it, but, listening more intently to the music, I know that it is more domestic and more solitary, that it is a reverie or meditation, for I can sing over the tune of it to myself, it is more of a devotional rhapsody upon some pious thought or sentence, the music, indeed, could be played at another speed and with another expression and it would have the exultant incisive statement of a rhapsody, it could be stated, set forth, 'laid out' as a rhapsody, but in its true form, undistorted, it is devotional and personal. It is an act of adoration to a holy individual, the expression of love for this individual, and the thought of what sufferings this individual has undergone for the sake of others.[1]

But I have no religion. I envy, but cannot enter into those feelings. Perhaps their aesthetic expression is all the more beautiful to me because of my deficiency. All that I know is that the chorale makes me want to weep. And, of course, it recalls to me the time of my life when I had it so much in mind, the summer month when I left London and went to Holland, and arrived in the little town of Leeuwarden, the capital of Friesland, and used to sing this chorale over to myself every morning when I woke up, and looked out of my window over the roofs of the town and down to the placid canal, tree-shaded ; and had no book to read, and at last the letters came, forwarded from Amsterdam, and enclosed in one of them, a feather from the firebird's wing.

[1] "Mein Jesu, was für Seelemüh", one of the hymns Johann Sebastian Bach wrote for the hymn book compiled by Georg Christian Schemelli in 1736. It is a meditation on our Lord's agony in the garden of Gethsemane. I heard it played upon the clavichord by Violet Gordon Woodhouse.

VI

Escalera Dorada

WE promised " a masqued or false beginning ". This whole episode was to be " a flourish or a flight of fancy based upon a phrase or a part of a sentence that comes later ", a promise which now fulfils itself, for the mosque of Córdoba and its court of orange trees now fades away or disappears — in just the same way that the palace in Murano has vanished or sunk of its own weight of years into the waters — and we find ourselves coming down the ' Escalera Dorada ', a double staircase with gilded balusters, into the transept of a cathedral, a transition which is nothing less than our arrival into this land, of fact and of imagination, and our descent into it by means of one of the best known and first-seen architectural landmarks of that kingdom, but it resembles nothing else so much as the openwork iron staircase coming down from a high gallery under the roof, behind the stage in some huge theatre, near to the proscenium arch, and climbing, down, down, under ropes and pulleys, among scenes and backcloths that we half-recognize, onto a huge and empty stage. In this manner we enter into Spain, " for it is Spain, but another country of the mind, like Spain seen in a feverish dream ".

The experience, or act of magic, is that of waving aloft the golden feather or the lock of hair. Waving it in the air for the fulfilment of vow or promise.

And now a moment of waiting, a rustling of feathers, a

clapping of her wings, and the firebird runs out onto the gilded landing. It is the balcony, high above, from which the double stair descends ; and the firebird, the bird-of-paradise, runs out to the balcony upon her points, comes to the gilt balustrade, and begins to come down the stair.

A staircase, remember, that descends into a cathedral from a door, high up, on the sloping hill outside ! And the door can be open or shut, it is of no importance. We are not to know how it is that the firebird runs out onto the balcony. It could be a little figure coming out of a clock at the moment when that strikes the hour, one of those old clocks in cathedrals which people linger to see until the hour is struck. The branches of the stair part, and go asunder, have a pause or landing to each side, and lead down again into each other, join and mingle, come down together, unbroken, in one long descent. This is the manner of the 'Escalera Dorada', the golden staircase of Burgos Cathedral, and in the last flight, when it debouches, when it comes out upon the floor, it turns from gilt metal to marble, it has winged monsters or gryphons upon the balustrading, and the marble steps open fanwise, grow broader until they reach the pavement.

But now something happens that can only be described in terms of the shifting of stage scenery : for the balcony, at top of the double staircase, lowers itself, comes down lower to our level, not too high above the level of our eyes, not too low to see the ballerina's feet and legs, while we feel ourselves raised up, lifted, as it were, from pit to dress circle or grand tier, all of which takes but a moment or two and is accomplished in semi-darkness, which is no longer in duration than the time it takes to read these words, or than the act of getting our eyes accustomed to the glitter and brilliance when the lights go up.

And now we are ready to begin.

The firebird, as large as life, and nearer to the footlights, descends to our astonishment, in the same person, down both branches of the double stair. Down, down, a step at a time, down both sides of the staircase, but with so light a foot that, like the fountain foot, it leaps and you do not know the moment when it comes to earth again.

The motion of the descent is that of a bird-of-paradise stepping down, branch to branch, bough to bough, from top to bottom of a golden tree, for the birds-of-paradise prepare a dancing ground, a stage or ballroom at the tree foot, and in nature, the dancers alight from all directions dropping through the leaves.

Down, down, to both sides, in simultaneous vision, like the figure and its image in a looking-glass, down, down, and outwards, for the first flight of stairs to the double balconies or landings, where the firebird, the ballerina, turns in her paces and the double image coalesces, merges into itself, and becomes the living person. This beauty of going up or down, from step to step, is one of the beauties of the world since I was young, and a recognizable trait of person and of the individual. And it is as though, in ecstasy or hallucination, the stair began to lift or climb, of itself, in order to keep the dancer level before our eyes, and so prolong the moment, for it is the immortal moment, there can never be anything more beautiful than the dancer coming down the stair. It is the transcendental moment, the exceptional or transcendental, that has no parallel, that has broken, of itself, into some superfetation of the ordinary, and that, if we are to think in terms of familiar images, only compares, where other Gothic tapestries are concerned, to the tapestries of the History of the Unicorn (in the Musée Cluny) which are upon a rose-coloured ground. That is why we " open " in a wood of primroses, but they are rose or red primroses, not primroses of the ordinary kind. The Cluny tapestries, too, are exceptional ; they are transcendental because of their colouring, because of their rose-coloured background, which puts them apart, makes them unlike other mediaeval tapestries which are upon an ordinary ground. But they are exceptional, as well, in technique and execution, and in the beauty of the ' millefleur ' ground sown with flowers and little animals, little birds, and rabbits.

Let us think for a moment of the Cluny tapestries ! There are six hangings, and in each the lady of the tapestry appears : playing an organ in a ' millefleur ' field ; standing before a blue and gold damask tent ; plaiting a crown of roses ; and (I cannot remember two of the themes) seated between the lion and unicorn, holding up a mirror to the unicorn, in accordance with the old legend that this animal " so loved chastity that the only way to capture it is to place a virgin in the place where it is accustomed to go to water. As soon as it sees her, it will run to her." Let there be a legend, too, attaching to the wood of rose red primroses, as there must be to all things exceptional and transcendental, not least to this phantom or apparition upon the golden staircase ; for it is either a ghostly person or a ghostly stair, and in the certainty that both exist, that I have seen both with my eyes, I have done no more than attempt the impossible, take the theatre into the cathedral and the cathedral into the theatre, and depict the firebird or ballerina coming down the ' Escalera Dorada ' onto the floor or soil of Spain.

Where we quickly lose ourselves.

To meet again, where ? At the shop in the Sierpes where they sell painted fans and *mantillas*, opposite to the tobacconist where the posters of bull-fights are displayed. And the ghost seen sitting in the well of the assize court at the baize-topped table, among inkpots and bewigged lawyers upon an interminable afternoon, born of that ennui, now gazes at a poster of a *torero* in a green *traje de luces*, in particular, and at another of a matador waving his cyclamen cape, and avoiding a gigantic, surging bull.

The ladies in *mantillas* and spotted crinolines resemble Phœnician goddesses and come forward fluttering in all their flounces. The panpipe of the knifegrinder sounds at the street corner. There are climbing roses upon palm trees, the magnolia, and the high acacia. What a world of little courts and patios ! And the persons we meet in Seville, whom we will never see again ; driving to the old convents in an open carriage, while the rest of the world was at the bull-fight, when there was that slight accident, something happened to one of the rubber tyres, and the niece of our friend, the dark beauty in the huge, black flopping hat, the hat of ' La Belle Strasbourgeoise ' in Largillière's painting, but a Spaniard, and a Borgia (Borja), shaded her face with her hand so as not to be stared at by the crowd.

What a world of indescribable, ineluctable sensations, at the mere mention of driving in a carriage round that city, in the hot afternoons, in the glorious, high midday, in the scented evening ! There is probably no other city in the world where you can drive in an open carriage and meet so many cavaliers and amazons, and in fact it is better to go in a carriage. You are unpopular if you drive in a motor down the *Paseo de las Delicias*, among " plantes et arbres d'essences variées, principalement des palmiers, des orangers, et des mandariniers, très fréquenté le soir par les promeneurs et les équipages " (somehow this sounds even lovelier in French than English !),

towards the " vaste plaine appelée Tablada ", and the Venta
de Antequera " où l'on enferme les taureaux la veille des
corridas ".

It is the thought of what beauties have gone, or could
drive under the feathery acacias, to the turn of the avenue in
view of the Giralda, and so back again, for it is the point of
the promenade to pass and repass the same persons, to see
them come by once more, and again. A marvellous instance
of which is the midday procession of carriages during the
Feria, so close on one another that they have to go at walking
pace up and down the double avenue of pavilions or *casetas*
in the blazing heat. But this episode has to keep to its condition of being a vision or an hallucination ; it must not be the
Feria in a particular year, and hardly in a particular city, unless,
by Seville, we mean the totality or epitome of all that is
implicit in the name of Spain.

For there are, or were, the other cities. Till the fall of the
Kingdom (ninety years ago) there was this procession of
carriages every evening at Naples up and down the Toledo, a
street named after Don Pedro de Toledo, the Spanish Viceroy,
going slowly, slowly, at a walking pace, through the middle of
the old town, and it is impossible for me to write these words,
who have known them, who was inspired by them for the
first book I wrote, and not to think of the frescoes of Solimena
and of the double geometrical staircases of the architect Ferdinando Sanfelice ; of the white horses of Solimena in the sacristy
of San Paolo Maggiore and his history of Heliodorus in the
Gesù Nuovo ; the cloister-vineyard of Santa Chiara with its
walks of majolica ; San Gregorio Armeno with its coloured
marbles and its nuns in red and black ; the mummies of princes
and princesses of the house of Aragón upstairs in the sacristy
of San Domenico Maggiore ; and the flashing white cloister

of Cosimo Fansaga in the Certosa up above the town, looking down on Naples. It is true they would mean little or nothing to the persons driving in the carriages, but Naples is more than tinged, it is deeply tainted with the blood of Spain. The more curious the scene, therefore, when the carriages emerge from the Toledo and come out onto the Chiaia, in view of Vesuvius and the siren bay, among the *lazzaroni* ; Capri in the distance as in the haze of a Claude painting, and the yellow banks of Sorrento ; and looking the other way, past the tomb of Virgil, to Posillipo, and to the far islands, Procida and Ischia, passing the ruins of the Palazzo di Donn' Anna, built out into the bay, with wide balconies, haunted by the notes of the lute, and in our imagination, by the embodiment or reincarnation whom we have in mind.

Not content with which, we must transport ourselves to other cities of the Spanish Viceroys : to Lima, where we would find ourselves taking the air in open carriages, where the old houses have projecting latticed balconies, and the pedestrians are the *tapadas* (veiled ladies), but veiled in bright colours. Here, in Lima, and in Mexico, we pass the bull-ring ; and the gold and silver of Mexican mines glitters from the saddles, the stirrups, and the bridles. They are the horsemen in *charro* dress, in black with much silver embroidery, and the *sombrero* ; and the ladies wear, not the *mantilla*, but the Mexican dress called *china poblana*, as Madame Calderón de la Barca describes it : " a white muslin chemise, and a petticoat, shorter than the chemise, and divided into two colours, the top of it, yellow satin, with gold fringe, gold bands, and spangles ; the rest of scarlet cashmere embroidered with gold and silver ; an under-petticoat embroidered and trimmed with lace to come below it. The first petticoat is trimmed with gold up the sides, which are slit open, and tied up with coloured ribbon. A long, broad, coloured sash, something like an officer's belt, tied behind after going twice or thrice round the waist, into which is stuck a silver cigar-case. Silk stockings, or no stockings at all, and white satin shoes embroidered in gold." Such is the *china poblana* dress, difficult to describe and coming from Puebla, much worn in Mexico, but resembling nothing so much as a dancer's dress from an old ballet. There is some story or old legend connecting this costume with a Chinese princess supposed to have been wrecked on the Pacific coast of Mexico in a galleon from Manila,[1] but the *china poblana* dress is not in the least Oriental in effect. It is more like a multi-coloured Columbine from an old ballet. The sensation of driving in a carriage with a person so dressed would be that of seeing a theatrical company promenading round a town in travesty, and it is thus that we imagine ourselves on the avenues to and from Chapultepec, among the *charros*.

[1] The tomb of the *china poblana* is to be seen in the church of La Compañía de Jesus at Puebla. She became a Christian under the name Catalina de San Juan, and threw aside her finery for a red flannel skirt. The people revered her memory and imitated her dress. Hence, the *china poblana* costume.

VII

En Sanguine

Now this present book has been concerned, so far, with the 'sham emotions' of the theatre, if false they be. It is the school of anti-nature, of night turned to day. The theme of the embarcation need be no more than an advertisement or an invitation into these pages. Once launched, and sailing from left to right across the stage, the voyage is no longer of factual or geographical significance. We shall leave *Gilles* standing, as in the painting, motionless, his hands to his sides, not moving or stirring. He is in the sacred trance of poetry, a mood I have known, myself, though it has not attacked me for some time.

But why does the trance of poetry strike its hierophants so that they stare dumbly, and neither move nor stir ? Why is it that *Gilles* is so awkward and wooden in his attitude ? Could it be that he, too, upon that spring afternoon, saw the figure going into the red-brick house, passing under the rose pink magnolia tree ? And another rose pink magnolia, at the back of the house, below the bedroom window ? Of which no more said, now. But no, I cannot let the chance go by. I am near-sighted. I could not make much of the leaves, and only saw the rose pink, swan-like blossoms. I do not even know their shape. I could not see them clearly. Whether they were open cups, lotus cups ; or thin and narrow, like the white swan, like the ibis ? But I believe this rose pink magnolia was like a lotus, like a waterlily, that it had pointed petals, that the rose pink cups were nearly naked on the branches.

I have known the white ibis roosting, in numbers, on the bare branches of a tree. They were like white magnolia flowers, and in the dawn they spread their wings and flew away. They were the scavengers of the city, feeding on the open drains and sewers. Who would think it, to see a white ibis upon a bough, or walking in a field ! But the rose pink magnolia is of another creation. It is rarer of nature. For there are white flowers, and snow, and white swans, but this is rose-petal, of a particular rose. The tree is " pyramidal in habit " and the flowers are cup-shaped, they are like goblets, and in ignorance one could call it a pink tulip tree. It is " the giant Himalayan magnolia ", though it would never grow so tall in London, and one has to imagine for oneself what a wonder it must be when it is as high as oak or elm tree and loaded with many hundreds of the rose pink flowers.

More could be written of them. For they will not ride the spring gales. Now, a few days later, the blossoms may be lying dashed upon the paving stones. They are at the mercy of the wind and rain. But what a miracle of beauty in their few days, which, to them, are so many months or years ; when the sun comes to them and the rose pink petals open in warmth and admiration, like a career that is soon over, that is quickly ended, fed on adulation, while the magnolia for a whole lifetime is neither younger nor older in its flowering season, for the miracle of the rose pink magnolia plays every year ! How curious to meet the rose pink magnolia before our opening in the wood of primroses ! For the one is symbol of the other and significant of the same person. As though, even in little things, there was something extraordinary in the attendant fates. To find growing there, not by design, but as though planted in forethought and anticipation, this most beautiful of flowering trees, which takes twenty or more years before it blossoms!

Nothing else but the rose pink magnolia tree ; the rest is brick wall and paving stones. But listen to the magnolias! One, is " the Chinese Yulan or lily tree " ; another, " flowers, greenish - yellow " ; most, " creamy white and lemon-scented " ; another has " upright, canary-yellow, scented flowers, and at the least touch the wood and leaves emit an aromatic fragrance " ; " goblet-shaped, pure white flowers " ; or " ivory-white and like huge tulips " ; some, " a lovely shade of rich purple, white inside " ; others, " bell-shaped, white-suffused, wine-red flowers " ; another has " small egg-shaped flowers " ; another, " pure white with crimson stamens " ; and another, " white, and stained with purple ". Among the magnolias there is a multitude of persons.

But none so beautiful as the rose pink magnolia, which now speaks to us for other reasons, and not its beauty only. We have explained, already, that the pink magnolia is like a human being in its period of blossoming, that it comes to maturity like the maiden, not sooner or later, but outlives the mortal. When I saw it, upon that spring afternoon, and only for a moment, the rose pink magnolia looked so beautiful that it could have called a school of painters or poets into being, which happened in the Orient, for over many centuries there were painters who did nothing else but paint the blossoming trees. But nothing of that sort is here intended. The rose pink magnolia is but outward symbol for the being whom we now see for the first time in another setting.

Let me think, in order to console myself, of the methods of other artists! This is what de Caylus, who knew him well, has to say of Watteau's method of composition. " He

sketched with no immediate purpose, for he never made a
preliminary draft or jotted down an idea for any of his pictures. Usually he made his studies in a bound book, with the
result that he always had a great many ready to hand. When
moved to paint a picture he was sure of finding in his notebook things he had approved ; then he assembled them in
groups, usually to fit in with a landscape he had visualized or
got ready." So it comes to this : Watteau, at least, is not to
be numbered among those artists who must have everything
ready in their heads before they can begin. There have been
painters, writers, musicians of that kind, in plenty, but their
output has been small and it is never, perhaps, stressed sufficiently how important a part improvisation, or we could call
it the gift of sudden and spontaneous creation, has played
even in those works of art which are most celebrated for their
preconceived and perfect form. The instances of this truth
are most patent where they might be least expected.

But listen, further, to de Caylus ! He writes of Watteau's
dissatisfaction with his own paintings. " It might be thought
that his brilliant success with the public would have flattered
his self-esteem sufficiently to save him from such annoyances.
But his temperament was such that he was continually sickened
by what he was doing. I believe that one of the strongest
reasons for this disgust had, as its motivating principle, the
elevated views that he entertained on the art of painting. I
am in a position to affirm that he conceived the art more nobly
than he practised it, an attitude of mind that was unlikely to
prejudice him in favour of his own productions. . . . The
exercise of drawing had infinite charms for him and although
sometimes the figure on which he happened to be at work was
not undertaken with any particular purpose in view, he had
the greatest imaginable difficulty in tearing himself away from

it. I must insist that in general he drew without a purpose.
. . . He possessed cavaliers' and comedians' costumes in
which he dressed up such persons as he could find, of either
sex, who were capable of posing adequately, and whom he
drew in such attitudes as nature dictated and with a ready
preference for those that were the most simple." Theatrical
wardrobe he had none, other than the short coat and breeches
and the hanging cloak. And de Goncourt, editing de Caylus,
continues : " *Sanguine* was Watteau's favourite medium ; he
loved it, French-Venetian as he was, for the warmth of its
tonality ; he may even be said to make use of a *sanguine* all
his own which is crimson in colour rather than the reddish-
brown of the type generally employed and which derives its
charming colour, its flush of life, from the artist's skilful
opposition of blacks and whites. This *sanguine* was, I am
inclined to believe, that English red chalk whose superiority
is vaunted in the technical manuals. The *sanguines* of Watteau
are miraculous works. . . ." [1]

Watteau was a draughtsman who excelled in drawing
separate figures upon the same sheet of paper. Not, therefore,
to be termed groups of figures, for they have no co-ordination.
They are the same person in different attitudes, looking to
right and left, or seen from back and front, with another person
altogether, it may be, filling the corner of the sheet in order to
waste no paper. But what is inimitable in his drawings, beside
his miraculous handling and his rendering of materials, is the
merging of one figure into its neighbour, whether they look
in both directions, or the figures are of different persons but
have the degree of connexion of flowers of two sorts grafted
upon one stem.

[1] (The passages quoted are from E. de Goncourt, *Three French Eighteenth Century
Painters*, translated by Robin Ironside: London, The Phaidon Press, 1948.)

Now, at least, the drawings of Watteau are taken from the living model. They are drawn from life, unlike the figures in his paintings. And there is this same difference in the moment of the rose pink magnolia tree. It is no longer the school of anti-nature, of night turned to day. These are no longer the ' sham emotions ' of the theatre, if false they be. Instead, it is the same person encountered in the other sphere of her existence, for that has a dual nature. One is the shadow life, one the real, and in proximity to either there can be no certainty as to which is which. They intermingle : they haunt each other : they throw their shadow each on each.

All of which remarks are contingent to our theme and purpose, for the figure entering the house and passing the rose pink magnolia tree had direct and unequivocal resemblance to Watteau's red chalk drawings. She is one of his *sanguine* drawings to the life, or indeed, the totality of them, except that nowhere in the entire body of his paintings and drawings is there anybody who resembles her. There is no such phantom among the red chalk masquers, sister to *Le Grand Gilles* or glittering daughter : ghost among ghosts, and a ghost among the Columbines : I know : I have compared them.

You may look in vain among his drawings. And not only in his *sanguines* ; but in what de Goncourt calls his " painted drawings ", done in *sanguine*, Italian (black) chalk, and white chalk, " on that tinted paper which has been christened *papier chamois* in the sale catalogues ". But there is no sign of the ghost for whom we are searching. The resemblance is there, but not the person. Neither in his paintings nor his drawings. One may look, in particular, among the Columbines, for it is there that you would expect to find her, among the drawings of " female heads in flat caps ". The drawings are lovely and exquisite, but there is no sign of her.

There are drawings of hands, which could be the hands of Columbine, and indeed, we would know her figure by her hands. There could be no mistaking those : her long, thin wrists, flower-like wrists, for they ride upon the air like flowers ; the back of the hand is long and narrow, it curves and dips, the fingers bend down from it while she is dancing, which gives to the back of her wrists a resemblance to the head and forehead of a bird, to the head of a bird-of-paradise, or to the Amherstian pheasant which has a tiara or crown of feathers on its head, and this must come from the way she holds her fingers when she dances, the index and little finger lifted and apart, and the two middle fingers lower and yet separate, the thumb lower still, making her wrist and fingers like the head of a bird, a bird-of-paradise or painted pheasant, itself dancing. But look at her wrists and hands a moment more, and you will see them like white lilies. They are pale and flower-like, and yet they have something of the serpent. There is a cobra in a bird-of-paradise, and a serpent, a hooded rattlesnake in a temple dancer. What is the bayadère but the naga, the many-headed serpent, dancing ? The serpent god, the lily god, lily-wristed. We look in vain in the drawings ; there is a wrist or a hand to remind us of her and nothing more.

But happily, or unhappily, we see her face. We recognize her. She is the phantom of *L'Embarquement*, and the person on account of whom it was painted. But she has not come down to go on board. She waits in the wings and will come on again. She is absent, like a ghost, from every painting, every drawing. And yet inhabits the world of Watteau, so that we look for her in each picture, in each *sanguine*. There may never have been another instance of such a haunting.

VIII

Spell

AT this moment we hear the wheezing of a hurdygurdy.

We meet a man wearing a black patch over one eye and with a wooden stump instead of a leg. He is carrying a violin. He is dark and swarthy, and so tall that we shall notice him again and again and wonder who he can be. I saw him at a fair in the nineteen-thirties, in the outskirts of Paris, near St.-Denis.

There is a bigger circus or fair population to be met with upon the road in France, even now in our own time, than in any other country, nomads of the *piste* for ever on the move down the long corridors of poplars ; where the old mare grazes, where there are blackened circles in the dog-grass. The scene could be one of a hundred provincial towns in France, or the Foire de St.-Germain, or the fair of St.-Denis.

And we still hear the wheezing of the hurdygurdy.

Now the tirra-lirra of the *musette* or hurdygurdy has its aristocratic origins. It has come down in the world and was once played at Court. It has survived the French Revolution and is one of the few things left to us of the shepherds and shepherdesses of Arcady.

There are booths selling all kinds of goods, and people are eating and drinking at the counters. And now there are lines of trees down the middle of the pavement and tall houses with many rows of windows. And it is gently raining, but only for a few moments, as it does upon summer afternoons after a thunderstorm. When it stops, a blue mist or steam is rising from the puddles, and something drops with a crash — it could be a trestle-table tumbling to the ground. A little later there is the loud sound of another, falling in the distance.

Among the curiosities of the fair are the painted signboards to advertise the strolling players. And it is here that we recognize *Le Grand Gilles* of the Louvre. Who, that knows the painting, has any doubt of his beginnings? His pose shows how entirely he is borrowed from the strolling players. He stands with both arms held stiffly to his sides, in the attitude of one of the figures painted on the canvas hoardings. If this wonderful painting, Watteau's masterpiece, were to be cleaned and the accumulation of two hundred years and more of dust and dirt and deterioration removed, what would the effect be? Would *Le Grand Gilles* emerge from his twilight? Would he be, once more, the white pierrot of the hustings? For we do not believe that his hat and ruff, his short coat and pantaloons, were yellow and parchment-coloured when they were new. Look at his sleeves, which are so wrinkled at the elbows! Look at the pink ribbons in his dancing shoes!

It is the portrait of a young man who was a friend of Watteau, or vaguer than that, the son of a doctor who was one of Watteau's friends. He is the pierrot of the early years of Louis-Quinze, painted, in all probability, in 1720 after Watteau had come back from London, and only five years after the livelong reign of Louis-Quatorze had ended. It is the portrait of a pierrot, many years, perhaps a hundred years, before his time, and it is only when we look closely at him that we can read the period in which he lived in the cut of his coat and trousers. And how essentially they are a Frenchman's clothes! *Gilles*'s trousers are cut like the trousers of a French workman or a railway porter. The trousers of *Gilles* are the premonitory ghost or warning of the Zouave. Nobody but a Frenchman could have designed or made the Zouave's trousers.[1]

Gilles stands before us in the manner of a dolt or giant, one of the freaks of the fair, ordered to stand still and not to move, but, also, it is the stance or pose of his mental state. And, as well, this is the wooden attitude in which the painters of the fair have rendered him in their incompetence. He is one of the daubs of the fairground ; the dolt or zany of the tents. And the miracle of this work of art is the poetry and sensibility imputed to *Gilles*, despite his expressionless face and the woodenness of his attitude. *Gilles* has stood there for two hundred years, and more, and is never a day older. He is not intended for the light of day, but for the lit airs of the theatre. There is in his mood something that is equivalent to when we see the full moon burning in broad daylight. It has cleared a space for itself in the firmament, but, all the same, it ought not to be there at all. He is not a rich man, nor a poor one, nor the member of any serious profession. His father, the doctor, will not approve his means of livelihood, which is hopeless, and can lead nowhere. It is not work. It consists in standing about, doing nothing. Take one more look at him before he burns out in the morning sky !

His ruff is nothing but the collar of his time. It would be wrong to read any other significance into that moonlight expanse, unless it be, simply, that it is for Sunday best. His feats are not dangerous. And he is no dolt or zany, but poet and acrobat of the company. His are feats of poetry, not of intellect. He has the appearance of standing quite still in the moonlight. He is like a person who stands quite still, out

[1] Général Lamoricière in 1831.

there, and never moves. Moonstruck, to all intents and purposes, but not looking at us with a silly stare. He is in the
sacred trance of poetry, and while it possesses him he cannot
move or stir. But, as we look at him, he fades out, like the
moon going behind a cloud. And for the moment it is cold
and lonely here without him.

Not for long.

A moment later we are walking in a long street leading to
a bridge connecting the old and the new parts of a town. A
railway runs below, and the bridge goes over the glass roofs
of the railway station. Even the guide-book remarks that " the
view of the city from the bridge at night, after the lamps are
lit, is very striking ". And the whole town is " prepared for a
festival ". There are floodlights on the Castle and on the
Grecian monument upon the hill, opposite, and every night
there is dancing to pipe music in the public gardens.

How beautiful this city looks from a distance ! It has two
or three spired buildings, nothing when you come up nearer
to them, but they stand out like the towers of another Kremlin
in the northern mist. The grey grain of the Castle, for the
stone is cut and dressed in a foreign, perhaps a Gallic fashion,
has a surface like the grain of stoneground bread. The long
street below the Castle has shops only to one side, and the
railway runs where the moat, or even an arm of the sea, should
be. And there is a street, parallel to, and behind that, with
severe Grecian buildings in blackened stone, one of them an
early nineteenth-century publisher's office, as stern as the
premises of the weekly legal newspaper would have been in
Ancient Sparta ; and coming to the corner we behold the
Castle, once again, upon its green baize hill.

This is a town like all other towns and a town not like
other towns. How tall the houses are ! There are buildings,

down below in the side-streets, that are ten or twelve storeys high, tall grey tenements with stygian windows. In the new part of the town are the squares and circuses, the iron railings and honeysuckle ironwork of the balconies. I was born in a Grecian crescent, facing the same ocean, and played as a child in a crescent garden near a laburnum tree. But this long street in which we are walking cuts straight across the old town. The bridge leads from the old to the new part, or from the new part to the old, whichever way you look at it, and the bridge was rebuilt in 1897, the year that I was born.

It is trying to rain. But it is midday, and wind rattles the framed photographs that hang outside the theatre. Rain runs down the windows of the bookshop and of the tobacconist over the road, the same rain we are all used to. And when you look round again the sun is out. The spires of the town stand out in beauty, even the monument that is like a giant drinking fountain, of granite, halfway down the street of shops. And we cross the cast-iron bridge into the new town.

So now, the significance of this place of waiting, that is the long street leading to the theatre, can lose itself in the flowers of imagery. Why is it that we led up to it with mention of the northern auricula ? Or of the hooded flowerseller whose knotted handkerchief all but hid her face and hair ? Why but because the direct description would identify, and in one respect, alone, there could be no question of mistaking the flowerseller for any other person ? The little flowerseller who is, herself, the stage auriculas that she sells at her flower-stall and the carnations *Jenny Lynch* and *Prince of Denmark*, in virtue of their colour and of their complexions or ' carnations ' ; ' pink and white ' ; or ' painted on a ground of pink and white ' ; flaked, too, which means touched or marked with red, as in the world of travesty ; glittering inhabitant,

therefore, of that other or alternate world, of the theatre of
artifice, which, now, and for a long while to come, may be the
only reality.

" The floral clock immediately beside the statue (works in
the pedestal) is worth a glance ", and so is much else, besides.
There are the fisherwomen of Newhaven and Musselburgh in
their striped dresses ; but, more than all else, it is the northern
air that shapes the accent, paints the pinks and roses, and tastes
delicious in the cream of Corstorphine. It is in the smell of
a peat fire ; in the smoking of the haddock ; above all, in the
mists hanging over the waters, hiding the far side, where I
longed to be, always lifting in the evening, when it was too
late ; but the mists themselves were beautiful, and so was
the thought of the phantom born there.

Next morning, again, the sun was like a lovely bird upon
the window-ledge. It had red-gold hair and bird-like feet.
And it inhabited the house. It lay on the sofa in a blue
dressing-gown next to the breakfast table. It moved from room
to room and spoke upon the telephone. A red-gold bird, not
the wintry robin, and it sang and danced of another world,
but miracle of miracles, of our own flesh and blood and in a
language that all can understand. For this phantom, born
again, is many other persons. A spring evening, smelling of
spring, or the lovely dawn bird upon the window-sill.

In the July evening, when the fire was lit, we looked at
the little boys skating in top-hats, in a spelling book, and drew
the curtains, and took down the Magical History of Mother
Goose. Oh ! the beauty of her thatched cottage under the
trees, with tall hollyhocks and honeysuckle, and we see the
crone in her steeple hat, sitting in the kitchen, her black cat
beside her ; the kettle is boiling, the tall clock is ticking, and

the old chapbook turns into a pantomime. The beautiful glittering daughter touched with her wand, and turned the page, and the magical history knew neither youth nor age. Oh ! the beauty of the tall house, and the magic of it, in the panelled room ; the fire flickered, the cat purred, there was magic in the room.

That summer I held in my hand the golden chain between youth and age. O rose that has known the violet, stay with me, here, at ' the gate of heaven ', where deep flows the river and dark lies the shade. O the river that runs along the smooth lawns, running like music through the green demesne ; it could be one of the rivers of paradise, within the grey walls ; and here, at ' the gate of heaven ', a rustic cottage stands high, and hanging woods behind ; thatched roof, white walls, and antlered balconies ; it has a room with little paintings from Canton of beauties as fragrant as the jessamine or gardenia teas ; the thatch is soft as moleskin, cut and sewn ; the hanging woods are like a backcloth or a painted drop scene ; we are waiting for the hunting party and the Prince of Courland ; or it could be the cottage where James sits by the fire, dreaming of the Sylphide ; but nothing of the kind, it is the meeting-place of the anglers. Does never a fisherman, casting his line in the late evening, when the woods are unreal and there is late light upon the mullions, when deep glides the river and the shades are long, cast again and again into the pool, and catching the little rainbow trout, flecked and spotted with vermilion, that dies and lies gasping, feel the poetry and magic of the enchanted hour, and know that this is the maiden of the dancing waters, the maiden of the river, and the ghost of the Swiss Cottage in the green demesne of Cahir ?

Upon the wet rocks, out in the west, the women are walking in red petticoats, dyed red from the fuchsia hedges in front of their white cabins ; they call out in their own tongue in the steep fields with the loose stone walls.   That land is the sister to this other shore, to the house with turrets among the silver birch trees, that I never saw, sister to the rocks and rain ; this is the sister to the Gothic drawing-room with the harp and the rushing river below, to the holy well, the beds of watercress, to the ghost upon the stepping stones, to the barefoot figure under the white damson bough, the black waters and the gallery of yews, to the haunting, dead, dead, dying, not quite dead, but dead like the generation of swans whom I saw settling upon the flat waters ;   now, so many years later, other swans, other jackdaw princesses in the dark tower, upon the winding stair.   Come away, then, do not look back, nor count the clutch of eggs upon the rushstrewn floor, for it is as much the keep of dead thoughts as the leafless woods of BallyEdmund which I passed, that February, like a secret and a mystery, all day and every day, in midst of the hunting, while the deeper mystery was preparing.

IX

Vision

WE open in a wood of primroses.

But not primroses of the ordinary yellow-flannel sort ; they are the double primrose *Madame Pompadour*, of extreme rarity, of glowing ruby red (few collectors of old primroses have more than a plant or two growing in their gardens) which has seeded and naturalized itself over some acres of the woods along a river, and I have not to tell the reader exactly where it is, but the scene is in Co. Clare, along the Shannon. (I have been told this. I have not seen it.) How beautiful it must be !

And I suppose, growing there in profusion in their hundreds and their thousands, that in a certain mood of ignorance or of reflection it would be possible to walk some way into the wood of primroses, admiring them, glade after glade, dell after dell, lying wine red (the synonym for *Madame Pompadour* is *Crimson Velvet*) into the little distances between the tree stems, only for those few days and evenings of spring, and not know that this is something different, that it is one of the miracles of nature, to be seen nowhere else in the world, and never again but here, in this far-away and remote place, lying out into the Atlantic. Or one could be seized, at once, as I believe that I would be (as I have been !) at first sight of this wonder, and never be able to forget it.

Let it be one or the other, it matters not which, so long as
we can see it ! The primroses have ' escaped ' from an old
garden into the woods, and it is like walking into a theatre,
the sight is so lively, once we have left the green lawns of the
demesne and hear no more the flowing waters. It is like the
début, the first appearance of a phenomenon that is to alter
the image in the poet's eye. You may look behind you in a
moment, and see nothing else, be shut in entirely by the trees,
and by the crimson primroses growing in their tens of
thousands. Why *Madame Pompadour* ? It seems that no
one knows. No one can tell how old this primrose is.

But it is known for the most beautiful of the primroses.
Persons who have seen it growing tell me it is a sight not to
be believed. The entire wood loses its identity and is taken
over by the crimson primroses. It is as though some other
flower that grows in woods, the anemone, the bluebell, ' went
over ' to another civilization, root and flower. Come deeper
into the primrose wood ; the rose red, wine red primrose,
the crimson, the vermilion among the primroses, making the
multitudinous woods incarnadine ! Painting Titania's bower ;
or, it may be, dyeing it to match her hair ! The double crimson primrose ; some with clustered polyanthus heads, the
candelabra primroses with their lights all burning, at once,
in the soft woods of spring !

The woods are carpeted with cloth-of-roses. You tread
on primroses. The honey breath of the primroses sighs upon
you, and there are little gales of primroses, soft lulls again,
heroic deeds down in the vermilion, crimson laughter, and
soft sighs like dying sounds of music. It is another country,
another continent of flowers ; walled in like a theatre, lit
with its own lights ; with its own stage-hands, firemen, door-
keepers ; its own carpenters and engineers, nurses in uniform ;

programme sellers, intervals, refreshment of dew; and, now, the lifting of the primrose curtain.

For in intoxication of the red primroses, and in enchantment, we hear a knocking, knocking, like the prompter knocking in his box, like the three thumps before the curtain goes up; or it is some bird, a woodpecker, knocking on its tree. And another bird calling out, like laughter, as it wings its way.

The world shrinks, in little, into the primrose wood, with a sweeping of the strings, with a sweeping of the golden wires. Touch the strings, loved genius of music, once, and three times! We need no more till "Time runs back to fetch the Age of Gold".

The curtain lifts and we behold a world of beauty in a nutshell. It is 'the wood near Athens', or our own Blue Man's Bower; a scene so old that no one remembers what it means, born in a raindrop, no bigger than that, and as quick to die. The Queen of Elfhame, wings of gauze upon her shoulders, sits on her chair of state; long gloves and sleeves of gauze, a dress like the frill of a double primrose, no longer, not to hide her legs, but of black and violet among the crimson primroses to be the queen of them; and now comes down from her throne, and we see her crown or little tiara, her necklace, and her bright hair hidden in a net or snood; and dances on her points; and in the end, walks as light as the fluff of a dandelion upon the heads and backs of men.

And, immediately, in an act in a raindrop:

Titania, lying asleep, in 'another part of the wood', and the hand of Oberon squeezing the juice of Love-in-Idleness, 'a little western flower', upon her eyelids.

And in an act in the golden eye of a flower:

Bianca Cappello making love to the Duke of Florence; walking on high pattens in Venice; in the house of her father, upon the balcony, bleaching her red hair ; marrying, moved to Florence, become the mistress of the Grand Duke, dying in mystery.

Supping in the hot garden ; braiding her red hair with pearls ; haunting the long passage over the Arno ; and in the ilex woods of Pratolino.

Whence spring other visions :

As the queen, in her closet, while the Italian who is to be stabbed and murdered, sings to the guitar. And a hundred years later, as the poetess whom Milton attended to hear play the lute, in the Palazzo de Donn' Anna, built out into the siren bay, looking on Vesuvius and the islands, with wide balconies.

Or as the dancer, Florinda, in her pink satin *basquine* with flounces of black lace, and a white rose behind her ear; leading to other metamorphoses, for it is Spain, but another country of the mind, like Spain seen in a feverish dream.

Or as I first saw her upon that afternoon :

One of the beauties of the beautiful world, since I was young ; the only being of hope and promise since the second disaster ended ; born at the house with turrets among the silver birch trees, thence, to the theatre in the flower market, where the meteor burned in daylight and sweet dawn broke in the afternoon ; deer-footed like the red fawn, Aurora and meteor in one, the red fawn of the glen, running or dancing like the deer, the red-haired maiden in the garden, like a reindeer turned into a maiden, and a meteor burning as a virgin.

Like a ghost running into the garden, down the colonnade or hemicycle, from left to right, behind the leaping fountain, and in a moment, with quick lovely steps running onto the stage, wonderful and lovely being, in rose and silver, with dazzling smile, coppery-red hair, thin waist, and flower-like wrists ; and as the music changes, dancing like bird or angel, but gone into the wings. . . . Later, in the chain of waltzes, in the waltz with the little glissando, with the great chords and the whirling coda, when the soaring, mounting music, apotheosis of the dance, begins, clashes its cymbals and its tambourines, and opens, like a rose, into the waltz of waltzes, like the whole of youth in the moment of the rose, dancing, turning, in the movement of the waltz, beautiful, glittering, in rose and silver, waltzing in the garden, in and out among the flowers, turning, turning, with high wide steps, and lovely wrists and hands, in sleeves and ballet dress of cloth-of-roses, waltzing, waltzing, with dazzling vermilion smile, till, in ravishment of the music, she pricks herself with the spindle and drops upon one knee.

Beautiful the moment when the spell is cast, and they fall asleep, and we are to imagine that the clocks stand still : I can think of nothing more beautiful than the sleeping palace, deep down in the sleeping wood ! And the plumed music, more plumed than any other, for the journey down the river to the enchanted castle ; the throbbing and trembling, in anticipation, in the orchestra ; the sleeping virgin, asleep for a hundred years ; the prince and hunter summoning his courage to kiss her ; the crash of the spell broken, and the immortal moment when she wakens, and opens her eyes, and lifts herself, and he holds her in his arms. . . .

And within a few days, in metamorphosis, among the skaters on the pond, to the slow adagio, like a ghost among ghosts, like a ghost among the Columbines ; there is no such phantom among the red chalk masquers, sister to *Le Grand Gilles*, or glittering daughter ; all in white, with long waist and coppery-red hair ; while the snow is falling, the lovely changeling lifts and floats down with the snowflakes, links arms in the long chain, and smiling and stooping low, goes, runs swifter than changeling snow upon the summer cheeks of the rose. . . .

Or the kitchen drudge, but not like that other Cinderella who is dead, who had for a broom a goose's wing, the ghost of whom I met, or thought I saw under the white syringa tree ; but this Cinderella sits on the boards (where she will dance) with long thin waist and long, thin Botticelli wrists and fingers ; looks, to strange music, at the portrait of her mother above the fireplace, bows her head and weeps :

Dances with her besom, plucking at its straws as if they were the locks of coxcomb princes, " the Morning Dream that hover'd o'er Belinda's head ; A youth more glittering than a Birth-Night Beau (That ev'n in slumber caused her cheek to glow) " ; is kind to the beggar-woman and, straight, is transformed into a princess, steps into the chariot, and is driven to the ball :

Which is in a garden like Vauxhall, with a flight of steps. The courtiers are dancing ; but magic changes the staircase into the dancing-ground of the birds-of-paradise, altering the sexes, for it is the cockbird who is the dancer ; or it would be better said that Cinderella, at the ball, dances like a bird-of-paradise, using the staircase as her perch to step down from bough to bough, and as light as one of the feathers of her own bright wings is caught up by her partner, and carried, head down, onto the dancing floor.[1]

But we have not done yet.

Who could forget Cinderella arriving at the ball, her pages and attendants and Prince Charming waiting ; appearing in the archway, coming down the steps in her short ballet skirt with long train held up by her pages ? A train that is a

[1] This dance was altered, subsequently.

golden cloak with a high collar like a ruff, a corolla looped with pearls, within which we see her head moving, and her smile, like intelligence and sensibility within the rose or lily ; and now comes, slowly, slowly forward on her points, down to the footlights, down into the galaxy of all the lights, nearer and nearer, facing the entire audience, with head erect, smiling, as it were, into their faces, her ruff or corolla like a halo, like an aureole of pearl and gold, coming, coming forward, on tiptoe, on those noiseless points, taking all the galaxy of lights, dwelling in them, herself glittering, coruscating, giving forth light and poetry, nearer and nearer, Prince Charming holding her by the hand, her matchless waist and legs, beauty itself, nearer and still nearer, coming forward, till no more :

And sheds her cloak :

And in a moment, dances, by herself, to the often changing time, looking down, as if to pick and choose her steps ; and again ; and now whirls, faster, faster, and spins across the stage. Who could forget her little short steps to that ever changing time ; or how she comes up or down the flight of stairs, stepping proudly and beautifully like a bird-of-paradise?

Her *pas de deux* is upon, and below the steps, as though but just alighted, and of half a mind to fly back into the branches. How lovely her movements ! The light liftings of the ballerina onto her partner's shoulders, riding upon his arms ; and then, like a tiger lily coming down, descending, swinging in the wind, held there for a moment, and back again for the point, the climax in the tigered air ; or, as the ballerina changes from bird-of-paradise into lily, in a particular light, the pink *martagon*, making fragrant, spicing the winds ; and again, the scarlet *martagon*, according to the light ; and now, the golden-banded, golden-rayed *auratum*, in the variety with the band of vermilion down the centre of the petal, and spiced, scarlet tigerings ; and another, pink-tigered ; and now the white, pure white *candidum*, the Madonna lily, the lily of the Annunciation ; and turning, *rubrum magnificum*, carmine upon a white ground, with crimson markings, with pistils of vermilion trembling, shaking, rubbing their vermilion upon the sugary, spiced, golden lights, and the dancing lily, the ballerina, is held still in ecstasy upon the top stair, and makes her bow.

And now, her dance ended, waltzes upon her points in enjoyment and ravishment, lighter and lighter hearted, so swiftly, that you scarce can see her steps :

And the clock strikes twelve, loud like thunder, like the swaying earthquake, and Cinderella runs out, but drops her ballet shoe.

X

Passe Virgo

WE are approaching a low shore, not much higher than a mudbank, but with sheds and tumbledown buildings that suggest a customs-house or douane. Or a mere landing-stage. And now the cupid at the prow announces Fusina, on the *terra firma* opposite Venice, port of embarcation for ' the Queen of the Adriatic ', and in the same breath, terminus of the tramline. You may look back, for the last time, at the domes and towers rising out of the sea. Those can stand for the world you leave behind you.

But we turn away and find ourselves among a crowd of persons paying a copper coin (obol for Charon) and passing through a turnstile. The barge of Venus has been metamorphosed into a paddle steamer, and instead of the rose-hung island there are telephone wires and a cast-iron latrine. And the whining tram tottering to a standstill under the hoardings. The mouth of the Brenta is a square basin crowded with boats and barges. The Palladian villas are inland towards the mountains. But this is a slum population inhabiting the waters, sleeping in the bows of boats and under awnings, more inclined to drowse in the sun and talk all night. And now the scene transforms itself and loses its identity. It is no longer Italian, and could be one of the water towns of China, where tens of thousands are born and die in junks and sampans, but is now an endless and desultory fair held upon both banks of some canal or inland water.

It reminds me of the dreadful town of Hotin, that I saw upon the borders of Romania and Russia, on the Dniester. Hotin is a town to which I have been, in person, and to which I have returned before as to an earthly purgatory. Probably there is no town, anywhere in the world, that is more dreary and depressing. It is impossible to eat in this fearful place, and the most familiar gesture is the pushing away of cup or plate. The glasses are so dirty that one dares not drink from them. The long street ends in nothing at all. It just dies out on the brow of the cliff above the yellow muddy, awful river. That was the end of the world (in 1937) and it was of no use to look over the water into Russia. It must be worse, now, with no frontier. The agony of the spirit is such that it will not allow us to remain in any one place for long. Never for long enough to get accustomed to it. And it is a new sort of prison, to be continually upon the move. Not a journey to an end ; not a transportation ; only an aimless wandering. It is here, in this dreadful place, that we meet the ghosts of the travelling circus company. I heard of them, many years ago, at Marseilles, in the year after the first war had ended. They were stranded there, and had pawned their suits and had to walk round in their tights and spangles. I have seen them before, too, in my imagination, but they are only ghosts, imaginary companions to meet, and think of, in the loneliness. Not that we ever speak to them, for that would not be possible. They are not here at all. But it is as though a company of actors was left without its ' lead '. I have known this thing happen. I have seen it with the great company of Russian dancers, first one, and then another. I have lost the girl harlequin, the phantom of *L'Embarquement*.

I shall describe, later, how the sight of a dress belonging to a female dancer of the Comédie Vénitienne, in the Musée

Carnavalet of Paris (preserved by some miracle, for it seems
almost impossible that it should have survived), was the birth
for me of a whole series of visions, or of the same recurring
theme with variations, for I have grown to prefer such things
and to find more poetry in them than in most paintings, or
indeed in the majority of objects in museums. This silken
dress, old and frayed, in the colours of a harlequin, green,
black, and yellow predominating, seemed to me to be inspiration enough for a school of poets. I saw this dress for the first
time not long ago, and have been haunted by it ever since.
When I think of the person, or persons, who could have worn
this dress, I could cry out with ecstasy. In the garden in the
style of Portugal, below the formal parterre, below the balustrade at Queluz, under the palace, where there are orange
trees and bay trees planted alternately, where you look down
from the stone balcony towards the canal that is lined with
tile pictures (*azulejos*) in blue and yellow, for it was there I
felt a foreboding, in the late afternoon, while all the birds were
singing, when there was the particular light of evening upon
the fountains and the pink-washed walls, when there were
roses in bloom, and the geraniums of Portugal, and the carnations, when there was glitter from every sharp leaf, from
orange, from myrtle, from *Prunus lusitanica*, in their formal
planting, when I thought of the mask that could be worn
with it, not an ordinary mask, but cut like the leaf of a tulip
tree, and I could hear in imagination the music of Queluz that
Beckford heard, or said he heard, the warblings of Italian
singers, the oboe and flute players posted " at a distance in a
thicket of orange and bay trees ", not forgetting the soft
modinhas of Brazil, that Beckford loved, that Beckford wished
to learn . . . " languid interrupted measures, as if the breath
was gone with excess of rapture, and the soul panting to meet

the kindred soul . . . with a childish carelessness they steal into the heart . . ." he goes on, and it was now I knew this thing had happened, that the blow had fallen ; it was a movement and a feeling like the closing of a fan, like the painted world closing, shutting back into its slats, like a world closing, like the shutting of a heart, but, in fact, a heart in flower, in blossom, most happy, but a soul and person that cannot be again, that will not be born in our time.

the kindred soul . . . with a childish carelessness they steal into the house . . ." he goes on, and it was now I knew this thing had happened, that the blow had fallen; it was a move- ment and a feeling like the closing of a fan, like the painted world closing, shutting back into its slats, like a world closing, like the shutting of a heart, but, in fact, a heart in flower, in blos- som, most happy, but a soul and person that cannot be again, that will not be born in our time.

RECUEILLEMENT

AND so to that most poetical of all theatrical relics, the dress of a female harlequin of the Venetian Comedy in the Musée Carnavalet in Paris. How could I ever forget this ? Who, that has loved what I have loved, could look at it but with heart beating and the blood rushing into his eyes and ears ? I only saw it for a moment. But that one moment was enough for me. One thing is certain. I need never look at it again. For the sensation was that, entirely, of falling in love. As always, one remembers the impression of the whole, and certain sharp bits of detail — and forgets the rest. I wonder how it came to the Musée Carnavalet. I expect it arrived in a collection of old dresses, and that nothing more is known about it. And so much the better. The dress is not even shown in a glass case. It stands on a little wooden platform at the foot of a stair. You can touch and feel it with your hands.

I discovered it upon the afternoon of the day I was to catch the night train to Barcelona. I had never seen or heard of it before. You might think there would be photographs of it in theatrical histories ; but there is none. So far as I know it has come down unnoticed. Old and frayed, in the chequers of a harlequin, green, black, and yellow upon a dark green ground. And I remember some detail that suggests black grapes, not bunches of grapes, but grapes, singly, more resembling black plums or cherries, or mock suns, parhelions, such as you see floating in the sky if you look closely into the light. Not quite the pattern upon an ordinary

dress, but the chequers sewn together so as to leave no doubt
that they are the patches of a harlequin. The stuff of the dress
might be French, or could be Venetian, there is no telling.
But of the Italian Theatre ; of the Comédie Vénitienne. The
dress seemed to sing to me of Italy and of the Comédie
Vénitienne.

I was upon my way by the night train to Barcelona and in
a sad and horrible condition, made ill again with nerves. I
had been to Barcelona the year before, ill also, and now I
was starting to have pains once more ; having emerged the
previous year, weakened, after a horrid diet of milk, and now
dreading to begin dieting again. Nothing serious, but an
illness that wearies and that is brought on by the conditions
of our time. I suppose that ' nerves ' are an inseparable part
of the life of any person of sensibility in every age, past,
present, and to come, that they are indeed the battery of
which the discharge and the accumulation makes the artist, in
all the arts, and the man of energy. If this be so, then my own
forces of creation were at a low ebb and needed to be re-
charged with electricity. This is a process that can be accomplished by contact with ideas (objects), and with persons.
There are living persons who revitalize and give out force
and inspiration. Such fountains of fire, now idle, now
" turned off " for ever, now in full play, have been before and
will be again. But never the same. Ah ! never the same
persons, for such individuals and founts of inspiration are
immortal, in the human sense, which is to say, they are death-
less and so cannot be born again. They live in what they have
given birth to. The recharging can be the work of weeks and
months, or of a moment. And, in this instance, as quick as
the touch of a hand upon a trigger. I felt, indeed, not only
that I had been sent to the dress, but that this dress of the

Venetian dancer had been sent to me. I thought that there could be no other person in the living world to whom it was so necessary.

I had only to stand before it for that one moment. There was no point in looking at it for longer. No need to mention it to anybody. I looked at it and passed on. It was there to give a message to me ; now, that moment, in my climacteric, in the moment when I did not know which way to turn. For I had gone there in the rainy afternoon, feeling like someone lost. I had lost something or somebody, no matter what or whom. It was falling from my hand. The painted world was closing, like a world closing, like the shutting of a heart. There was nothing left for me among streets and houses of dead souls, where every corner was upon the way somewhere, to a meeting or a parting. And with it I had lost the world I had laboriously constructed, no one brick or stone of which, in that moment, had any meaning for me. For they had lost all meaning.

But this dead dress of the Venetian Comedy was like a message and a change of mood. It was a living ghost, an emanation of that world I had thought was dying. Its beauties were reborn and breathed again in that brief moment. I was not to be separated from them. They were not to be taken away from me. They were there, once more, and in brighter colours than before, brighter, in that moment, than when I first saw and felt them as a child. It was a return of affection from the scenes and things I loved. It was the person, the breathing image, the ghost-dress of the female harlequin, inhabited and filled. Like a letter long waited for, and come at last ; and when I say that there was no need for me to look at this old dress that had saved me, that spoke to me of the world I loved, for a moment longer, that the one glance, the mere recognition was enough, and more than enough, to start me upon the courses that I knew, it is as though I took up that long awaited letter, looked at it, and put it unopened in my pocket. I knew the handwriting, and I would read the letter some time later when I was alone. So must those in prison feel when a letter comes for them. It is a return of affection from the world they once lived in and from those they love.

So we disembark, and find ourselves among a crowd of persons upon a quay. A huge Venetian mooring-post, cut in spirals like a barber's pole, to which to tie up the bigger sea-faring gondolas (of our imagination) that bring passengers ashore to the mainland, the *terra firma*, is the first object that we notice. An instant later we are among the bird actors. But a step further to hear them chattering and talking ; about eight or ten of them, all told. Cloaks in three tiers or storeys ; cocked hats with rolled brims ; bird masks. One of the bird actors smokes a long clay pipe under his mask ; but what is odder still, two of the men are carrying muffs. One of them comes towards us, head down, as if thinking. Another carries his hat in his hand so that we see the hood or cowl covering his whole head. A young woman has a huge hooped skirt lifting in the wind. We see her open fan over her shoulder, and her white bird mask stuck like a glove into her hat-band.

Walking a little further, we are in the outskirts of some town upon the Venetian mainland. There is a small boy dressed like an itinerant cook or chestnut seller, in a ruff or flat cap, and a long, thin-nosed mask. Everywhere in the crowd are black-cowled figures, in black *tricornes*, wearing the white bird mask, the *bauta*. They are watching a charlatan upon a platform ; and now we see another carnival figure, a bigger replica of the little cook boy or scullion, in the same mask and ruff, but coming up and talking to a young girl who is of small height and dressed in a bodice and short skirt. She has a little basket on her arm, wears a plain black mask that hides only her eyes, and her feet are a dancer's feet.

There are trees ; umbrella pines, and boughs of fir trees like green saws hanging on the air. And we come a little nearer still, to where a coach is drawn up. Some fashionably dressed ladies have got out, with their greyhound ; while, not far away, a large old lady sits upon a chair to watch what is going on. And her companion ? All we see of him is his head, and a bit of his white ruff. But no mistaking him. A black mask and smooth black skull-cap. We see the white line of his forehead above his mask, his eye of mischief and intelligence, and a square inch or two, no more, of his bright colours.

Under the high trees, by a stone wall with an urn, behold many hands raised in dancing ; the mouths of brass instruments under the boughs ; and a band of violins ! And three figures more. A very young girl, fifteen years old, foretaste of what is to come, fan in hand, dressed like a dancer, wide-hooped, in a short yellow skirt trimmed with double flounces of black lace. And a great tree trunk. A tree trunk that is like the column of an Indian temple, festooned with leaves, that is stout as the mainmast of a ship, that climbs up and up into the green world of its own branches; and a ladder leaning against the tree trunk with a familiar figure climbing the rungs. A figure that appears to be running up the ladder into the green heavens, into the high scenery, so that perhaps he will drop down holding to the curtain ; that has the attitude of an acrobat, a wire-walker running up the rope ladder to his perch, to his shaking platform ; and who, yet, stands still, but only in order to be better seen. A hat like a tramp on holiday, a suit like a tramp's suit but elegantly cut, a mask like a tramp's black face, like the blackened face of Jackson,

" the original tramp cyclist ", his hat or wand sticking out of his pocket, for both his hands are on the rungs, a light and springy step upon the ladder, tireless, ready to run up or down for ever, and so, a kind of Mercury, a messenger, someone for ever running in and out in comedies of intrigue and, upon occasion, muddling the messages. But now, and for this moment, caught like a bright bird in a cage.

A man in striped sleeves, in a short cloak, dances with his back to us. But we have no time for him. For with heart beating, and blood rushing into our eyes and ears, we recognize with whom he is dancing and know her again, immediately, for we are given a vision of her looking at us out of the scenery, head and shoulders only, as a portrait of a young Venetian woman, could we but see her Venetian-coloured hair, muffled up to her chin in a black silk domino, a black *tricorne* put coquettishly upon her head, holding a closed fan to her lips to keep her secret, the line of her domino making nearly a circle with the curve of her hat and showing her face, moon-shaped, like the young moon nearly at the full, nothing but her mouth and eyes and nose and forehead, like the face of Pierrot, like the face of the woman in the moon, but known to us, and at once extinguished, as though the spotlight was turned off from it and we must look for her to come on again from some other corner of the stage. Which happens before there is time to think, and we see her in the galaxy of all the lights, coming slowly, slowly forward on tiptoe, on her points, down to the footlights, her beautiful, slim legs and matchless waist, her hair coiled at the back and gathered into a net or snood, diamond earrings in her small ears, and wearing a tiara of many spires, all glittering, and throws herself, alive, into the tumult of all the music, vanishes, or fades, and is no more seen. . . .

196

BOOK III

THE JASMINE KINGDOM

I

Delphinium : Iris

WERE it the time of year I would go out and look into the
blue delphinium, for it is a new sensation, that of losing yourself among its lily towers. The blue delphinium is one of the
inventions of our century and something there has never been
before, younger than the aeroplane and older than the temples
of Angkor which, indeed, are suggested, are even simulated,
when you see a whole bed of blue delphiniums growing together, nodding, bowing, above the forest of their leaves, but
now it is early in April and there is nothing more than the
formal foundation for the towers. They are lily towers, no
doubt of that ; but I mention the aeroplane because it is a
quick way up into the skies and there are sky blue delphiniums
with a white eye ; azure blue with a faint rose flush and dark
eye : such as you might see, looking out onto the clouds ;
gentian blue with a white eye splashed with blue : this, passing
over the mountains ; brilliant sky blue selfs : the pure empyrean ; deep cobalt blue ; delicate, pure silvery blue, high, high
up between the cumulus and cirrhus ; outer petals sky blue, inner,
a soft rose ; cornflower blue with a white eye ; sky blue with
inner petals rosy mauve and edgings of gentian blue : as blue
as the evening around the evening star ; or wistaria blue with
light heliotrope flush and dark eye for the scented morning.

These are, all, kinds and colours of the blue delphinium ;
but you need only come up close to one of the blue spires and
wonder at the satiny deepness of the petal ; they are the blue

towers of the delphinium, lily towers which I compared to the temples of Angkor, and so are they, growing together in their varying florescences and differing altitudes ; some of them eight feet high, over all, with a flowering spike of five feet or more ; heavy pyramidal spikes ; bold tapering spikes ; long, open ; long, symmetrical ; long, well-clothed ; broad, tapering ; massive, well built ; pyramidal, and well furnished ; nicely placed, and well-formed florets ; they do, indeed, suggest the towers of Angkor Vat and Angkor Thom ; they are like no other kind of architecture ; blue towers of the bayadères, blue cups of the honey bees, strung out like bells that diminish, that grow smaller along the flower spike ; they are like carillons, or peals of bells of pure note ringing in the wind ; as, also, the wand or thyrsus of a blue god, a god rubbed with sandalwood, as the pollen shakes out from the dark eye of the delphinium, or from the white paste eye of the delphinium ; and looking into the blue face of the flower, there is nothing bluer ; the blue satin petal is blue as the eternal, awful zenith, straight up, overhead, into eternity ; dark, dark blue, when the main is deeper blue than the sky ; or blue to please, loaded, light blue, flawless, not altering, or shading . . . and wistaria blue for the harlequin I saw drinking wine from a *fiasco*, under a pergola in Florence, on the hillside.

Thus and thus, the blue delphinium which is one of the perfections of our time, and it would not be difficult to write of the iris in the same strain, for we are living in the golden age of the iris, or in the rainbow age of the iris. It is now, before our eyes, that it prinks its colours and fulfils the promise of the spectrum. There are the clear ice blues ; the mid-blue or cornflower blues ; the azure blues ; and the dark purples. There are the dappled plicatas pencilled with bright blue upon a white ground, pure white edged with fawn, or boldly stitched and veined with deep yellow ; the yellow ground plicatas, white falls etched and edged with rose ; lemon cream dotted with faint blue giving a green effect ; yellow, with standards heavily sanded russet and cream, falls marked evenly with dark sienna ; indeed, speckled like a bird's egg ; and the new red irises, and pink irises with tangerine beards.

They are something there has never been before. And they are flowers which in their formality lend themselves to painting. There are irises (and a lily) in an earthenware pot in the foreground of the huge Portinari triptych by Hugo van der Goes which hangs in the Uffizi. Beside them are dark purple columbines in a glass tumbler. And there is a drawing of *Iris trojana* by Dürer, attached to which there is a mystery touching, of all improbable iris localities, on Venice.[1] There are a pair of screens of dark blue irises by Korin, but it is the ordinary purple or dark blue flag upon a ground of gold paper (probably *I. tectorum*, usually lavender, sometimes purple, which grows upon roofs in Japan) and never, in any instance, either in Oriental or in Western art, is it other than the common iris, for the reason that the improved iris, like the delphinium, is the invention of our time.

I would like to see what the great school of decorator-painters of Japan during the sixteenth and seventeenth centuries could have made of the iris or the delphinium in its modern development, as displayed before our eyes, for perhaps they, and they only, had the genius to paint these formal flowers. I have the vision of a series of rooms with sliding

---

[1] *I. trojana* was not established in European gardens until 1887. It has been suggested that Gentile Bellini may have brought a rhizome of this iris with him from Constantinople and grown it in his garden, and that Dürer may have made his drawing of this flower when he visited Gentile Bellini in Venice in 1506. As against this, Dürer was not in Venice at the time of year to see it in flower. Cf. *The Art of Botanical Illustration*, by Wilfrid Blunt: London, Collins & Co., 1950, p. 24 (footnote); and an article in *The Burlington Magazine* for April 1947, by K. R. Towndrow.

walls painted with the plicatas of Sir Cedric Morris which I saw growing last summer in his garden in Suffolk in shades of vellum, salmon, chamois, and soft fuchsia or petunia, mostly, but, also, there were some blue selfs, a wonderful sight, for it is a new race of flowers growing in that red-walled garden, they have never been seen before ; [1] or the yellow ground plicatas grown by the brothers Sass in " cold Nebraska ".

There are the sensational iris introductions from America ; *Lady Mohr*, standards pinkish oyster white, like the light shining upon an iridescent oyster shell, and with chartreuse-green falls, brown beard, and a violet signal patch upon the falls ; *Spindrift*, seashell or coral pink with deep tangerine beard ; and the already famous *Loomis V*. 20 in tones of apricot and orange. Or by all accounts the most extraordinary of all, *Night and Day*, not yet flowered in England, with almost black standards and clear or milk white falls, an iris of enormous size, as big as *I. susiana*, but not sanded, etched, or chamleted, like that Oriental iris from the Lebanon.[2]

[1] The *Wave Screen* of Korin (1661-1716) is probably his masterpiece and the most finished example of his powers. Too often, what he draws are caricatures of figures, trees, or animals. In the words of the *Encyclopædia Britannica* (1911 edition): " The *Wave Screen* is reproduced here in order to give an idea of what this school of painters could accomplish in the way of decoration, and from this it may be imagined what Korin's greater predecessors, Koyetsu and Sotatsu, could have achieved in flower painting if allowed the opportunities here created for them ".

[2] *I. susiana* — together with its Oncocyclus and Regelia relatives; *basaltica*, large flowers so closely veined and dotted dark blue, blackish grey, or dark purple that the white ground is almost invisible ; *Naʒarena*, white with violet veins, falls cream, thickly dotted with dark violet ; *paradoxa*, falls strap-shaped, light crimson, densely covered with thick velvety hairs, with a pink bar, standards milk-white veined bluish purple, styles brownish yellow with dark purple spots; or the marvellous *var. Coschab*, paragon of the Oncocyclus group, from the shores of the Caspian, probably shaken out of its marshes, now, by the explosion of the atom bomb in Russian 'experimental stations', an iris closely veined with purple on a white ground, narrow falls, pale pink ground so closely covered with purple black hairs as to look and feel like velvet — these irises of the Oncocyclus family are ancestors and progenitors of the plicatas of our day.

But now discussion begins and the opposing schools take up their argument. There are opinions that prefer single to double flowers and extol the selfs or pure colours above those that flaunt themselves in many hues. For such there is *Great Lakes*, a Canadian iris, a pure blue, clear blue self, and other irises of the same origin that have nothing in them of the Orient but suggest balsamic airs and Northern skies. There are the mid-blue, cornflower blue selfs, washed with silver ; ' black ' irises, like *Sable*, blackish violet mixed with dark claret like a ' black ' pansy, and as ' black ', in importance, as the ' black ' tapestry of Zamora ; and magnificent yellows like *Olakala* which is orange yellow, or another iris which is ice lemon, frosty white with clear lemon edges.

The argument is the same, in theory, as that between lovers of the Florentine and Venetian schools of painting and I have continued it, confined to my own two opinions, within the long walls of a camellia house, comparing the single crimson flowers with golden stamens, to the wax-like white, as perfect of form as gardenias, but scentless, like a beautiful young maiden dying, and no ghost ! Or it could be put in another way, that the young girl of *Le Spectre de la rose* who has come from the ball, holds, surely, not a rose but a camellia in her hand ; and yet she holds the rose to her face, she breathes the scent of it, and it is the scent that puts her asleep and comes in her sleep to dance with her ! Was that a white or a pink camellia, for there are single pinks and single whites, and there are camellias that have petals like shells, that are arranged neatly like a flower made by nuns out of seashells ; and others shaped like a convolvulus, a trumpet flower, single, and like a cup of coral ; or those that dangle upon the bough like roses, but roses were never so thick and thornless ; they are semi-double, and the dark green leaves are dense with them. The rose pink camellias I am thinking of lie in such heavy clusters upon the branch that they hang down from the wall ; they make a roof or thatch of roses ; or it is like lying in the waters of an enchanted lake and looking up at roses. And it is another kind of virginity from the nun-like, white camellia ; this is the demi-virgin, as of the South Sea maiden, daughter of the triton, garlanded with flowers, who comes to you, swimming, and is not innocent ; the many camellias are a shoal of maidens, and you do not see the water upon their bodies. Their waxen limbs or petals are unencumbered, which is the beauty of the camellia, that it is a flower naked upon the bough, and the rose pink camellias in their dark leaves are so many maidens, as alike as sisters, all in the clear water of the atoll pool.

But the iris is not like a human being at all, of any age or clime. The camellia is a face, or a naked body, but the iris is a tiger flower, a tiger or leopard among other flowers, whatever its colour. Even the white iris is the snow leopard of the flowerbed ; and it is not a ghost, it has its markings. There are the snow white and the ivory white, all of them veined, and with striations and faint pencillings in their petals. There is a screen of white irises by a Japanese painter of the generation before Korin, but, again, it is probably but the white form of *I. tectorum*, described, though, as " an exquisite white, with a delicate touch of pure gold on the crest, and with all the beauty of the rarest orchid ". There should be, I speak ideally, and as though the anachronism was nothing to argue about, individual iris studies and great iris compositions by these painters. But certain of the irises resemble towers ; they are the lily towers of Florence and Siena, towers of the Palazzo Vecchio and Palazzo Pubblico, within which latter are the marvellous frescoes of Simone Martini ; or the lily tower of Montegufoni which reminded me of a lily, which grows out of the valley like a lily.

I have seen the fields blue with *I. tingitana* round Tangiers, and a flock of white ibises not far away ; or could anything be more beautiful than the dark violet and gold *I. reticulata* flowering in February out of the snow ? But what I would wish to see is a meadow of *I. hoogiana*, clear blue with bright golden beard, an iris from Turkestan and one of the most beautiful of all irises, and to compare it with *Great Lakes* which is of another world, or, at least, of another hemisphere, just as I have imagined and arranged a meeting in some celestial fairground or natural green circus in the hills, far from any town, between the horsemen of the Huns or Mongols, of whatever Horde, at the time of their swarming when they set out to take the world, and the feather-crowned warriors of whom one may read in Catlin's *North American Indians* ; the Crows in dresses of white deerskin with long hair, black and shining as a raven's wing, a foot or more of which would drag on the grass as they walked, now lifting in the air and floating out behind them as they rode, wearing the crest of quills of the war eagle on their heads, and upon their horses' heads another crest of equal beauty and exactly the same in pattern and material. The Mandans, another tribe, wore crests of war eagles' quills falling from the backs of their foreheads down to their feet, and as well, with a chief or warrior of particular renown, a horned headdress, formed from a pair of buffalo horns, shaved thin and highly polished, the horns but loosely attached, so that by a skilful and almost imperceptible motion of the head they could be made to work, one backward and other forward, like a horse's ears. I have even imagined a meeting between these Red Indian warriors in their horned headdresses and the knights of mediaeval Japan in their lobster armour, with a pair of steel horns, more like antennae, coming out of their helmets ; [1] and with the horned Vikings, who are too Wagnerian for my tastes, except in so far as they were poets, or would listen to poetry. In the case of the Red Indian warriors we have to think of the rustling and rattling of their eagles' quills as they walked or rode, as though they had alighted out of the winds, and not unlike in note to the wind in the swords of *Xiphium*, the division of Spanish irises to which *I. tingitana* belongs, which I saw growing in Morocco.

The Red Indian warriors I would have invited into Turkestan, and there, as though letting birds out of a window, I would let them loose to wander over the plains, and would have had them present at the banquets of the Mongol Knights, as witnessed by Clavijo, the ambassador of the King of Castile to the Court of Tamerlane, in the great encampment or summer town of tents. The circus ground was a part of the plain outside Samarcand, half a league in extent, " with a number of great wine jars set round the field, each at a stone's throw, and

---

[1] The horned helmets worn by Japanese knights from the thirteenth century onwards were in imitation of a deer's antlers. In later instances they were like a pair of buffalo horns. Or they wore crests of steel sunrays like a bird's spread tail ; or they could be in the form of a pair of minutely fronded ferns. It is fascinating to compare the knights of Japan in their lacquered armour and antlered helms, their coloured lacings of twenty-five and more sorts, imitating such textures as wistaria flowers, water plantains or jays' feathers, and with their swords which were miracles of watered steel, with the blued and etched knights of the German mediaeval armourers ; or sometimes they were etched in black and gold. Their suits of armour are, in fact, sculptures in blued or blacked steel ; and not only the knights of late mediaeval Germany in pointed visors and lobster-claw shoes, but, more curious still, those that imitated the slashed and puffed costumes of the German Landsknechts. Those, certainly, are among the extreme fantasies of the German armourers. Of the first sort, who that saw him, during the Vienna Exhibition at the Tower of London Armoury in 1949, will forget the giant figure of Ulrich IX, Vogt (Bailiff) of Matsch, and Count of Kirchberg (1408–81), whose gigantic armour, six foot nine inches high, stood facing the door as you came in ? Ulrich IX was grandfather of Barbara Matsch, who married Jakob IV Trapp, thus bringing the Castle of Churburg, in the Tyrol, into the possession of the present owner, Count Trapp. Cf. *Japan's Ancient Armour*, by Hatiro Yamagami :Tokyo Board of Tourist Industry, 1940.

two tripods made of wooden staves painted red. Hung on each was a huge leathern sack that was filled with cream and mares' milk. This, the attendants with wands in their hands kept on stirring, rocking the milk backwards and forwards, while time and again they threw in many loaves of sugar." The town of tents was of pavilions, looking like castles in the distance, stayed with ropes dyed red or green, and with high doorways so that the Mongol horsemen could ride in ; some of them with battlemented walls, and a turret with a gangway, so that in a high wind men could climb aloft " walking afoot on the canvas " to repair the damage ; some tents with ex-terior walls of silk woven in bands of black and white and yellow, " like silk sarsenet " ; others with no pattern, their only ornament being bands of white with spangles of silver the size of an open hand ; interiors of linen, set over in loose small pleats like a woman's gown, " and as the wind blows, these wave to and fro ". Or of silk stuff, woven as though it were the pattern on a tile. Or of red tapestry " like shag velvet ". Or of white satin (zaytuni). One tent with outer walls of grey squirrel fur ; another of red stuff with inlays of various colours, and inner walls lined with skins of ermine. And in midst of this town of tents the white deerskin lodges of the Crow Indians. " All being now in order and arranged ", for I cannot forbear quoting further from the narrative of Clavijo, who is more inspiring, even, than Marco Polo, we would see the Great Khanum " coming from one of the neighbouring enclosures ". Her gown was of red silk . . . her train held up by fifteen ladies walking behind to steady her huge headdress and enable her to go forward. " She had a thin white veil before her face, which appeared to be entirely covered with white lead or some such cosmetic, the effect being to make it look as though she was wearing a paper mask."

She sat behind Tamerlane ; " and as soon as she was seated, the second lady appeared coming from another enclosure ; then, issuing from another tent came the third wife ; and so forth, nine in all ".[1]

Whether here, at the Assembling of the Great Horde in the plain, or in one of the four or five palaces of Tamerlane in Samarcand, new building by Persian architects, all with fine tilework, orchards, apricot trees, groves of plane trees, and fountains such as that by the side of which Clavijo saw the Great Khan, a fountain with red apples floating in the basin, I would have the Red Indian warriors enter, rattling in their feathers, to be received in audience, and I think that some such thought or flight of fancy is inseparable from the notion of different species of the same flower growing in localities half a world apart from each other, that it is not to be disassociated from their differing features and appearance, that it is, indeed, implicit and inherent in their mutations of form and colour. Personally, I would not be able to see a bed or clump of the blue Turcoman iris *I. hoogiana*, and not far away *Great Lakes*, the Canadian blue iris from Ontario, and not feel the winds of two different worlds blowing upon me. To myself, they could not be just two varieties of the same flower growing, side by side, in the same garden.

I. hoogiana, and its wonderful speckled sisters of the Oncocyclus and Regelia group,[2] breathe of the great nomad

---

[1] Cf. *Clavijo's Embassy to Tamerlane*, translated by Guy Le Strange. Broadway Travellers Series : London, Routledge & Co., 1928.

[2] *I. gatesii*, the largest flowered of all, the falls being six inches in diameter, has purple lines and points on a creamy white ground ; or it is elsewhere described as greenish white, lavishly veined and dotted with purple. *I. lortetii*, from the Lebanon, is speckled reddish violet on a creamy or pale lavender ground, the signal patch being a solid splotch of crimson brown. They are very large, silvery pink flowers, with dark grey reticulation. *I. gatesii*, in short, is silvery grey ; while *I. lortetii* is veined and dotted with rose colour on a creamy ground. *I. Korolkowi* is another

plains where flower the most beautiful of the wild tulips, those
that were collected and brought into cultivation by the Turkish
flower lovers, no doubt because they were reminded by them
of their own ancestral wanderings in the flowering meadows,
and that influenced them, there is no question, in the shaping
of their wondrous turbans, while the blue irises of the other
hemisphere have no history, except what we allow to them in
pitching and taking down again after a few days, or a few
moments, the soft white deerskin lodges of the Red Indians,
painted, sometimes, with comets looking like toadstools, with
the night sky, or the signs of thunder. That which we get
from the Canadian irises is the colour of an unsullied world
blown to them, I like to think, from the clear skies of the Great
Slave Lake and Great Bear Lake, where the trees end, or along
the Alaskan Highway into the blue and white mountains, to
where the mists and fogs settle on the Aleutians, which islands
are where two worlds end, or where one world ends and
another begins, all in the habitat of the iris.

The plicatas with their Oriental blood are an imaginary
extension of the Orient. They are more Oriental, by far,
than the irises painted in Persian miniatures, or upon Japanese
screens, in just the same way that other creatures that are distinctively Eastern-looking, such as Arab horses or Afghan
dogs, have had their points and qualities further developed and
brought to perfection away from their native lands and in

Regelia iris, veined purple or chocolate or olive green on a pale white ground. It is
an iris from Bokhara. Mr. E. A. Bowles, in an article " Iris Memories " in *The Iris
Year Book* for 1950, writes beautifully of the " glorious golden beards " of certain
irises, particularly the blue *I. pallida dalmatica*, which he says resembles a " furry
caterpillar even more fluffy and brilliant than that of the Sycamore Dagger moth " ;
and writing of the exquisite markings on the falls of *I. unguicularis* he comments
upon " the varying amount of white on the lilac ground colour, and the size and
brightness of the central golden spot which marks the landing stage of the insect
visitor ". Mr. E. A. Bowles, an iris veteran, was discoverer of the beautiful pale blue
form *I. reticulata* var. *Cantab* which flowers in February.

other hands. What creature could be more Oriental in appearance than a white Arab stallion or mare, or red Afghan dog? The Oncocyclus and Regelia iris is pattern and prototype of the plicata; and I would like there to be accurate botanical drawings of it in its modern varieties done in all the excitement of this knowledge, and great decorative compositions or decorations into which could enter some of that quality of over-enthusiasm which is the distinguishing mark and secret of decorators like Sotatsu and Koyetsu, and which degenerates into caricature and vulgar impersonation in the hands of Korin. Even so, no other painter who ever lived has imitated and caricatured trees, waves, mountains, in his manner and at his high temperature of inspiration and made them into decorations, but Korin is the decadent of his own school. I believe that his greater predecessors and forebears, Sotatsu, Koyetsu, Kano Eitoku, could have made of these modern irises the greatest flower paintings there have ever been. They have qualities, alike the selfs and the plicatas, which would have particular appeal to painters of this school and which they, only, could assimilate and render into works of art; and it is their paintings I had in mind when I saw the irises of Sir Cedric Morris, and when I read the descriptions, or see the few solitary examples, so high is their price, of recent iris introductions from America.

II

Blue Gentian

THIS summer (1950), and never before, I saw the blue gentians growing upon the mountains. It may be in the experience of many other persons who have been to high places in summer, but it is not in mine, and I am delighted that in this instance it has been long delayed. We had left Rome to travel for a few days into the Abruzzi, a part of Italy where I had never been before. The road led through a hill town where they were filming *Fra Diavolo* and many of the inhabitants were dressed as ' supers ' in brigand costumes that well became them. We looked down from the piazza over the *campagna* in midst of a squadron of hussars in yellow uniforms, men in peaked hats, and peasant women wearing the folded head-dresses of the mountains. At about the point where stands the old abbey of Casamari with its Cistercian church we entered the former Kingdom of Naples and were among the *ciochiari*, wearers of thonged sandals. That night we came to Scanno, a precipitous mountain town, pouring in cascades of houses down the hillside, but being a Friday the women were not in costume. On Sundays they wear black cloaks and round red hats or tambours which have a mediaeval Albanian air. They must have Albanian blood in Scanno and be connected with the Albanian villages further south in Calabria.[1] Sulmona and Aquila we saw the next morning

[1] The Albanian villages of the Sila Greca centre round Spezzano Albanese, between Sibari and Cosenza. They date from the fifteenth century, the time of Scanderbeg. Splendid Albanian costumes are still worn at Lungro, San Giovanni in Fiore, and at Tiriólo where there is much weaving in the houses.

with their splendid churches. In Sulmona there was a market
with country women from a village in the Abruzzi who wore
huge white headdresses and stiff, white, stayed bodices, part
Oriental, part of the period of Holbein, yet distinctively
Italian in appearance.[1] We saw the empty chalk-white vessel
of San Clemente in Casauria with its porch of the twelfth
century and pulpit and baldaquin carved with winged angels
and great stone ornaments derived from the rosettes of the
artichoke, all standing in a garden, and passed over the huge
mountain mass of the Gran Sasso d' Italia in order to come
down to Ascoli Piceno, near to the Adriatic, with its distinctive
and charming buildings, and altar paintings by Crivelli which
I had long wished to see.[2] All that day whenever the road
climbed high enough I looked for gentians, but we went
through woods of green larches and much snow upon the
road, and there were no gentians. The mountain villages
were extraordinary ; one of them, below the road, crowded
along a knife-edge or backbone of rock, the flat-roofed houses
running up and down it like the rungs on a ladder, and stopping at a precipice edge, a village ruled over and administered
by the parish priest, a famous local character of brigand
affinity. More villages, later in the same day, would have been
a paradise for the Romantic scene painter, perched upon the
edges of cliffs hundreds of feet above the road, or miles away,
inaccessible, half-hidden in clouds. The mountain villages of
the Abruzzi must be as spectacular as those of Calabria,[3] and

---

[1] Pettorano sul Gizio, nine miles from Sulmona.

[2] The large altarpiece by Crivelli in the National Gallery came from Ascoli
Piceno and was painted in 1476.

[3] The most sensational of the Calabrian villages must be Pentedátillo (five fingers),
about twenty miles from Reggio, one of the Greek-speaking villages of the Aspro-
monte, a relic from the Byzantine Empire conquered by Belisarius in the sixth century
and ruled by a governor (Katapan) from Bari until the taking of that city by Robert
Guiscard in 1071. There are five or six of these villages in which mediaeval Greek is

they are as surely material for the background of Romantic opera as are the green 'demesnes' of Ireland for a proper setting of *Le Lac des cygnes*. I am remembering the leafless woods of BallyEdmund. . . . There was village after village of this 'bandit' character, but no gentians ; and so through a golden valley, and the sunset, into Ascoli Piceno where there was a beautiful motorless piazza, lovely architecture, and a banquet of Alpini singing their songs into the night.

Next morning, the road led over lesser mountains towards Spoleto and Perugia through the Monti Sibillini, and after Norcia climbs in banked curves a barren mountain side and comes through chestnut woods, past the last goatherd, to idyllic slopes of violas and pansies. Snow lay by the side of the road a few hundred feet below the summit. At about this height there was a wonderful lightening and exhilaration of the air and the mountain top came up out of the rock in the form of a heavenly meadow. There was a point where the road joined this meadow and the precipice fell away on the other side perhaps three thousand feet into the valley. And then the road lost its dangers and wandered in easy curves in and out of the pasture. We were a hundred feet, perhaps only fifty feet, from the top of the mountain. There were

still spoken : Bova, Condufuri, Roghudi, Galliciano, and Amendolea. There is a wonderful drawing of Pentedátillo in Edward Lear's *Journals of a Landscape Painter in Southern Calabria* : London, 1852, p. 190. " The appearance of Pentedátillo is perfectly magical . . . wild spires of stone shoot up into the air, barren and clearly defined, in the form of a gigantic hand against the sky, and in the crevices and holes of this fearfully savage pyramid the houses are wedged, while darkness and terror brood over all the abyss, around this, the strangest of human abodes." Pentedátillo is, certainly, a *locus classicus* for the Calabrian brigand, though, being Greek and not Calabrian in origin, whether or not they wore the green trousers, top-boots, bright yellow neckcloths with scarlet stripes, and the peaked Calabrian hat (*cappello pizzuto*) with many-coloured ribbons hanging down from it, I do not know. G. M. Orioli, travelling in Calabria in 1934, saw one old man, only, wearing a peaked hat. Pentedátillo must be a marvellous sight by moonlight.

yellow pansies and violas, and some form of wild auricula, and suddenly the blue trumpet of a gentian, and another and another, and as soon as we had stopped and scrambled up the bank, no gentians at all, and then, a few feet further on, we were in the middle of the gentian meadow.

It was a pasture right at the top of the mountain, not more than two or three hundred feet across, but continuing for some distance along the watershed, and I suppose during the greater part of the year covered deep in snow. There were places where the meadow was yellow with violas and pansies growing for protection under the stones, for the pasture had the appearance of having been showered with limestone fragments. Such was the antiquity of the flower villages. They grew up again in the same places, of slow increase, and were to be found there, year by year, sheltering in the scree. It would be beautiful to walk all day up in the mountains and take a helicopter from one pasture to another. I could see another of the heavenly meadows upon the next mountain. And I walked a little further into the blue gentian settlements.

The yellow violas and pansies were the foreground of a Botticelli painting, as beautiful as that, and of that ' period ', but the gentians were of a different feeling and I can only think that no painter of the *quattrocento* had climbed as high as this into the mountains. Innocence and honey breath are the quality of those other flowers but theirs is the ordinary colour of flowers in nature. They are not more beautiful than the cloth-of-gold of buttercups, than the wild roses along the Gypsy hedges. But the gentian is transcendental in that, living in the high places and feeding on the snows, and warmed by them, it is the embodiment of two other elements, air and water. It lay clustered, close to the ground, for as far as the eyes could see. But pick one of the gentians and look into its blue trumpet ! It is the dark blue of a mountain tarn upon a sunny, windy day, of a rock pool with the brown moorland round it. I have seen waters as blue as gentians in Galway and in Sutherland, and there must be such, in plenty, in Connemara and in the Hebrides. Probably in Iceland, too. But the gentian-pools are in localities where gentians never grow. These are the high mountains. This is the little sea blue gentian, the colour of Arctic and Antarctic seas, and of the terrible, open heavens.

The gentian is the solemn flower of the mountains and does not often descend lower than the snows. Not one of the flowers of the *Primavera*, for you must prepare to spend the night in cold. Or to come up the mountain again at four or five o'clock in the morning in order to see its blue trumpets blazing out of the half-light, while the rocks are full of shadows. It inhabits the tops of the mountains and you could think it came down to them out of another element, that it touches the high places of the earth and is gone again. That is why I said I would like to fly in a helicopter from one high meadow to another in order to come down in no space at all where there is a field of gentians. This was *G. verna*, the spring gentian of the mountains, with a huge Alpine population found everywhere, all through the Alps and down the Apennines, and much further, in the Baikal and Altai mountains, in the Caucasus and in Afghanistan, so that it varies much and a number of forms and varieties are known. My one and only experience of this blue flower growing in nature was of the ordinary kind, but plant collectors have found white flowered forms, ghosts of the blue gentian, there are violet purple types, and there is a form from the Caucasus which has yellow flowers. It grows, too, with flowers twice the size of the type in Irish meadows. One collector states that the most beautiful colour variation known to him is from the Val d'Isère with flowers of an exquisite pale powder blue.

And he goes on to describe an albino form of *G. acaulis*, shading from pure white to ivory, with speckled throats of lizard green. *G. acaulis* is the great trumpet gentian, or gentianella, which has been grown in gardens for hundreds of years, is of unknown origin, and does not exactly match with any wild species. The lizard markings in its throat — or are they more like a thrush's spottings ? — are more visible in the snowy trumpets of the white form than against the blue flesh or integument of the gentianella. There is another form spotted with olive green. And other gentians with funnel-shaped sea blue flowers — but the colour of which sea, and in what mood ? — a gentian from Burma ; and the sapphire blue *G. bavarica* which I now remember, only as I am writing this, to have seen growing in the wet meadows round Kloster Ettal, one of the most fanciful of the Rococo abbeys in Bavaria, where there is even a liqueur for sale that is made from gentian roots ! So that I have seen gentians growing before, in nature, but only in the lush meadows, not high up in the mountains. I read of another gentian found in Kashmir at altitudes of ten thousand feet or more, with clear blue flowers marked with white and deeper blue stripes ; and of a sky blue gentian from Yunnan ; and have seen, of course, the clear, icy Cambridge blue *G. farreri* grown in gardens. Another gentian from Siberia is described as turquoise blue ; and there is a deep peacock blue from Western China. The autumn-flowering *sino-ornata*, a Tibetan, is the most loved gentian of all and it will grow in box-edged beds in Derbyshire but will not flower at all with me because of the lime in the soil. Who does not know its five-pointed trumpet flowers of pure azure blue, striped, outside, with lines and bands of purple blue and ivory ? Grown in those beds it is a sight not to be believed, like a sudden descent or invasion from the mountains. It is wonderful to think there are even gentians from South America, including a scarlet gentian *G. scarlatina* from the Andes, which has hardly appeared yet in gardens, and other types from Peru and Chile with yellow and scarlet flowers that are not in cultivation. What a huge population breaking out of the snows and peopling the mountains !

If you had the liberty of the mountain meadows and were allowed to choose what flowers should grow so as not to give the landscape in its simplicity the look of an innocent spring pasture before the flocks have been turned loose to graze, you would ask for there to be azure blue, sapphire blue, dark sea blue flowers. Let it be the day after the flowers have opened and before there has been time for the goats to come up the mountain ! But by no ingenuity or feat of inspiration could there be a shape of flowers more suited to their position upon the tops of the mountains than the clustered bells, or solitary, funnel-shaped, and erect trumpet. The gene or germ of the gentian could be the snow crystal, for its colours are mutant from the thick mass of snows. The dirty white edelweiss — a flower of flannel — even when it is lemon-scented and comes from China (*Leontopodium aloysiodorum*), is no daughter of the snow. But the gentian could have fallen out of the heavens between the clouds. It is mirror and icy principle of mountain and of ocean. And of no human connotation ; not like the viola or other flowers, even the saxifrage, which simulate the eyes of human beings or the human countenance. Such are the flowers of which the petals are the face, and the stalk the body. But the gentian is a blue throat, or a bell, or star. It is one of

the miracles of nature that it should be blue and found upon
the mountains.[1]

[1] The sky blue roses found growing in the high plains round Leh, capital of
Ladakh, on the borders of Tibet, by the American explorer and naturalist Suydam
Cutting, have roused little speculation among flower lovers and botanists, and the
importance of this discovery does not seem to have received due recognition. It has
been suggested that it is a colouration due to the high altitude, and that they would
flower differently at lower levels. Nevertheless, the mention of these light blue roses
is a matter of much interest, for probably they could be induced to have their sky
blue flowers if conditions were carefully studied and reproduced for them. Some
botanists would deny that this colour is possible to the rose. Cf. *The Fire Ox and
Other Years*, by Suydam Cutting : London, Collins, Sons & Co., 1948, pp. 11-12.

Archipelago of Daffodils

THE bluebell woods of Derbyshire are of another mythology. I mention those, in particular, because I have been told that an older and paler form of bluebell grows there. The whole wood is dyed blue with them at my old home and their honey breath brings poetry and the sharp-shadowed image. When I think of them, now, I remember the Venus of the bluebell wood, which was what I called the stone fountain of Bolsover Castle when I was little more than twenty years old, and my mind fills again with the images of that time. I must turn my head away and not look back on them. Instead, and for the moment, I would think of other places, even if I have not seen them ; of the furthest site to the North where lilies of the valley bloom in May and June out of the sandy shore of the Baltic ; of an inland lake in Sweden where the only red water-lilies grow in all Europe ; of another lake where three thousand swans breed, where a flight of wild swans is for ever passing overhead. . . . I have not seen lilies of the valley growing in a wood, which they do in some parts of England ; and the lilies of the valley sold in the streets of Paris have been gathered in the woods. Do the same women and children pick the wild strawberries later in the year, and later still, the autumn mushrooms ? Are there lilies of the valley growing in the woods of Aranjuez as well as strawberries ? I have seen arum lilies growing at Ninfa in the *campagna* ;

under pine trees in Andalusia, almost in sight of Africa. And in how many other places ? But neither the lily of the valley nor the arum is a true lily. They masquerade as lilies. They are mistaken for lilies. They are not lilies at all. Any more than the wild garlic which was the original of Pope's " lily-silvered vales ".

I have seen the paeony growing wild in the woods of Rhodes, and in the forest of Azrou, near Meknes, under the cedars of Atlas. In both instances there was snow not far away. But who could see this flower in nature, and not think of its thousand years of cultivation in gardens in China ; in Imperial gardens and the gardens of mandarins ? There is a paeony temple in Peking, with a green paeony, perhaps no more interesting than the green rose ; and there are descriptions of the Dowager-Empress in her garden, surrounded by eunuchs, directing the planting of her paeonies, and according to one account knowing by instinct what colour the flowers would be. It is the paeonies with ' cockatoo crests ' that particularly appeal to me, and it is their Oriental blood come down to them from ten centuries of hybrids that gives them the resource and stamina to perform like this. Beautiful and extra-ordinary forms must be lost irretrievably, for the paeony, it is well known, was the ' rose ' of Chinese gardens. It is not possible that in the most skilful Western hands this flower could rival its own millenary past in the lifetime of two human generations. For a sight of that, one would have to see the Imperial gardens of the Ming Dynasty in the sixteenth century. The single paeony in the woods of Rhodes, under the cedarn shade, or wherever in nature, is but remote ancestor or abori-ginal compared to what has been brought out of China and further hybridized ; double paeonies with outer guard petals like a cup of shells, of another colour, loaded with cream or

rose or golden petaloids or filaments of the paeony; milk
white, with lemon or canary yellow petaloids, in this form
like a rosette within a starry shell; or a rose paeony with
petals in three tiers or storeys. There are the rose and the
carnation paeonies, rose or carnation scented, and others with
paeony scent of their own; or those that in shape and colour
are like nymphaeas or water-lilies; paeonies that are bright
Bengal rose or light silvery rose; some that are dark amaranth
purple, nearly black, smelling of a tea rose; or pink apple
blossom edged with silver, spice scented; or those few that
are red carmine cups or rose cups and have the 'cockatoo
crest', that are so loaded, heaped with filaments or petaloids
that the cornucopia overflows. These are but the herbaceous
paeonies of the garden, and the tree paeonies may be the most
beautiful of all the family. They have been as long domesti-
cated and are as old in origin. There are tree paeonies that are
aged a hundred years and that renew their youth in flower;
larger and more decorative, more the painter's flower than is
the rose; and more beautiful of leaf. The foliage, alone,
suggests a Chinese flower painting and the flower is the shape
of island, cloud, or mountain. These are the flowers seen
often in Chinese paintings and upon Japanese painted screens.

I have seen meadows of white narcissus in Dauphiné, not
far from La Grande Chartreuse, in that part of France for ever
associated with Hector Berlioz to his admirers, and have
wondered whether or not that wild flower grew there in
abundance in his childhood. Nearly all of Berlioz is to be
found in the impressions of his early years. The red cup or
crown of the narcissus in the meadows nearly in sight of the
Alps has become implicit for me with the image of this most
extraordinary genius among musicians, in all things unlike
any other artist who ever lived, to the degree that a learned

critic has suggested that with his violent red hair and eagle features he may have been a throwback to an earlier race.[1] And I have seen meadows of anemones ; and the wonderful spectacle of fields of red poppies in Norfolk in the month of July, with the lark climbing high above, but invisible as a scratching diamond in the cloudless sky.

I have written, in another book, of the fairy daffodils or narcissi and the miracle of their coming up through narrow fissures in the granite rock. This was *Triandrus albus* or *Angels' Tears* on the Sierras of Portugal. For its home is Portugal. To my mind this little narcissus more resembles the ghost of some antelope or gazelle and I would never have named it *Angels' Tears*. The little *Hoop-Petticoat* daffodil *N. bulbicodium* grows in the marshy meadows of Portugal ; and in the multitude of miniature daffodils there is one so rare that it has only been found growing in two places, entrances or posterns to Queen Mab's Kingdom, or a way in and a way out, the second of which was only discovered in 1946, in the first flowering after AntiChrist had gone down in smoke and horror to the shades. There may be more, and unknown, forms of the little narcissus in the mountains of Portugal. It has been told before how a collector went forty years ago to the Ile Drenec, one of the Glénan group of islands lying off the coast of Brittany, an uninhabited, rocky island which is the only other habitat of *Triandrus calathinus*, in order to find this daffodil, but the islet had become bare rock, great seas having passed over it and washed away the soil. How can this little daffodil have got there, to this one rocky island ? I would like to think that ships of the Phœnicians carried it

[1] His contemporary Legouvé writes of Berlioz : " Such a head of hair ! It looked like an umbrella of hair, projecting like a movable awning over the beak of a bird of prey." And, in another place, Legouvé says that the hair of Berlioz was like the edge of a precipice and gave him vertigo.

there and to Cornwall, the new world of daffodils, and to the Scilly Islands. And I would have it grow on the Skelligs, and on Great Blasket, and upon the Aran Islands. But it only grows, out of Spain and Portugal, upon that one little Breton island (for it has been found growing there again) and seed of it must have been blown over the Bay of Biscay, or washed ashore.

N. cyclamineus is another inhabitant of Northern Portugal with its trumpet in the form of a long narrow tube and its perianth curved back, and high-peaked, like a cyclamen. To my mind, the most beautiful of all is the *Hoop-Petticoat* daffodil *N. bulbicodium*, which never fails in enchantment with the little spurs upon its wide-blown trumpet, all that is left of the perianth. Growing in quantity, this little daffodil resembles the Court of Elfhame, taken to the crinoline, and there are moments, as in Leech's drawings or comic prints of the 1850s, when a wind, of the pier, of the promenade, tilts the crinoline, lifts its circumference, and if the flower was human, like the young women of the period, we would see her white-stockinged legs and black-kid bootees, but the crinoline is pulled down again and it is only a *Hoop-Petticoat* daffodil in its reed-like leaves among the fairy meadows. But perhaps *N. bulbicodium* is not like a hoop-petticoat or crinoline at all, and resembles the fashionable bonnet of the 1830s, of Gavarni's drawings for *La Mode*, and of the dancers in Schumann's *Carnaval*. I have left till last *Minimus asturiensis* growing in Northern Spain in " shallow stony loam soil among gorse ", surely, where the ground opens and the witch, " a young woman of pleasant appearance ", takes us into the Fairy hill. The scent of this little daffodil is of unimaginable sweetness, a jonquil smell, but the honey of unearthly flowers. You may stoop down to it, not believing it could be a daffodil, and it is the perfect daffodil but like an image seen in a drop of water, no bigger than that.

I have often wished that I could write the catalogue of some daffodil grower and have stood entranced for moments together before the cut flowers in the R.H.S. Hall in Vincent Square. The all-white trumpet daffodils and narcissi are pure white, creamy white, white as milk, or ice white, with the nearly imperceptible differences and gradations upon which I would like to exercise my pen. *Namsos*, a huge milk white narcissus ; *Beersheba*, a magnificent daffodil of white vellum ; *Chinese White*, a pure white narcissus, with an eye that is just touched with green ; are some of them. But there are subtler distinctions. The white narcissi are not all ghosts of the golden flower. *Cushendall* has a white perianth, and a creamy frill with moss green eye. *Frigid*, an ice white narcissus, has an eye of emerald. There are narcissi with pure white petals and pink crowns ; cream white flowers with greenish lemon crowns ; ivory white or waxy white with sea green deep in the crown. There are the different shapes and beauties of the trumpet ; those that are frilled or rolled back at the mouth ; others shallow and fluted ; or strongly and boldly flanged in terms of an architectural plinth or pediment ; bell-mouthed ; or like a shallow cup or bowl. No less, the beauties of the perianth, derived from the shape and overlapping of the petal, forming almost a perfect circle, star-crowned, or like an architect's plan for a twelve-sided hexagon within a circle, with pointed, rounded, blunted petals, and never-ending delight in their nice placing.

The yellow trumpet daffodils are never to my mind so beautiful. They may have enormous vase-shaped trumpets like garden ornaments from a period of bad taste. I prefer the old double, almost green daffodil from Ireland which begins and ends the race of daffodils, in the same way that the paper white pheasant's eye narcissus is the primitive of all narcissi, down to the bunched Poetaz hybrids, polyanthus-headed, smelling of heaven and the clear sky, and to the wonders of our own time like *Wild Rose*, not a big flower, but one of the new ' pink ' daffodils, for it has a cup of apricot, a colour never seen before in the flower ; it is apricot flesh, broken down, macerated with rose red brick dust. A famous music hall comedian has told me that in his youth, touring the provincial theatres, he has known " troupers of the old school " who spoke *parlare*, the ancient theatrical language, to each other, and who would search for, and take back to their dressing-rooms, some piece of old red brick from wall or building, saying that its dust was better than any rouge paint. I can think of no other way to describe the colour of *Wild Rose*. It is red brick dust, made into rouge, and mixed with apricot. Another ' pink ' narcissus has a cup of salmon rose, a colour which it is more easy to see in the mind's eye. There are narcissi that are ice white with deep green perianth tubes, or milk white with primrose crowns ; and so to the new race of the golden narcissus, of which *Chungking* is typical, of beautiful golden substance, as you could say a fruit is golden, and with deep red crown. The petals are broad and full, even and un-blemished, of a new shape of flower.

How wonderful it would be to see large plantings of the new narcissi ! Their price is so high that they sell individu-ally, a bulb or two at a time, but this new race of flowers must, little by little, be passed on to the public. Is it too fanciful to think that their shape and colour have something in them of the air of Cornwall and of Northern Ireland, where so many of them had their origin ? The most beautiful plantings should be, of right, in the Scilly Islands, which could become a daffodil and narcissus archipelago. Perhaps only upon those shores, and nowhere else, do the ' pink-crowned ' daffodils flower in their true colours ; crowns of apple blossom, shell pink, pink primrose, peach, or apricot, and in another climate they come faded. The fairy daffodils and narcissi, they, too, are ' little Western flowers ' ; they are flowers of the Atlantic. The giant milk white daffodils, white oxen of the meadows, and the ice white narcissi ; they, also, inhabit an Atlantic region. So does the golden-fleshed narcissus. They are in flower upon a spring morning while the rest of our world shivers, or is shut in with rain, and I can think of no more inspiring experience than to walk among them and make note of their new persons.

The crocus is another legend. Its stem snaps like glass, which sound is in the first syllable of the name. So is its bright yellow cup. But say both syllables together and the crocus turns to blue or purple. In Greek it was a term for saffron-coloured hair. Yellow crocuses are so many jockeys in yellow caps and shirts in my own mythology. I have never been able to see more than something gay and bright, and a little vulgar, in the yellow crocus.

But the blue crocus is the Orient on its way down to the Mediterranean shore. And arrived there first, before the Greeks or Latins. The crocus with purple feathers (*C. etruscus*) was in flower before the painted tomb. The cream crocus streaked with purple (*C. imperati*) blooms in January at Naples. There are blue crocuses from the Levant and from the Balkans. There are lavender crocuses, long-pointed ; or silvery white and veined with lilac. But the crocus of crocuses is the wide open blue cup with bright orange red stigmata. That is the crocus. And it must have the stain of the pollen at bottom of the blue cup. It should be as though bruised with its own pollen.

The autumn-flowering crocus, however beautiful, is of the nature of those persons who arrive at a party at four o'clock in the morning and you cannot decide whether they have arrived late or early. If you have seen it growing in Bavarian meadows on the way to some Rococo church or monastery, perhaps to Rottenbuch, a tinselled church gay as a Christmas tree, or in the Tyrol, you will ever associate it in your mind with that late feeling that winter is approaching, you get the wet smell of it in the woods, and that it is time to go home. *C. imperati* blooming in January on the hills round Sorrento in sight of Capri, and the white crocus *Fleischeri* with scarlet stigmata, when the pink almond clouds the earth, are the true crocus. No Dutch hybrid grown in the garden can ever equal the crocus in Greece or Southern Italy or the Levant. It has so many connotations ; the flower of Romulus and Remus when they dragged through the grass at the dugs of their wolf-mother, and Faustulus, the King's shepherd, found them ; the crocus of black Tarquin and his queen Tanaquil building the walls and aqueducts of Rome ; such are the crocuses of the Alban hills. The flower of the Crusaders' kingdoms is another matter. The white crocus of the Levant with scarlet stamens should be called *Bohemund of Antioch*, not *Fleischeri*. I could never see the crocus in the Levant and not be reminded of the Crusaders' principalities, for those nobles coming out of the North must have been astonished at the crocus. I have thought of them riding in the woods in early spring when the fields were bright with crocuses. In Southern Italy and in Sicily the crocus is connected in my mind with the Arab or Saracenic craftsmen who worked for the Norman Kings. It was they who made the wooden ceiling of the Cappella Palatina and who wove silken stuffs not inferior to those of Byzantium. In Southern Italy I think of the crocus as the flower of the Hohenstaufen, and expect the fields to be blue and white with crocuses round Frederick II's Castel del

Monte, an octagon of two storeys with eight rooms upon each floor, and round Lucera where he settled the last twenty thousand Saracens from Sicily and enrolled his bodyguard.[1] It is not surprising that another crocus, *C. susianus*, and a golden yellow crocus at that, comes from the Crimea and from South Russia, for it seems to be implicit in the gold and silver treasures, now in the Hermitage, which were made by Greek workmen for the Scythians. By the same token, of Hellenic influence, it is only natural that there should be crocuses from Kashmir and Kurdistan.

There are the flowers that are of no mythology at all. Ixias, for an instance, or moraeas, both of which are Iridaceae, relatives of the iris, from the Cape. *Ixia viridiflora* with electric green flowers as strong and violent as a neon sign, touched with Prussian blue and with a purple eye, must be incomparable, in nature, and of no known image. A new imagery would have to be made for it. And there are ixias with pale blue, or rose scarlet flowers, orange with a black heart, mauve and white with yellow anthers, yellow with dark purple throat, or pink lilac. I have flowered *Ixia viridiflora*, but a solitary plant gives little idea of what it must be in nature. Only the electric blue green flower spike of *Puya pygmaea cerulea*, a Chilean relative of the pineapple which is, at once, a flowering impersonation of the taste of that fruit if you had never seen or heard of it before and had come to it for the first time, and an image for the Araucanian Indian, is as violent and intense of colour as *Ixia viridiflora*. But there is no legend for it, and if I could spend a few years of my life among ixias I would invent one.

---

[1] In the cathedral at Lucera there is a marble altar supported upon six pilasters. This marble slab, according to Mr. Norman Douglas, was once the dining table of Frederick II. Cf. *Moving Along*, by G. M. Orioli, London, Chatto & Windus, 1934, p. 208, where it is illustrated.

Moraeas, the African equivalent to the iris, which were grown in England more than a hundred years ago in the time of Mrs. Loudoun and make a tentative appearance in her drawings, have only revealed themselves in peacock colours in the hands of one grower of our day. He alone in England has found their secret. Moraeas have three large, rounded petals and their peacock eye. They are, in truth, unlike Cerberus in every other way, three-headed and three-eyed, for the peacock eye is on each petal.

The eye of the moraea is pale green or blue or indigo or velvet black, with a claw of green or yellow or orange, and a ring of the same colour round the eye. The petals are white or lilac or bright red, yellow or lavender or purple. It is *Moraea villosa* that is most beautiful of the peacock irises, that comes in so many colours, but mainly white, mauve, or lilac; that opens its three peacock eyes, and grows upon sandy foothills at the Cape in September, the Antipodean spring. But the moraeas grow much further inland upon the thundery, rolling grasslands in Basutoland, where the Basutos have their round beehive huts and wide-horned cattle and wander in their red blankets, and here in scattered colonies in the enormous terrain there must be ungathered moraeas of new varieties, and the starry many-coloured rhodohypoxis, and many other flowers. Moraeas may be one of the most beautiful of the little-known flowers of the world ; wide open, as though worked with springs, they look like the marriage of a three-petalled poppy and a three-winged butterfly. I do not know, but I would surmise that the moraea is short-lived and during its flowering period, like the tigridia, opens a new flower every day. It should be a flower of as many associations as the lily or the tulip, but it is unpainted and unsung.

IV

Magnolia and Rhododendron

I HAVE attempted in *Sacred and Profane Love* to write a description of a tree of the rose pink magnolia *M. campbellii*, eighty or a hundred feet high, in full flower in some Himalayan vale, and of the felling of this same tree still in flower for firewood, which has happened, for the ignorant Sikkimese or Burman peasants attach no importance to it and chop it down, first, because it is the heaviest and largest tree. The rose pink magnolia, even in the twenty- or thirty-foot-high specimens which is all that this tree has had time to grow to since it was brought to Europe, is one of the wonderful sights of the world. Anyone upon seeing a magnolia of an ordinary kind would wish that it could have rose pink flowers and this has been granted, although it may be thirty years before *M. campbellii* comes into flower. I do not know of any other writer who has thought of, or attempted, such a subject, which certainly could not be painted or set to music. Neither, for it calls for exact description, is it suited for a poem. It is a theme that can only be done in prose. Admiration for magnolias, and agreement that they are among the most beautiful and sensational of flowers, has made it that if an old flower book has drawings of magnolias it at once goes into another category of price. A single magnolia flower or a spray of magnolias can be drawn or painted but not the entire tree. Still less, the toppling and crashing of that tree of flowers. I have achieved this, but no one has ever mentioned it to me.

I would like to write, too, of the carmine cherry. This was found by Kingdon Ward in Northern Burma where, to paraphrase his words, he noticed one evening close to his camp a big cherry tree about to flower. " Two days later, quite leafless, it was in full bloom, a mass of blossom ", and for a full minute he stood before it, " unable to speak a word, drunk with the glory of it ". This wonderful vision was a carmine cherry tree ninety foot high, Ward's *Carmine Cherry*, *Prunus cerasoides* var. *rubea*, a sight which few Western eyes have seen but a tree which grows, too, on mountains in Siam. The flower buds are crimson or ruby red in colour, first appearing in the middle of March towards the ends of the branches, which is the moment of seeing the giant carmine tree " about to flower ", and a day or two later it is in full bloom. It would be wonderful to see it, and try to write of it ; and I have imagined paintings ninety foot high of the carmine cherry, taller by as much again as the hugest canvases of Rubens or of Tintoretto, done by painters of the Kano school, Kano Sanraku or Kano Eitoku, who alone of all the artists there have ever been had enough of mental excitement at seeing such a sight as this and the particular technique to carry it out and communicate it in their paintings. It would not be possible or conceivable that it should be copied, flower by flower ; the only method, as practised by the painters of mediaeval Japan, would be to try to convey the excitement of beholding this glorious and astonishing flowering tree. In humbler vein, in this present book, I let the rumour that had reached me of a wood of crimson primroses so affect me and take me where I willed.

Not the shadow of the carmine cherry, but its image in

the sharp evening on the golden ground. And that of a little tree with blue green leaves, silvery beneath, with big creamy white flowers that have orange spottings. Near by, a taller tree with narrow, deep green leaves and flowers of the shape of blue butterflies, but not all of the same blue.

Or we can be wandering in a near valley to find a tree that grows like a tent of beautifully formed apple-green leaves, with lily-shaped flowers that have green or wine-coloured staining in the throat, and a delicious scent. It is a valley in Hupeh in Western China and the silver pheasant dances in the brilliant evening.

Here is another apple-green rhododendron, bright green, with waxy scarlet flowers in great trusses, tubular-shaped, and it needs little imagination to know we are nearing the display grounds of the satyr tragopan. There are shrubs of bell-shaped flowers of pale to deep orange, marked with scarlet ; others, deep crimson with plum-coloured bloom upon them ; or black crimson turning to blood red when the sun shines through them. The tragopan was born for the blood red rhododendron with spatulate leaves and stem of cinnabar.

But there are small trees or shrubs with willow-like leaves and butter-yellow flowers ; and those that have aromatic leaves and pink apple-blossom flowers freckled with rose madder. The pale pink with a faint rose stripe ; the brick red, the salmon red, the Indian red, the terracotta ; for whom are these intended ? The geranium scarlet, alone of rhododendrons, from the Salween ; those that have glaucous green, or box-like foliage, or rounded blue-green leaves and scarlet flowers ? Are they for the crested fireback, the eared crossoptilon, or Amherstian pheasant ?

There are white flowers like honeysuckle, with honeysuckle scent ; or white butterflies with lilac markings and dark eyes ; there are creamy yellows with a claret eye ; those with sage-green leaves and salmony flowers, orange-throated ; and those that are rose pink or rosy crimson, but there is always yellow in their throat, and the young leaves are glaucous blue.

Some have crinkled dark-green leaves with brown indumentum ; or bright orange indumentum on the under surface, and the young growth is covered with gold hairs.[1] There are leaves that hang in a stiff collar below the flower ; and the metallic rhododendrons, those that are orange yellow in flower, with a wash of red or pink metal upon the petal ; deep blood red bells ; or trusses of waxy flowers that could have been hammered out of scarlet metal. And again, the bright scarlet, black spotted ; or crimson, black spotted, shining blood red in the sun.

But most lovely of all is the white lily-like rhododendron with the scent that is as delicious as the flowers. And the bright pink and white azalea, or the yellow smelling of wetted honeysuckle ; and again, the huge rose and white rhododendrons that have the speckled throats. They can be twenty or thirty feet high, or but a foot above the ground ; a little prostrate shrub, a flower in a pot, or a magnificent flowering tree. They have arrived from Western China and Tibet and Burma during this century ; they grow, perhaps, better in Wales, in Western Scotland, and in Ireland, than they do in

---

[1] Mr. James Russell favours me with the following note on indumentum. " Many of the big-leaved rhododendrons have this orange or gold wool beneath the leaves, and as the young leaves grow the whole surface is covered with soft golden hair which glints in the sunlight. The *cinnabarinum* series have beautiful leaves which, when young, have a blue bloom like grapes. *Ferruginosum*, a rare plant sent here (to the Sunningdale Nurseries, Windlesham) from the Himalayas by Hooker in 1850, has leaves like washleather, when new they are the colour of verdigris which appears on copper. Many *triflorum*-leaves are so highly scented that one's coat will smell of them for weeks after touching them. They are full of a scented oil."

their own mountain valleys ; and the modern hybrids may be more beautiful than the parent plants themselves. Never before in history has there been such an invasion of plants, and there are more yet to come if there is still time to find them. The *Rhododendron Year Book* contains nearly ten thousand names of species and their crosses, even if the most recent arrivals are only known by numbers. In addition, there are, sometimes, six or seven forms of the same rhododendron.

So the great massed armies are not unmanageable. The poetry of numbers has its play in gardens.[1] The invasion of rhododendrons coming from Western China, Tibet, and Burma, and their multiplication by hybrids into so huge a population, is of novel nature because they have arrived in such numbers in so short a time, and by reason of their variety of colour. The rhododendron may be the last and latest thing to come out of Asia into Europe. What is not so certain is whether this most flaunting of the flowering trees has a

---

[1] I have before me, as I write this, an astonishing list of carnations, picotees, and pinks grown by Messrs. Youell of Great Yarmouth that occupies an entire page of six columns of small print, and overflows onto another, in *The Gardener's Chronicle* for 1843. They march down the page in ranks of scarlet, crimson, pink, and purple bizarres ; scarlet, rose, and pink, and purple flakes ; red edge, purple edge, rose and scarlet English picotees — picotees on yellow grounds, sixty-five of those, only, to choose from ; and " new and superb pinks " ; a grand total of seven hundred and thirty-eight in all. Somewhat of a military eye would be needed among the flakes, bizarres, and picotees. My half-trained glance falls upon a crimson bizarre, Hufton's *Squire Sitwell*, but I know no more of him. . . . The present-day list of James Douglas of Edenside contains the names of two hundred and eighty-six carnations of all kinds. But it is said that early in the eighteenth century there were one hundred and sixty sorts of *Painted Lady* pinks alone. There are close on ten thousand daffodils registered and classified in the *R.H.S. Year Book*. But, to the uninitiated, they are not easy to tell apart. It would take as long an apprenticeship among the daffodils as I have been told by a French officer in a military post in the Atlas mountains is needed before you can tell one Senegalese rifleman from another, all of the same colour and belonging to the same tribe. At the close of the auricula period about the beginning of this century, there were eight hundred named auriculas in commerce. There are American collectors who grow the same number of different camellias in their gardens ; and I have some hundred and fifty varieties of old roses in my garden, and hope for more.

place in art. It would seem impossible to paint it. And it would be as difficult to make any kind of design or pattern out of it. The rhododendron is too informal. And the nomenclature, the naming of the new rhododendrons, belongs to the worst period of poverty of the imagination. At a time when language and the sound of words had any meaning it would have been impossible to give such names to flowers. *L'Œil Noir, Menelaus, Faunus, Curion* (old names for ranunculuses) ; *Pluto, Camusetta, Golden Fleece*, and *Golden Grove* (old tulips) ; must always be better names for flowers than *Naomi*, or *Lady Chamberlain*. It is not, therefore, the fault of the flowers, but, in part, that of the period of natural gardening in which they were discovered. One would like to know what one of the masters of garden design would have made of the rhododendron. Were there rhododendron plantings as old as the cypresses of Villa d' Este or the canals and formal groves of Versailles the rhododendron would long ago have entered poetry and been a part of formal prose. But it is so recent that I do not know of any writer who has attempted it. With the formal garden it is as drastic a change as the introduction of electric lighting into the theatre. Now, at last, there are great colour groupings to be used for distance. The glitter of the ilex was all the old gardeners knew. Their colour was in their parterres.

Let us consider those. The parterres of Le Nôtre were of four kinds : *Parterres de broderie*, in which the box lines imitated embroidery ; *Parterres de compartiment*, consisting of scrolls, knots, and borders ; *Parterres à l'anglaise*, grass plots all in one piece or cut into shapes, and bordered with flowers ; and *Parterres de pièces coupées*, only formed of box without either grass or embroidery. Nearly all of Le Nôtre's elaborate parterres, upon which he prided himself, have disappeared. The most magnificently conceived of the *Parterres de broderie* was probably that of the Grand Trianon. Here, for the *soirées de Trianon* during the summer, a thousand gardeners were employed and the flowers in the parterres were changed almost every day. Dangeau says that on one occasion the King and the whole Court had to leave the gardens owing to the overpowering scent of the tuberoses. Would that other defeats suffered by Le Roi Soleil had been of this character, and as little harmful to the French nation then in the zenith of its powers ! [1] The flowers used for the parterres of Le Nôtre were chiefly roses, tulips, jasmines, and carnations. Scent was contrived but not much colour, for the flowers mentioned, and others such as hyacinths and auriculas, would not carry far from a visual point of view.

The great luxury was in orange trees. Louis XIV was an ardent collector of those. Hence the Orangerie at Versailles, one of the masterpieces of French architecture with its great outer stairways, conceived upon a truly Roman scale, being to Versailles what the colonnades of Bernini are to St. Peter's. Hence, too, the orangeries in German gardens, such as that at Herrenhausen. There, some of the orange trees stand in huge green tubs that have to be drawn by horses, and are five hundred years old. John Claudius Loudun, the Scots landscape gardener, describing the gardens of Enghien in Belgium in the early nineteenth century, belonging to the Ducs d'Arenberg, says " the old orange grove . . . contains one hundred and eight orange trees in tubs, many of them, as is the case in different old family seats in the Netherlands,

---

[1] It has been calculated that a good deal more than half of the whole countryside within fifteen miles of Paris was taken over by the parks and gardens of Louis XIV, Louis XV, and their Courts. Versailles, St.-Cloud, St.-Germain, Meudon, Marly, Sceaux, Chantilly, to the west of Paris ; and Fontainebleau, Vaux-le-Vicomte, and others, to the east.

presents from the Kings of Spain two hundred years and more ago. The trees show straight stems of six and eight feet, and globular heads from which, according to continental practice, protruding shoots and blossoms are pinched off as soon as they appear, for culinary and perfumery purposes." The orange trees were so many rarities from the Orient, treated as such, and with splendid pavilions built for their accommodation. This being so, it may be imagined what would have been their reception of the rhododendron.

If we could see the gardens of Versailles as they were in 1688, at their apogee, when the waters of the Obélisque, eighty feet high, fell, as intended, in snow-white flounces owing to careful adjustment of the pipes ; when the Bassin de Latone threw its hoops or colonnades of waters, and must have looked in the distance like the grand armada of the whales, a-blowing ; when the marvellous Théâtre d'Eau showed its dancing columns invading an oval space in hundreds of jets of water down the path of three cascades advancing to meet each other ; we would know that colour was the one thing missing from their gardens. Absent from the huge open spaces of Versailles in spite of their green groves and *bosquets* ; and from Marly with its twelve pavilions, six to a side, before the palace of the Sun King, in a sunless valley, and its marvellous Rivière d'Eau, one of the wonders of the century, consisting of sixty-three steps so nicely adjusted that the waters flowed down them and looked like a solid sheet of falling water. We may wish that it was possible for us to accompany the Sun King on one of his progresses down the long broad avenue that led from Versailles to Marly, a reminiscence of which, there is no doubt, is to be seen in the broad walk connecting the palace of Sanssouci at Potsdam with the Neues Palais, about three-quarters of a mile away, and a wonderful moment it is when you look back at the low, pavilion-like Sanssouci up its rows of hothouses arranged in terraces like the flashing tiers of some glittering cascade. The unnecessary extravagance of two palaces so near to one another, of Sanssouci and the Neues Palais, of Marly and Versailles, is part of the accumulation of magnificence. So are the orangeries. So were Marly, and the original Trianon de Porcelaine, begun at the end of winter and completed in the early spring. Seven years later it was demolished to make way for Mansart's Trianon de Marbre, but it was at the Trianon de Porcelaine that Le Roi Soleil had to take flight from the tuberoses. Colbert, in charge of the Royal palace, wrote to his agent at Marseilles : " You know that for the ornamentation of the Royal gardens we must have a large quantity of flowers. As there are so many varieties in Provence I beg you to buy all the jonquils and tuberoses that you can find, and also any other curious flowers that would contribute to the adornment of the Royal gardens."

Rarities from the Orient were treated with as much deference as ambassadors from the Court of Siam, whose reception by Louis XIV was made the subject for a splendid Gobelins tapestry. Orange trees had palaces built for them. It may be imagined with what enthusiasm the formal garden designers of that age would have fallen upon Japanese ornamental cherry trees, had those been known to them, and how they would have seized the opportunities given to us in our own day by the invasion of so many flowering trees and shrubs from China. Now, at last, the dream of the lacquerer is come true, when it is too late. The wild fantasies of the Western mind let loose in an Orient of the imagination have been realized. But they have come at a time when we no longer see them in that light of poetry, and when we cannot even think of names for them. How much more would they have been

appreciated at the Trianon de Porcelaine ! Listen to Madame
de Sévigné writing in 1675 of the gardens of Clagny, which
had been given by Louis XIV to Madame de Montespan :
" We have been to Clagny. How can I describe it ! It is a
veritable palace of Armida ; the building is growing visibly ;
the gardens are made. You know the manner of Le Nôtre ;
he has left a little dark wood. There is a grove of orange
trees in great tubs ; you walk there, and they form alleys
in the shade ; and to hide the tubs there are rows of palisades
high enough to lean on, all flowering with tuberoses, roses,
jasmines, and carnations ; it is surely the most beautiful, the
most surprising, and the most enchanted novelty imaginable."
The *Mercure de France* adds the information that " there are
beautiful palisades of myrtle arranged to hide the tubs, which
hold oranges in such a way as to make it appear that orange
trees are planted in the palisades ". The *Mercure Galant* describes a fête at Sceaux in 1685 given by the son of Colbert
in honour of Louis XIV and Madame de Maintenon, and tells
how the Royal party rested an hour in the Pavillon d'Aurore,
and then went through the Salle des Marronniers to a little
wood " fait en labyrinthe " and sparkling with fountains,
whence they passed to the Allée d'Eau, not far from the great
canal which was half a mile in length. The accounts of such
festivities read like descriptions of another world, and if only
that other world of the Far Orient of which themselves were
dreaming had come to meet them, as it has come towards us in
our time, what wonders there would have been. . . .

So I come to the shutting and closing of the jasmine kingdom, which is as though someone has just died, and it leaves
a sense of loss. It led on like a dream and like a distraction
rising out of things that had come before, and of which the
shadow or the puppet play has been projected upon these

pages. Why do I write, or rather, why do I go on writing, except for love of this world and of the wonders in it, which are enough for all the hours of every lifetime since the first human footprints upon the tawny sands ? But I must explain that I have no religious feelings of any sort whatever, and that in my instance the place of religion is taken by the things of which I write, for good or evil, further than which I will not betray myself, or reveal more of my own religion.

In this world one of my delights has been the shadow or the double image. This would seem to be in entire and utter antithesis to the fixed image. There is no space, here, to talk of the inimitable pencil drawings done by Ingres. How marvellous are those ! They are the masterpieces of the single image. The caricatural exit of Picasso out of static reality by means of his invention of the double profile is but the rude gesture of a Spanish anarchist of genius, for Picasso has it in his powers to rival Ingres as a draughtsman. Only in certain of his drawings for the *Metamorphoses* of Ovid does the doubled profile of Picasso emerge from caricature into a thing of beauty, a blurred vision induced by the glitter of the seashore, or a mere trick worked by playing with the muscles of the eyes. But the metamorphosis of the person is as rare in literature. I do not want this book to be like any other book that has been written before. Its transformations of the theme are more akin to those in music. Sometimes there is but the hint or echo of the theme. What is it all about ? Why those long passages, they are connecting passages or corridors, of flowers ? The composer of music is not asked to explain himself ; nor, in our day, the painter. They have the licence of their profession. No one questions them. Here, in this book, I write to please myself ; and I am my own best audience. I have watched myself ever since I began to write ; and I know that

I write best when I write to please myself. Then, there is no other motive. I can practise my own religion, or lack of that. Writing, in such circumstances, is a profession and an act of faith. When I write of flowers it is to praise the beauties of the world, and with no other object. I would wish to have that Western wind and those fragrances blowing upon me yet again. Here, it is so still and sad and little happens. It comes. I feel it coming. I am seized and taken up by it, and at the same time, cannot move or stir.

BOOK IV

DREAM OF THE TWO SISTERS

I

Dream of the Two Sisters

THE two sisters whom I knew long years ago were dressed, but not alike, in some shining material that could be cloth-of-silver to match their fair colouring. I am trying to remember in more detail. For it was in a dream; that is to say, I saw them in my sleep, which if you stop to think of it is of universal experience, is common to all humanity, but no explanation whatever makes it the less mysterious. You come into the room and look at the sleeper, and you have no idea what is happening behind his or her closed eyes and only know that this is one thing that makes sleep different from death, that you can wake him. It is sad and annoying, we all know it, to have a broken or interrupted dream, but this particular dream had a melancholy or poignancy of its own. For the figurant in my dream was twenty-two or three years old, and now it is many, many years ago. Time to be born, and live, and die again. And all the while I was conscious of that. Some part of my mind was whispering in my ear that this was so. Could there be any sensation more terrible; or that tears with more violence at the heart and memory? Yet the experience was entirely of its time and moment. It was not as it would be to-day; or, put differently, I was young, in my dream; I had the feeling and sensation of being young, but perhaps only as I would know that now, and did not know it then. For certainly with some natures it is an aftertaste. We live in the moment ; or suppress that, and think of it much later.

Both sisters, I have said, were dressed in some shining, silvery material, but not dressed alike, any more than they resembled each other in feature or character, or in any other respect than that both had fair hair. One of them interested me more than the other ; and it was the elder sister. They were dressed in my dream as a brother and sister, Prince Charming and Cinderella, or an Arcadian shepherd and shepherdess, it does not matter particularly, but the younger sister wore a hooped skirt and I think the reason for this was because there had once been an ' Arcadian ' party in the country, and because upon another occasion, a previous summer, I knew that the two sisters had danced a minuet upon an island in a lake in the middle of a garden. I wrote a poem about it. In my dream they were as they were, then. The elder sister was as in the poems that I wrote to her. But the only inconsequence was that the sisters were of no special importance in the dream. It was as though I only saw them and passed by.

For they were in a crowd of persons. And that was what was terrible. I was so near her that I touched her. I saw her moving in front of me and she looked round. Among many persons moving from one room into another ; a ghost from early memory, for the two sisters must have been very young, must have been little more than children, to be dressed as a pair of sisters at a ball. How am I to describe it ? I felt a young man in my dream ; and yet it was as though they were brought in to see me when I was very ill, or dying. I knew them ; but I had scarcely the strength to recognize them. And now that something else was dead in me, both sisters were of an equal importance to me so that I was as pleased to see the younger as the elder sister. I even felt, perhaps, that she was nearer to me than the other one, though she had put no mark upon me. It was as though there was no time left to remember anything, only time for recognition, to see them once more, and yet, no deathbed scene, for I was not in the least dying. I felt young, and more as though they were figures I remembered out of my childhood. But no. There was that indefinable feeling or taste of youth. I knew it in my dream. And it is more like a scent. If ever I think of it, or try to recapture the sensation of youth, for it still comes to me, I am reminded of the scent of lime trees. It makes me remember the smell of an avenue of limes upon a still evening; something drifting down upon you, and it is shed forth or powdered upon you, it drifts onto you, and you do not know from whence it comes. You are only aware of it. It is in the air. And the air belongs to it. Sometimes the wind carries it to a little distance, and you look up, wondering what it can be, and see the lime tree like a tall green tower and hear the bees in the lime blossom. It takes no longer in time than to feel young, but chiefly, it seems to me, it is a scent you remember afterwards, or that reminds you of things past. You do not know it in its moment. And the season of it is immortal; and by the same measurement soon over.

Well, the green lime tree was then growing in that room. In the ballroom, or in some high anteroom or corridor. And it seemed to me in my dream that all were conscious of it; that everyone knew it and was permeated with it. Do not think I mean that a veritable lime tree, as it might be a Christmas tree, stood in a corner of the room. Nothing of the kind. But everyone had his or her youth shed upon them by magical influence, and were unchanged; those of long ago, and of now, of the blossoming lime branch. And I had the sensation

247

that the two sisters had been living for a long time somewhere
of which I had lost the address ; and even, within the dream,
I had other short dream sequences in which I went to see them,
but remembered little about it, and knew all the time that it
was not true ; just as I have, often, a recurrent dream that
someone whom I want to see, and want most deeply to see for
a particular reason, is in London and that I have lost the address
and telephone number, and forgotten the name, for the name
has changed, and in one dream that I remember, or am I
making it up, now, in order to flatter my imagination ? — I
had to go round, at some sort of fair or fun-fair, asking at every
booth for news of the person I wanted to see until I found
myself in the situation of Heine's *Florentine Night*, where there
is that recurring episode of the street dancer who is seen upon
London Bridge and comes again and again into Heine's
fantasmagoria and is in a sense the action or pivot of the story,
but there is no plot and it is a poetical fantasy written down in
prose.

I even remember, or so it seems to me, a dark house with
a long passage hall in some remote square, that I even feel I
could set out to find, where I have been again and again to
enquire, where this person is living, having come back after long
absence, but it is all a screen or defence for something I do not
like to admit to myself in my dream, which is that she is dead.
Curiously enough, this fact, for it is fact, is the one thing held
back from me in the dream. No voice whispers the truth to
me ; and at infrequent intervals I am allowed to go on searching. This person I will apostrophize under no other name
than as the ghost of the white syringa tree ; and I behold her,
not in my dream, where it is to be noted she hides herself in a
little and obscure anonymity of her own making, sign of her
selfless character, and perhaps knowing that she was to die

young, but, I use the phrase because of its double meaning, in the full limelight of the flowering lime bough, shed down upon her by the green lime branch, as I saw her in her doubled life, for she had two lives or sets of appearances and the fascination of this dead person was in the contrast and interplay between them, and in the mystery as to wherein lay the truth that met the eyes. I have heard her voice, like the voice of Xantippa coming up out of the well-head to speak to me, in a most wonderful and beautiful dream I had at Hammamet, wherein I dreamt of everyone I have ever admired in my life, a dream induced by the North African heat of August and by the all-pervading scent of jasmine — Tunis is, during August, a kind of jasmine kingdom ; they give you, every morning and every evening, a buttonhole or posy of jasmine made by the Arab women during the long siesta hour, the white florets are pulled apart and made into a little bouquet, the Tunisians are never without a wand or sceptre of jasmine in their hands, a whole memory of a summer in Tunis can consist of the hot weather and the jasmine, and in 1939 the bunches of jasmine were flown over to be sold in the streets of Paris.

I say that the heat of Tunis supplied this food or nectar for the imagination, and I have often noticed the counter irritant or compensation in a dream. It can be an entertainment ' put on ' to lull you in a time of dullness, for instance, in some quiet hotel abroad where you have gone to work during the winter, if you are a writer (for such things used to be, and there is no particular extravagance attached to them !). There is nothing else to do in the evening except to go to bed early, and read and put out the light, and I have known what was no less than a continuous entertainment, then provided, and I am unable to believe, as is supposed to be the fact, of only a few seconds' duration, indeed, it appeared to 'play' the whole night through. I have dreamt, thus, of imaginary foreign lands, an entire Balkan Peninsula, for an example, as full of paintings and architecture as Italy or Spain ; I have visited picture exhibitions of artists in whom I am interested and have 'created' each painting in its frame ; and have even stated, before witnesses, that I would appreciate a dream in the form of an early Wild West film, complete with sheriffs, cowboys, Red Indians, and shootings in saloon bars, and been rewarded with my wish granted and the dream 'running', continuously, for three nights on end. Such are instances of dreams made to please, their purpose being to amuse and interest and keep your attention fixed upon them, so that you go on sleeping. The heat of Africa, I say, required, evidently, another form of soporific, for it was so hot that unless you were given some inducement to sleep you would lie awake, all night, sleepless, turning from side to side in your bed. It was the occasion for the casting of a spell, for music or poetry that would make it that you would lie still, as in the sacred trance, and not move or stir. Thus, and thus, the voices and ghosts rising out of the well-head, and of the blossoming lime bough.

But there is another cause, and one which it is not so easy to explain. Just as ghosts are supposed to appear upon particular days in the year (I have not seen a ghost) in ghostly celebration of some anniversary or occasion, so there may be dreams, as it were, of special performance, of unique performance, of circumstance born, and never to be approached or repeated ; the dream of 'Gypsy' Lee, when he dreamed, the night before his execution, that they would try to hang him, in the morning, three times, and fail, and the dream came true. This is an example ; or one can imagine for oneself what may have been the last dreams of Charles I, Marie-Antoinette, or the Russian Royal Family ; less so, in the last instance, because they had no means of knowing it was their last night on earth and that they were to be murdered on the morrow. Then there are the dreams of prisoners, and of those who are ill and dream they are in health ; and the conducing circumstances of which I am thinking have something in them of all these causes or factors working together as though in combination. But what they are, strictly and entirely, is the shadow or reflection. That is to say, they are a balance or a compensation ; ghostly comforters or advisers, but not, of necessity, giving consolation. On the contrary they may be as sad as, or sadder than, the circumstances which gave them birth. But always, I say, they are the shadow of the event, not disconnected fantasies, leaves blown over, like those other sorts of dreams which are haphazard or sent for entertainment. If, this is my theory, there is something which has made you miserable and unhappy, you will dream, not of that, in further prolongation of its miseries, but of the next problem or unhappiness coming after or before it, which you may have nearly forgotten in the anxieties of the moment. It is as though those regions of the brain which govern and supply these fantasies can vary the melody but not change the key, which means they have the power to alter the direction or object but not the purport of the mood. They have some powers of substitution ; they can put one shadow in place of another but they cannot lay the ghost. It may hark back to other features, and wear that travesty, but it is the spectre undisguised. This is no more than to mistake the player for the person. Soon they coalesce or merge together ; the ghost fits the ghost, and the mistake is rectified.

There are fixations of incident, of a kind which the person

concerned must have dreamed of continually, at recurrent intervals, or not at all. I believe it to be absolutely true that the ' censor ' in the brain, to use a favourite term of the psychologists, ensures that the doubled or shadowed apprehension is veiled and hidden and that no hint of it comes to disturb your sleep or repose. That would explain the calmness of so many criminals in the dock, a calm that can even be, in itself, incriminating ; and I think it is also the reason why you scarcely ever dream of dead persons you have loved. The more portentous the circumstance the more completely it is obliterated. I do not believe, but it is distasteful to mention so disgraced a name in this context, that Lord Alfred Douglas dreamed of his friendship with poor Oscar Wilde. I think that Madeleine Smith never had her sleep troubled with visions of Émile l'Angelier.

I am not interested, here, in the dream interpretations of the psychologists and in the huge unknown territory that they have opened to discovery and investigation. I have always been able to interpret my own dreams. I am only using the form of a dream as a literary medium in order to create, if I have the power to do it, a work of art. I have set out to examine the shadows or reflections thrown in dreams, and the form I have chosen gives me the liberty of what may seem inconsequence but is, really, the direct result of one image trying to obliterate another. It is the balance or compensation of the subconscious. Someone is dead ; and you dream, immediately, not of the dead person but of someone else in life. And the person need not be dead, in *rigor mortis* ; it is sufficient that, for the plural must be used with shadows and their overtones, they are removed from you by some condition of the spirit akin to illness or imprisonment. Neither is it necessary for the cause or fountain of these transformations to be themselves affected. They may be prospering and perfectly happy. So, also, may be the percipient. It is but a spur to fantasy and to the imagination ; to be regarded in the light of the tongues of fire in the background of Nicholas Hilliard's miniatures against which languish the Elizabethan gallants in all the vigour of their manhood, and we are not to believe that they are really dying in the flames. Yet they chose to be so painted, and we must allow to them that they may have been singed in the fire.

A bonfire of green lime branches, a slow fire, for the sap is high in the tree stems and there is more smoke than fire ? Or a fire of apple wood which makes a scented smoke ? A fire to sit in front of, " while the rest of the house is asleep, thinking of the past and remembering times gone by ". No ! No ! Pile more boughs upon the bonfire until the smoke climbs like the column of the stylite into the still air ! And let us tell the future out of the shapes of smoke ! For the moment we are back in the ballroom where the two sisters appeared like ghosts or spectres of the music, not long ago. Now, they are nowhere to be found. What if so many different figures are all travesties of the same person ? But the ballroom empties, immediately. It is not true that the same ghost inhabits so many transformations. There will be travesties enough, in store, and not yet realized.

II

All' Italia

PASSING in front of the long red Roman building, I do not know quite where it was, but somewhere near the Pantheon, at about nine o'clock upon a spring evening when it was nearly dark and a hooded wine cart came by pressing me against the wall, a wine cart with a dog walking between its wheels, bringing wine into Rome from the vineyards of Frascati, and beyond, where the nymph parts the Golden Bough and treads the wild strawberry plant upon the banks of Nemi.

Those wine carts are nearly gone now. You never meet them in the streets. You may be a month in Rome and see no more than two or three of them in the suburbs, but at the time I am thinking of they were frequent and to be met with at every corner, and one of them pressed me, I say, against the wall somewhere between the Pantheon and the Roman fountains. Ah ! the goat-god rode in the tumbril, the goat-god who stood with his front hooves against the trunk of the olive tree, leering obscenely, moved from tree to tree, and walked away erect on his hind legs among the herd of goats, now coming round at dusk from house to house in a wine cart upon a temporary stage, his face and beard daubed with the lees of wine. I was twenty years old and he butted against me with his pair of horns.

Another time, in February, having got up at four o'clock in the morning to catch the little steamer that went along the coast to Capri, and in the early morning as we were rowed ashore we picked jonquils and narcissi growing out of the cliff at the level of our hands and were stormbound for three days upon the island and shut in by white mists, and I remember the white cubical houses, like the houses of Mykonos in the Cyclades, and the air and light of the goat-isle and how a wooden chair, a wooden table, was the altar of the goat-god and a stone wall or a crook of the fig tree a place of debauchery. Or I remember the little bowers or garden pavilions of Bolsover Castle, their window-sills and embrasures and stone seats, a place in which to listen to the lute and look out in the moonlight upon the Venus of the fountain, the stone statue of Bolsover and Venus of the bluebell wood, a pale, a moonlit shadow to Italian " isles of fragrance, lily-silvered vales " ; and were I to choose the most lovely place of the physical beauty of nature in all Italy or in all of the world that I have seen with my own eyes, I would name the gardens of Villa Lante, at Bagnaia, with the twin pavilions or casinos (and nothing inside them), box parterres, orange and lemon trees in terracotta pots, bronze fountain of four naked youths by John of Bologna, camellias, chiming waters, and faunal ilex shades. It is a place nearly to convert one to the goat-kingdom ; and I saw it again, now, not having been there for many years, upon a Sunday afternoon ; the men and women of Bagnaia were walking in the ilex woods, of timeless beauty, but there was no one in the locked gardens.

The wheat was so tall at the top of the garden that it stood above my head, for token of physical abundance in this promised land. I have never known such tall wheat. A Poussin, a Samuel Palmer would have delighted in it. Below that are stone seats, stone tables, o'er-arching shade. And the long musical descent of the waters, in their bed of stone ; a trough contrived like a stone chain of dolphins, head to tail, till the waters tunnel into the earth and come up in the bronze figures. A wall and hedge surround those, and beyond are the tiled roofs and houses of Bagnaia, an area not bigger than the garden of a London square, pagan, not belonging to the saints and martyrs (built by Cardinal Gambara, it is true) ; but the lichen has come upon the statues, the wheat has grown so tall, in obedience to another and older dispensation.

There is nothing to equal Villa Lante for this pagan quality ; not the fountains and cypresses of Villa d' Este, nor its huge archway, a triumphal arch giving onto the empty, Claudian *campagna*. That is in emblem of the theatre sense of the Italians, and a setting for the carnival of the waters. There is only the highest terrace of Caprarola (again with those two goat-syllables in its name !) to approach Villa Lante ; the top terrace with the caryatid figures of fauns and faunesses carrying baskets of ripe grapes upon their heads to crown their goat-locks ; single figures, but in the corners of the terrace, and at the steps, they are in pairs and talking together or holding communication by signs. Only the fauns of Caprarola are of the order of Villa Lante.

When I went there again I was overcome by the beauty of the place. Nothing, nothing had changed there in all the years. It was pitiless, and cared not what had become of its admirers. You can return to it, the wreck of what you were before, and it is no different. It is no older. It is cold, cold. But touch the warm stone with your hand ! See the bright lizard run along the wall ! The moss'd stone sings out aloud to itself in the sunlight. I had heard of this garden before I was ten years old. I must say, too, that it seemed to me to be haunted by my father who had told me of it. Were he alive now he would be ninety years old. When I thought of him in this lovely place it made me want to weep, and I remembered the Italy of my childhood and of how I saw Puccini followed by a great crowd of citizens walking on the walls of his native Lucca. Then the camellias of Villa Lante took on the tints of women's complexions of the time and I fell to imagining what could have been the beauty and fascination of persons I recollected when I was young, but too much of a child to comprehend such feelings.

This made me sing over to myself the tune of a Viennese waltz called *Luna*, by Paul Lincke, that I remembered hearing at San Remo in 1904 when I was five or six years old, for it is a perfect picture of the young women of the day in their large hats, and I am singing it to myself, now, as I write this, and it is wafted to me through the roses and carnations of the Italian Riviera and the palm trees and the painted sea, where the railway runs like a toy line along the seashore, all the way, or I like to think so, from Genoa to Monte Carlo. The *bersaglieri* rode through the town on their bicycles, in their feathered hats, playing tunes on their bugles as they went by. I can hear them now. But the waltz *Luna* comes back again, a ' restaurant ' waltz, certainly, for it is suggestive of eating in some outdoor place underneath the trees, but dining at a table apart, some little distance away. It was a popular tune at the time I remember it, and typical of Viennese musical comedy, bearing with it other associations, I have no doubt, but, to me, it is tinged with Italy ; it is as though one was dining in some restaurant in Italy, and had asked for it to be played, and they would play it badly, for they do not understand the music of Vienna. The camellias of Villa Lante, I say, took on the hues and texture of the human complexion that can be more beautiful than any petal, but I was thinking less of that than of how in comparison with this garden that is timeless and static, in which time stands still, something that is of yesterday, or the day before, is lost and gone for ever. It was no longer ago than that when I was first told the name of Villa Lante. It was only yesterday when I came here, and now and again at long intervals of years, and here and now. When would I come back again ? And that familiar person, enclosed within himself, who had told me of it ? What had become of him ? In what Elysian Fields was he wandering ? Where else but here, for some part of his soul or spirit must be at rest ? But, like myself, and I have inherited it from him, he was a person of no religious beliefs. All you can say when considering a work of art (Villa Lante is as much a work of art as any poem, painting, piece of music) is that some portion of its weight of aesthetic comes from the other souls that have attached themselves to it in admiration. This, some may think to be the sum final of survival and that you may leave no more than this behind you, which, if it be true, takes little or no account of those many spirits that are inarticulate and would mean that the passage of a work of art through time dragged after it as heavy a burden as ever slowed down a galleon in weedy Sargasso when the turtle-footed winds were stilled.

The box walks and ilexes of Villa Lante, I say again, were haunted for me among the lemon and orange trees in terracotta pots. This is one of the beautiful places of the world ; as lovely as the gardens of the Generalife at Granada. It cannot have been much less beautiful when laid out new. They leapt, as ever, the blue dancers of the Roman fountains and the colonnades ; as they leap, still, and the striped Switzer, halberd in hand, shows against the travertine. What is appalling is that we are helpless and cannot delay the shrivelling of the petal. I do not see it yet. I only know that it is near and cannot, now, be long delayed. The thought of that made me walk apart at Villa Lante ; and the thought of all that had happened, two horrible and hideous wars in a lifetime. But I could not dwell upon those. I went further back in my mind to the tuberoses of the flower market in Florence which are among my early memories of Italy, and to the little horse carriages in which one drove about the streets, sitting, probably, upon the small uncomfortable front seat from which one had to be careful not to fall out upon the pavement. Or the Roman flowerstalls which I had seen again ; the flower-stalls of the Piazza di Spagna below the steps ; or in nearly every street. The arts of Italy were utterly remote from us, but to be seen on every hand ; and it was as though the cut flowers and the green umbrellas of the cabmen and the coloured postcards were all that was left of Italian arts, Italian graces. All else was dead ; dead as everything is dead up to the day that one was born, or later, till one can remember. The masters, the makers of light, Piero della Francesca, Mantegna, Botticelli, Giovanni Bellini, those were inconceivably distant. They had died out of the bloodstream of the Italians.

The mediaeval towns of Italy — trams, motor horns, and the wireless excepted — were every bit as noisy as they are now, and with the same types of inhabitants. For the population has not altered. It is to be argued that the physical types portrayed in Italian paintings of the grand epoch are an attempt on the part of the painters to escape from their environment. The dark, unshaven, Dominican monks among whom Fra Angelico passed his days were of another creation from the fair-haired, rose-and-white-carnationed Virgins and children of his pictures. As much as any Northerner who ever lived in Italy in his imagination Fra Angelico dwelt in an imaginary world which resembled St. Augustine's England. The

"Angeli, non Angli " of Pope Gregory are the young people of his paintings. They are of the same race as King Richard II and the angels of the Wilton diptych ; but upon the hillside of Fiesole and in the streets of Florence such fairhaired types were few and far between. They would be rarer still at Foligno and at Cortona where Fra Angelico spent his early years. From those hill towns he got his painted houses, his lights of sunrise falling aslant upon colonnades and inlaid churches, but not his inhabitants, who were of another longitude. Fairhaired angels and children were an obsession with the Italians. When we come to Botticelli there is a little difference. His models are more closely observed. This is no imaginary population ; they are fairhaired Italians. This is to be seen in the complexions of the young women in Botticelli's *Primavera*, and it is no exaggeration to say that you can hear them speaking in Italian voices. If the angels of Fra Angelico, his heavenly choir and angelical players of musical instruments, consorts of viols and violas, and blowers of the high-toned, shrilling trumpet, were to converse at all in the intervals of their celestial harmony, it would not be in the *lingua Toscana*. With Botticelli it is a world of adults, Italian adults. Lucrezia Tornabuoni is reputed to be the figure of Venus in the *Primavera*, and you can see that she has the sallow skin of the Italian to go with her burnt brassy hair. I call it that because the fairhaired Italians, if they go hatless in summer as was apparently the custom with young daughters of rich Florentines of the late fifteenth century, get their hair not so much bleached in the sun as burnt to a hard brassy gold, the colour of brass wire. I suppose theirs was the generation born in 1460–70 (the dates of Lorenzo il Magnifico are 1449–92 and they would be a little younger than he and his brother Giuliano de' Medici), and that the spirit which animated them and makes them appear timeless, or, in fact, contemporary to whatever decade in one's own life is the most spiritually receptive and intelligent, died out entirely, and never came again.

They are bareheaded, the nymphs of the *Primavera*, but I began to think of them, as the sun burned hotter, as June turned into July, wearing the high-crowned, wide-brimmed straw hats that you see being plaited by the women at the door of nearly every peasant house in this part of Tuscany. It would be when the grapes have come upon the vines, when it is impossible not to stand quite still and look out at the fireflies that are dancing like sprigs of fire all over the night for as far in every direction as the eyes can see. And earlier, in the late evening, when the frogs croak in their deep voices in the water pools. I wonder, as they grew older, if the nymphs were famous as beauties who had been painted by Botticelli in their youth. He cannot have invented their clothes for them. The nymphs must have worn dresses of that pattern, but probably only among a few families and in that group of friends. It must have been, in part, the imagination of the painter. Did they keep to these dresses as they got older, thin muslins and flowered cottons that were the fashion of a decade ? But, in fact, the change would be imperceptible. What would decide it would be the flimsy nature of such thin materials that did not last, that could not be stored away as could silks or brocades. Or was the whole scene of these youthful figures in a grove of orange trees the fantasy of the painter, and did they bear but an emblematic likeness to the persons they are said to represent ? I think this is more probable, and that there is but the hint, no more, of a resemblance ; that as the painting became older, in the lifetime of those who knew its history, legends grew up about it and persons were tied to it by anecdote. It is likely, too, that they all died young. I believe that this is implicit in the painting and that one has not to think of them when they grew old.

When I was eight or ten years old I was taken for one Easter holiday to live in Florence in a hotel in the Piazza Santa Maria Novella, and for two years afterwards during the Easter holidays to stay in a flat in the Via dei Bardi. How well I remember that dusty square of Santa Maria Novella with the two obelisks in the middle round which they held chariot races under the Medici Grand Dukes ; and the porphyry figure of Justice standing on a column in the Via Tornabuoni, near where one ate ices ! Or walking down the Via della Vigna Nuova to fetch our letters and passing in front of the Palazzo Rucellai, which is a fifteenth-century building by Rossellino ; and the square stones and rustication and the giant, golden bulk of the Palazzo Strozzi, and its great unfinished cornice and *fanal*; (corner lanterns), link holders, and iron rings ; or upon Sunday afternoons walking in the Boboli garden, a name so reminiscent of a bubbling fountain, and coming wearily, for it is a long walk down an avenue of cypresses, to the Isolotto, a round basin with stone causeways across it and locked gates, which I regretted, for I had been reading Prescott's account of the battles of Cortez with the Aztecs upon the causeways leading to Mexico City. But, here, the causeways had stone balustrades upon which stood orange and lemon trees in terracotta pots, and on the stone island in the middle there was the statue of Oceanus by John of Bologna.

His was a name I knew (for some reason, though a Fleming, he is one of the only painters or sculptors of the Italian Renaissance, except Titian, to have an 'Englished' name) ; and indeed I had already been taken to Bologna, and I admired the arcades of Bologna and the marble statue by John of Bologna in the square. I can see the statue now, as I first saw it in 1908, and I have a distinct impression of the giant snowy form of Neptune, and the smaller figures of *putti* and of sirens riding upon waves. Of what would the town of Bologna, " where nearly all the streets are arcades, with red plaster walls ",[1] remind an intelligent child of ten years old, I ask, and it is little wonder that when I found out many years later that there had been a famous Pantaloon with the name of John Bologna upon the London stage I at once wrote a poem about him ! I have often wished there were statues by John of Bologna in Venice and have imagined a giant Oceanus standing in the lagoon in front of the Doges' Palace, somewhere near the island of San Giorgio Maggiore. He could be kneedeep in water as though to wade ashore ; or in a stone chariot scudding the waves ; and I have thought, too, of a line of heroic statues along the Giudecca. John of Bologna was used to working in the giant canon. Is not the sixty-foot-high, crouching stone figure of the Apennines in the gardens of Pratolino attributed to him, gardens that were laid out by the Grand Duke for his mistress Bianca Capello ?

Returning to Florence, how well I remember crossing the Ponte Santa Trinità where you come to something so typically Italian, or so it seemed to me when I was a child, two streets converging and meeting at an angle in front of you and the knife edge of the central block or backbone of both streets was decorated with a fantastic lion mask spouting water into a great scallop shell ! The Italians could so easily have done nothing, have left it alone, for it was curious enough in itself, but they could not resist the opportunity and put a wall fountain (I suppose a drinking fountain) at the corner. The lion

<hr />

[1] A phrase in a letter written to my brother, 14 May 1908, from Bologna. Cf. *The Scarlet Tree* : London, Macmillan & Co., 1946, p. 273.

mask was pointed out to me whenever we went by and I could see even at that age that the meeting of the two streets was like a theatre scene. From the lion mask at the street corner, the meaning and import of the word ' mask ' being perhaps but dimly apprehended by me, it was no great distance to Jacques Callot whose etchings I knew, certainly, before I was twelve years old ; to the masqued men and women in Pietro Longhi's paintings ; and to the masqued figures of the Commedia dell' Arte. Were not the remote descendants of these playing in the summer as pierrots on the sands ? And I can remember having it explained to me why the actors of the Commedia dell' Arte wore masks, while we were walking one winter afternoon on the deserted Spa, and I believe I was told at that time that some of the masks had their origin at Bergamo, a town I never knew for a long while to come, but, somehow, that association was implicit in the syllables that spelt its name.

Now, many years later, a personal philosophy that resembles in spirit the airs and ensembles of the most melodious of operas distils itself and rules the day and night. It is the music of Mozart's opera, and not Beaumarchais' play. A philosophy of life, and an architecture, but it is only theatre architecture, being only calculated and built of instinct for the theatre, or for the extremes of sun and moonlight, and another architecture, altogether, is required for all other purposes. The buildings are for fanciful background ; and they are such as I have written of in some of my books, and perhaps in a few instances brought for the first time into literature. I have named the music, but not the paintings, nor the poetry of my predilection, for those are of another ambience, this was not their period. They are of another time. They are Venetian or Florentine and belong to the golden age of painting, but for our present purpose we cannot make play with the high ships and caravels of Carpaccio, his hooded chimneys (Venetian chimneys), young popinjays in round caps, and turbaned Orientals who are merchants of Grand Cairo or of Istanbul.

Nor could I write, here, as I would wish, of Giovanni Bellini, the master of dawn and of late evening. I would have wanted to write of his *Transfiguration* in the Gallery at Naples which is one of the beautiful paintings of the world ; and of his *Agony in the Garden* in the National Gallery. Some part of my personal philosophy, or of my idealized world in which I delight to dwell with the more insistence because it is un-realizable, must be to float round the canals of a greater Venice in those few moments before I fall asleep in the knowledge that I am on my way to see the lost paintings by Giovanni Bellini that were in the Doges' Palace. For the most important paintings by Giovanni Bellini are lost to us. His pictures in the Sala del Maggior Consiglio were entirely destroyed by fire in 1577. They must have been the greatest narrative paintings of the Western world. The present series by Veronese and Tintoretto in the Sala del Maggior Consiglio, the *Venice crowned by Fame* of Veronese and the *Paradiso* of Tintoretto, were done to take their place. Giovanni Bellini is known, now, from a few portraits and from his altarpieces. But his lost paintings in the Doges' Palace were his master works ; and where works of art are concerned there is a prime difference between projects that may have been discussed, and that we could wish had been put into execution, and those that were, in actual fact, completed and were then destroyed. After this manner Giovanni Bellini has probably suffered more damage than any artist, in any of the arts, whom one can recall. For Carpaccio, who survives in quantity, was an inferior painter and little more than an illustrator of genius when compared to Bellini. He is of the stature of Pinturicchio beside Raphael ; of Benozzo Gozzoli compared to Botticelli. Carpaccio would be among the pleasures and beauties of the world if we were not aware of what we have lost in the burnt, or conjectured, pictures of this much greater master.

The commission to paint the pictures in the Sala del Maggior Consiglio was given to Bellini when his brother Gentile, who had already begun work there, was sent to Constantinople. Sultan Mohammed II, who had conquered that city in 1453, wrote to the Doge asking for the services of a good portrait painter, and inviting the Doge to the wedding of his son. This is in curious commentary upon the relations of the Venetians and the Turks. The Doge could not leave Venice ; or there would have been the wonderful spectacle of his arrival on board a Venetian galley, escorted by feluccas and other craft, to cast anchor in the Golden Horn ; and the no less magnificent spectacle of the Sultan being rowed out with many banks of oars to meet him. The Doge could not go ; or decided not to for reasons of internal policy ; and Gentile Bellini, in a sense, was sent instead of him. The painter personified the talents of Venice, if not her power, or riches. He returned to Venice in 1481, two years later, having painted the portrait of the Sultan now in the National Gallery, and, doubtless, other paintings and drawings that have long been lost, and resumed work with his brother.

The subject of the pictures which covered three walls of the huge Sala del Maggior Consiglio was *The History of Barbarossa*, and the two brothers worked, in all, for nearly thirty years upon them. Giovanni, according to Sansovino, was wholly responsible for two of the paintings : a naval battle, with the Doge receiving the son of Barbarossa as prisoner upon the golden poop of a Venetian galley, a painting upon which Giovanni had worked for eleven years, and the reception of Pope Alexander III on board the *Bucintoro* by the Doge and Senators of Venice. His two pictures must, indeed, have been one of the culminating points of European painting, for Giovanni Bellini is a vastly greater painter than Veronese, or than Tintoretto. Certainly, where my own predilection is concerned, these lost paintings by Giovanni Bellini in the Doges' Palace are irreparable, and as one who has admired Venetian painting for as long as he can recall aesthetic emotions of any kind at all (I can remember the Doges' Palace and the Sala del Maggior Consiglio, as I can both the exterior and the interior of St. Mark's, from the time I was ten years old), I would surrender all of Titian, Tintoretto, Veronese, for a sight of them. To these I add, in imagination, another set of paintings which have for subject the meeting of the Doge and the Turkish Sultan upon the waters of the Golden Horn, and the Doge's attendance at the wedding of the Sultan's son. I am wondering, as I write this, whether the *Bucintoro* was seaworthy ; whether it could put to sea, or manœuvre further than the Porto di Lido, where the lagoon meets the open sea, and every year upon Ascension Day there was the ceremony of the Blessing of the Sea, the symbolic wedding of the Doge with the Adriatic, and the casting of the ring into the ocean.

There is some little evidence for what such paintings could have been in the picture of *St. Mark preaching in Alexandria*, now in the Brera, a painting by both brothers ; and in the crowd of turbaned Orientals in *The Martyrdom of St. Mark*, a painting begun by Giovanni Bellini and completed by a pupil, in the Scuola di San Marco. This is a crowd of Turks in gowns and turbans ; nothing more or less. But the huge composition, repainted, damaged in detail, marred from the beginning by its awkward shape to fit a doorway, could only be from the hand of a master. So far as the Turkish costumes are concerned he must have been primed with material that his brother Gentile had brought back with him from Constantinople. The dresses of the Turks are of the same period, and are closely observed, as in the very finest Persian miniature paintings that have come down to us. In fact, they are for Turkey what the paintings of Bihzad and his school are for Persia of the Safahvids. In those (for an instance, in the *Niẓami* of the British Museum, probably the most elaborate and perfect of all Persian painted manuscripts, with miniatures by Mirak, Sultan Mohammed, and other painters of the school of Herat) there are blossoming trees and cypresses, maple or plane trees, flowering oleanders and rock-roses ; blue irises in pots ; tiled pavilions of wonderful intricacy ; turbans as diversified as a bed of tulips, some horned, some flecked with gold, or the high turbans wound round long sticks (Kulahs) which were the headdresses introduced by the Safahvi house, further adorned with herons' feathers as a mark of princely rank (it is, always, a young unbearded prince !); glorious tents with white tops and sides, walled and floored with fine Persian rugs, and with blue and white striped tent ropes with which the illuminators make great play to divide and enrich their composition ; striped clothes of the nomad shepherds and their black goathair ' lean-to's ' ; and storks' nests upon ruined walls.

But this is Turkey of Mohammed the Conqueror. These are the Turks we see in *The Martyrdom of St. Mark.* This whole subject of the Orientals in Venetian paintings is one that, so far as I know, has never properly been studied. *St. Mark preaching in Alexandria,* of the Brera (by both Gentile and Giovanni Bellini), is much inferior as a painting. It must be, chiefly, by Gentile. Its interest is in the large group of women sitting, Turkish-fashion, in the foreground. How often, in imagination, have I not tried to compose and people this other pair of paintings that I am suggesting ! For it is the Oriental figures in Venetian paintings that are my particular predilection. They are not only Turks. There are Byzantine-Greek merchants, Phanariots, more simply, and beyond dispute, Sephardic Jews who have fled to Venice from Granada. In *The Martyrdom of St. Mark* there is just the hint of what is lost to us in the paintings of *The History of Barbarossa* in the Doges' Palace, burnt in the fire of 1577 ; and of what could have been had Giovanni Bellini accompanied the Doge of Venice to Constantinople to attend at the wedding of the Sultan's son. Carpaccio would be among the pleasures and beauties of the world if we were not aware of what we have lost in the burnt, or conjectured, pictures of this much greater master. To myself, one of the inspiring sights of Venice has been the so-called Mori, three carved stone figures " in Oriental garb ", described in the guide-book, laconically, as " probably portraits of Greek merchants from the Morea " (but they are wearing huge turbans, and, also, there is another stone plaque with the figure of a camel), which are upon the wall of the house once occupied by Tintoretto, near the church of the Madonna dell' Orto. There are some wonderful turbaned Orientals in Tintoretto's painting of *The Miracle of St. Mark*, now in the Accadémia in Venice. Somehow, and understandably, the Venetian painters found a particular inspiration in the legends of St. Mark. This picture belonged to a series painted for the Scuola di San Marco,[1] and they were made the occasion for those Oriental figures beloved of the Venetian school.

---

[1] Of which others are in Sansovino's Libreria Vecchia in Venice (*Transference of the Relics of the Saint from Alexandria*) and in the Brera (*Finding of the Body of St. Mark by the Venetians*).

Veronese, too, painted Orientals though, to my mind, never so successfully as the earlier masters.

The true follower and imitator of Giovanni and Gentile Bellini in this respect, was Carpaccio. In two of his paintings in the Scuola di San Giorgio degli Schiavoni in Venice there are Orientals ; in the *Triumph of St. George* and in *St. George baptizing the Pagans*. In the former picture, attending at the killing of the dragon, there is a king or nobleman on horseback wearing a brocaded gown and peaked hat, much resembling the high, peculiarly shaped hat worn by the Christian Emperors of Trebizond, a headdress which was known and famous all through the Levant. There are, also, figures on foot, and upon horseback, in huge turbans reminiscent of those still worn by Nigerian princes, and three men sounding brass instruments in shaggy fur hats of obvious Turkish dervish origin.[1]

For myself, the Oriental figures in Venetian painting have always been one of the attractions of this most improbable and beautiful of cities. I remember them, and the Orient gold of the mosaics in St. Mark's, for as long as I can remember anything that had interest for me. In a little painting by

---

[1] In a painting in the Louvre of *St. Stephen preaching in Alexandria* there are Orientals in turbans and brocade gowns, and in the left-hand corner a figure standing with his back to us wearing what appears to be a fox-fur hat of the sort I saw worn in 1936 by Jews in towns in remote parts of Romania. In perhaps the most fascinating of all Carpaccio's paintings, *The Miracle of the Holy Cross*, in the Accadémia at Venice, a picture which gives us the crowded life of the mediaeval city with the old wooden Rialto bridge in the background and gondolas innumerable (fourteen or fifteen of them) with gondoliers in piebald hose, including one negro gondolier, we see standing in just the same place, in the left-hand corner, under a projecting porch or colonnade, the self-same personage. I like to think he is a Jewish merchant from Granada, a new arrival in the city, for many Jews fled to Venice after the fall of Granada in 1492, and this picture was painted soon after that before the turn of the new century. Other Jewish merchants and bankers are to be noticed in Gentile Bellini's painting of *The Procession in the Piazza of St. Mark's*, which belongs to the same series and is in the Accadémia in Venice.

Carpaccio in the Uffizi (a fragment of a *Crucifixion*) there is a white-bearded Turk in a gown of brocade and a folded turban, and I remember at an early age thinking how different his Oriental figure was from the angels of Fra Angelico with their feather wings dipped in the fires of the spring morning, for it is my surmise that Fra Angelico got up in the night and pushed open the wooden shutter of his cell, and looked out on the morning, and thought he saw the fires of the Heavenly City upon the pale hills and far-off walls and towers, and other cities and pleasant prospects forming in the clouds, before the fires of sunrise faded and it became another day.

Carpaccio apart, and the lost Bellini, there are the Turks and Orientals of Tiepolo, in whom there is a mystery, for the same individuals occur again and again. There are white-bearded Orientals, which is no wonder, for such were to be seen upon the quays of Venice and they are probably merchants of Grand Cairo, of Smyrna, of the Bosphorus. They may have sailed from Tunis, or Tripoli ; but it is to be noted that no longer do they wear brocade gowns. Those splendid Renaissance patterns of formalized pomegranates, of tulips and carnations, have gone and, instead, they wear plain dresses of ample Oriental cut, but of white linen, or of yellow, just like the Turkish dresses which lie in a lacquer chest in the house where I write this, and which I know were brought back from Smyrna by a Barnardiston relation in the reign of George II. The dresses of Tiepolo are, in fact, true and contemporary to their own time. But there are other Orientals who are not so easily and quickly identified.

There is the red-haired man with mustachios and an aquiline nose in the *Banquet of Antony and Cleopatra*, in the Palazzo Labia. He stands behind Cleopatra, looking gravely on, and we see him in his turban and striped vest or tunic against a pillar of the colonnade or musicians' gallery, outlined against a white garden term and a clipped cypress, close to the halberds of the sentinels and to a white obelisk that flashes in the distance. The kneeling Turk in the scene where Cleopatra disembarks hand-in-hand with Antony from the galleon is of another race. So is the huge old Turk — the Turk of so many of Tiepolo's sepia drawings and paintings — at the head of the wooden gangway which the blond page descends. And the negroes in both frescoes, whether serving wine or holding back a greyhound, are negroes of convention in velvet doublets. But the red-haired Oriental is another matter. He is the same, but clean shaven, who looks on at *The Beheading of St. John Baptist* in the Capella Colleoni at Bergamo ; and he appears in other paintings. I have, sometimes, wondered if he could be Albanian. I have even corresponded upon this subject with Miss Edith Durham, who was the foremost authority upon Albania. But she could not help me. She argued, instead, an Albanian origin for Pierrot, advancing on her own behalf his loose white coat and trousers, and big buttons, above all, his white cap, which is still (a white fez) the national headdress of the Albanians ; and pointing out that his zany-like character could be derived from Albanian youths hanging about for hire at Venetian seaports down the Dalmatian coast, unable to speak a word of Italian, and therefore dumb and speechless and, in all respects where Pierrot's clothes and temperament are concerned, dressed for the part. Upon what I consider can be nothing other than Albanian bodyguards in Tiepolo's great ceremonial paintings she was silent, or, at least, had no information that she could offer.

Tiepolo is last of the great Italians, a scenic decorator, but the only Italian painter of the first order since Tintoretto. The Florentine and Umbrian schools had produced no one of

eminence for two hundred years. The art died in Venice.
There can be few persons who have seen Florence and Venice
to whom one or other is not the most beautiful city in the
world. It is, as I said in another context, a division of temperament, or two kinds of minds, and as regards achievement,
little or nothing to choose between them. They are the two
schools of Italy : one of colour, one of line, and you can prefer
one, always, or change from one to the other, and alter back
again. I suppose the images of one or other or both schools
of painting must occupy the minds and imaginations of nearly
all those persons who will read these pages.

Such reflections were all in the nature of a daydream while
I was walking, those few moments, in the gardens of the
Villa Lante. I suppose that the violent and extraordinary
effect upon me of seeing these gardens again was in the nature
of a climacteric, that it was the result of seeing Italy once
more, after having been away from Italy for so long. It made
one want, not to stand quite still, but to walk quicker, quicker,
quicker, which is the way it ' takes ' some persons when they
are unhappy and miserable, or get bad news. I suppose the
desire to be still, without moving, is outward sign of another
kind of unhappiness ; but this was of a different order, more
akin to the wounded hare running round and round in a circle
until it falls, not one of those suspended moments when one
cannot bear anything to move or alter, out of misery, when
one would have everything unchanged, in that same spirit
that leaves objects untouched in the room where there has
been a death, and the room is unlocked and entered, now and
again, at long intervals, and no sound comes from inside the
room, and the person who has gone inside is sitting or standing
still there, and not moving, and comes out again, without
speaking, after a long time.

This was violent, not static misery ; its desire for speed, its expression in that quick walking, was the symbol for catching up with time, for running down and overtaking time. No ! not time, only, but oneself, one's own person, that part of oneself which has lagged and been left behind, but in fact it is not like that, it is the contrary ; it is some part of the soul of which the bonds have been severed, and it rises in agony to the surface and is not to be comforted, for it is exposed to the light. I have known others, besides myself, to whom this happens. Perhaps the desire to stay still is of the nature of a dumb abasement before the face of time. I remember being so afflicted after my mother came down to see me in the prison house of school, when she had left and it was all over, but when one is older the wish to move quickly, I have said, like a hare running in a circle, must be in symbol for letting the event stand still and getting in front of it, but, alas ! only running round and round in distress and agony of spirit. It was the Roses of the South that I wept for, the flowerstalls of my youth, and I give to it that familiar name because this mood of nostalgia was induced, was brought on by this scene exactly as it would be if one could, by some act of magic, find oneself back again among living persons as they were when one was eight or ten years old, unchanged, but gifted, as to oneself, with faculties to take note and remember. What shall we choose to see ? But it is enough that we are walking here in the gardens of the Villa Lante, which are neglected, for there are not many flowers. It would be one's own childhood, but the youth of those others, and that would have its own scent or flavour which, I would have it, was bought at the flowerstalls. That was a time when the talk was all of flowers, so it could be the roses of Italy, which smell little and are nearly scentless ; or, if it is scent you require, the tuberoses of the flowerstalls ; but for the images of time past that are in my mind I prefer the camellia trees of Villa Lante, blowing white or red upon the bough, and just low enough for the hand to reach.

Upon no account whatever, where that past is concerned, must it be the scent of lime blossom. For those others lived in a world that is not the same as ours. Most, if not all, of them are dead now. But this is my own world as I have known it. So the blossoming lime tree sheds down happiness and well-being. The white peacock spreads her tail and dances. . . .

III

White Peacock

THIS, allowing for the transmuting of the sexes, is an experience I have only known once in my life when I saw a white peacock spread its tail and dance — upon the terraces of Isola Bella in Lake Maggiore. I only saw it once but it became a symbol, and as much of a symbol and an experience as that first time I saw the gentian. Perhaps it would not be lessened in my instance if I lived within perpetual sight of gentians, any more than I find the blue crocus monotonous and ordinary when it first appears after the winter. The crocus is ever miraculous and beautiful.

Coming out from the Simplon tunnel after the first experience of modern Italy at Domodossola, where the Alpini frontier guards wore hard bowler hats of shiny leather, with a feather at the side, and the guard blew a horn before the engine started, the train of old wooden *wagons-lits* rattled down through Alpine valleys above the roofs of houses that had great stones upon them to keep the tiles in place, and wooden balconies, and emerged at last down a long curve over a shingled river bed upon the shores of Maggiore, and in a few moments we saw Isola Bella floating in the lake, and had reached the old Italy.

We always stayed the first night or two at Baveno, just opposite the Borromean Islands, so that probably the very next afternoon, or even upon the afternoon of the same day, we would be rowing out in a boat past the Isola dei Pescatori with its fishermen's houses and eating-places under trellised vines, and past a little islet with nothing but a tree or two upon it, to Isola Bella. How slow and leisurely the rowing, a foretaste of being rowed in a gondola down the Grand Canal ! I have not been to Isola Bella, now, for half my lifetime, but how well I remember the little quay where one landed, and the big bulk of the palace looming above it ! There was nothing much in the interior. It was disappointing. I only remember some rooms done, grotto-like, with shells and pebbles, and empty state apartments ; and one half-length portrait of a young man with extravagantly embroidered sleeves and laced hat, and decadent pale features, by Fra Galgario. After that, one came out into the sunlight of the 'floating' island. The gardens rise in terraces to a hundred feet above the lake and have stone balustrades with orange and lemon trees in pots, and stone obelisks, and magnolia trees, and pink oleanders. Here, perhaps for the first time in years, one saw the lizard darting on the hot stone.

Here, upon the top terrace, I saw the white peacock, just at a time when I had in mind a series of poems called *The Bird Actors* and when I had lately heard Mozart's *Il Seraglio*, at the end of the summer in London, and was obsessed with its music and had the serenade and the 'Farewell' song from that opera ever in my ears. I think it was in 1921 or 1922. I wonder if any reader of this book can experience the obsessing, haunting violence of such association, with Venice only a few hours away. I knew that Mozart, when a boy, had stayed in Venice for the Carnival and seen the wonderful spectacle of Venice in its decay.[1] The serenade from *Il Seraglio* is Venetian music coloured by the Turkish and

[1] In 1771 when Mozart was fifteen years old.

Oriental figures to be seen upon its quays. That influence is heard, too, in Osmin's drinking song from *Il Seraglio*. It, too, is Turkish music of Venetian inspiration.

The white peacock of Isola Bella was to me an actor, or a character, of like origin. It was holding itself quite still, when I came upon it, still and rigid in an ecstasy of self-admiration ; and then would turn, of a sudden, sideways, with slow deliberate step, keeping that position long enough to be admired of all, or, more probably, to hypnotize ; then wheeled, once more, with its back to me so that I could see the stage machinery, the slats and ribs of its tail ; and after long interval slowly and purposely turned itself right round to face me. It took a step or two forward. It held back its long neck as though to bury that in the feathers of its fan, or to lie there with its living eyes among the mock-eyes of its tail, and lifted its head forward, its white peacock head with little crown or tiara of white feathers. Now, with imperceptible but quickening motion, it vibrated the feathers of its tail and shook them like a sistrum. I could hear the rattling of the quills. Again and again it held them still and quickened them. It was a long rattling and shaking, a Celestial or fairy thunder, long-drawn and shuddering.

The white peacock was, also, like a fairy galleon, and in metamorphosis upon this enchanted island became in imagination the skiff or barque of Armida in which to transport me to her garden, this, from evocation of snowy sails and crystal rigging, but in the guise of the craft with lilied oars that might carry the stage hero to his inamorata. The white peacock was, as well, in one, the serpent god and goddess. It was a serpent which had become a bird, and the bird had become a princess, and the princess was a dancer. The white peacock was a ballerina. In birds, except in warrior fighting-cocks, and owls and eagles, there is this transmutation of the sexes. I could no longer see the white peacock in any other sense than as a bird princess and ballerina. Her princess's long train, which should be held up when she walked and of which I knew the rustling, sweeping sound from the trains of other and ordinary peacocks when they walk upon the lawn or gravel, for they love to sweep their trains upon the pebbles for the sound of it which simulates waves breaking upon a mimic shore, by some feat of magic was lifted and held still, and spread open on the air to reveal that ocean of eyes, the only purpose of which was to hypnotize. By what deeper and more incarnate magic could it be that the bird ballerina had the gift of rattling and shuddering her quills in acted or mimic ecstasy? No bayadère danced like that; or had that Milky Way for train and fan, and for a mirror held to your eyes to mesmerize.

Her tread was a dancer's tread, that of a ballerina coming down the stairs upon a stage. And while I looked, the white peacock closed her tail feathers like the slats of a fan, and trod with her bird feet holding her long train behind her so as not to touch the earth, and took up position and spread her tail again, turning about, as though to feel a faint wind from the lake and set her sails in tune to that. She closed the spikes and filaments of her tiara, shook and brushed them to-gether, bird-like, and opened them again. But the little, quick darting movements of her head belied the ballerina and revealed the serpent in the peacock. The bird had no beauty of feature and only bird legs. In those it must yield place to a human dancer. It was a bird actor. It wore a mask. It had a little, pointed face. But it rattled and shuddered its lovely plumes, and was dancer again, and white peacock, in that moment; a beautiful being, spiritualized, perhaps held prisoner, certainly gifted with traumatic powers. For the white peacock now went into trance and ecstasy, dancing, not moving her feet, as do the bayadères, a magical being in any company, not needing to bow her head to the birds-of-paradise, who are dancers, too.

Here, on Isola Bella, I suppose the white peacock perched upon a magnolia tree, or perhaps a stone balustrade, and called out in the morning in raucous, Indian voice. We need only imagine to ourselves how lovely a white peacock must be to the dark Indians. The pale bayadères were admired. Their dancers had skins of creamy chocolate, or as though dusted with sandalwood. They rubbed their bodies with turmeric oil to make them golden. The white peacock would be a magical being, son and daughter of a god in one, and bird and serpent. In a world where the birds were dancers the white peacock would be most beautiful of all. It is as much a miracle of nature as the rose pink camellia.

This was at a time, as I have said, when I had the music of *Il Seraglio* in my mind and when I thought it to be some of the most lovely music in the world. It was, therefore, an adventure of a peculiar and beautiful kind to be rowed out to Isola Bella and to have that music inhabited by the white peacock. The garden is not one of the best of the Italian gardens. Late in date, it was completed by 1671 and created long after the gardens of the Renaissance ; much of its detail is grotesque and in bad taste. The gardens of Isola Bella cannot compare in poetry with Villa d' Este or with Villa Lante. Originally, it had been but a bare rock with a chapel and a few houses. The stone had to be brought across in a fleet of boats to build the palace. Or would a single craft have been sufficient, making several journeys in a day ; in any event, many hundreds of boatloads of soil must have been carried to that barren islet over a period of years to raise the terraces. Statues and obelisks had to be embarked in boats for the short water journey. But, after all, Isola Bella is in Italy. The gardens are ' laid out in old Italian style '. It may be, according to which way you enter Italy, the first Italian landscape that you see. And it is upon the way to Venice. It floats upon the waters. How many times has it not been compared to a stone galleon riding on the lake ?

Isola Bella, it has been said, is " frankly artificial yet entirely in keeping with its surroundings ". The terraces are raised above a gigantic water cistern into which water can be pumped from the lake. This is the core or foundation for the ten terraces of Isola Bella, and in that knowledge the island becomes a huge decorated raft or pleasure carrier. This is the explanation of the galleon-like shape of the island with that great water cistern in its hold. A model of the intended palace, in one of the shellwork rooms, shows the superb water entrance that was projected, but never undertaken, with huge elongated piers in horseshoe form, and great ramps of steps, for true landing-place upon Armida's island. Beautifully ornate models of galleons and landing barges float off that faery harbour on a mimic lake. Behind, rises the bulk of the palace, as it might have been ; and a little way to the back, after crossing a forecourt which more resembles a decorated causeway, the terraces and statues and obelisks lift themselves, in travesty, a hundred feet out of the lake, higher than the palace roofs, with the lowest walk at gunwale level, and ten decks or terraces climbing to the white peacock.

A stone obelisk upon one of the terraces supported a star that was cut out of iron or tin. In another part of the garden a statue holds up the motto *Humilitas*, in ironwork. Such are Italian faults, and inconsistencies. But are not Palladio's

buildings in Vicenza built of stucco ? Italy is a land of sunlight and of the theatre. For the waterworks in their old
gardens the Italians had hydraulic engineers. The fountains
and grottoes of Isola Bella " were carried out by Mora of
Rome ", says an old book. And why not ? The ubiquitous
Carlo Fontana had a hand in them. Isola Bella is half landscape and half theatre. And to my mind the magical inhabitant
of the island was a player on that stage. A new population,
all the same, for white peacocks were only brought to the
island fifty or sixty years ago. They were not known in Italy
in the seventeenth century, and are a recent importation, but it
is an ideal setting for the bird, close to magnolia and oleander.
And it is even true that, in a sense, the white peacock is
a prisoner upon the island, for its wings are pinioned. It
cannot fly to the mainland. Its wings will carry it from
terrace to terrace, but the shores of Lake Maggiore are too far
away.

My mind was full of that music. The bird dancer was the
person or spirit who was the subject of that serenade. It was
the white peacock for whom Osmin sang his drinking song
sitting, crosslegged, under the flowering tree. And the
' Farewell ' song in which the characters of *Il Seraglio* take
leave of the audience was farewell to the white peacock. The
mock-serious strains of that music which so wonderfully and
curiously interpret the feeling of saying goodbye are, indeed,
among the miracles of the art of music. For it is a stage
farewell. It is not entirely serious. We can see them again.
But only if the opera is playing and we go a second time.
That experience is not part of the ordinary run of life. And
if we go again and again to *Il Seraglio* we have that sensation
every time. So it is a farewell which can be repeated, and it
must not be the same in feeling as a goodbye said for ever.

But it can be for many years, and we may be much older when we hear *Il Seraglio* again, and all this is implied in the 'Farewell' song. I felt this, then, and I had its full meaning in my ears. Probably I knew that it would be a long time before I would hear that opera again. When I was twenty-three years old, and landing on Isola Bella, my obsession was the music of Mozart, even more than when I had heard *Nozze di Figaro* so often during its London production in the summer of 1917. I can still hear, and I dare say so can one or two of my readers, the noise of the anti-aircraft guns firing on the German aeroplanes during at least one performance of this opera. Their percussion punctuates for me the lovely music of *Porgi amor* and *Deh vieni, non tardar*; it breaks into, but cannot destroy, the immortal *Voi che sapete* and the not less heavenly *Venite, inginocchiatevi*.

When I say that Italy ' is a land of sunlight and of the theatre ' I believe that I am stating all that there is to be said of dual appreciation and of the two kinds of minds. So let us forget Isola Bella, which was never more than a stepping stone and floating island upon the way to Venice and to Venetian painting. It is a toy, of the kind that a child floats in his bath, bearing the same relation to the great masterpieces that celluloid swan or rubber duck do to the great carved galleons of the Armada, or to the flightless *Bucintoro* that had no sails but was pulled along with ropes and went with gilded oars upon the shallow waters. Nevertheless, Isola Bella is a thing of beauty if you see it when you are young and your mind is full of music. It is ' artificial ', but so is everything else that is mentioned in this paragraph, except the sunlight. Whence came the magnolia and oleander to Isola Bella ? And the white peacock ? This ' converted rock ' is not their natural habitat.

IV

Rose and Lily

WE will travel further.

And imagination takes wing into the tapestries, transported
as though by the feather of the firebird's wing. They are the
tapestries of the *Baillée des Roses* ; [1] three panels of knights
and ladies, " obviously portraits ", in a background of wide,
vertical bands or stripes of green, white, and red, the personal
colours of Charles VII of France (1422–61), strewn with rose
briars, and with trails of the rose sprays that he sometimes used
as his device.

Upon one of the panels there are eight figures, four ladies
and four gentlemen, disposed, as it were, in two storeys, which
gives an odd perspective to the rose garden. Down below,
two of the ladies wear the horned headdress, a headdress that
looks like a cross-section of the two humps of a dromedary,
and it looks, too, like a fantastic saddle upon which no one
would, think of riding for their seat would be so uncomfortable.
The piked-horn, as it was called, is supposed to have been
brought to England by Anne of Bohemia, queen of Richard
II.[2] So it was a continental fashion, and the French piked-

---

[1] Now in the Metropolitan Museum at New York City.

[2] Cf. the tomb of de Vere, ninth Earl of Oxford, Marquis of Dublin, and Duke
of Ireland, at Earl's Colne in Essex, with his second wife Lancerana Serjaulx, the
joiner's daughter, who had been maid of honour to Anne of Bohemia, wearing the
piked-horn ; and the alabaster tombs of the Ladies Benedicta Vernon at Tong,
Shropshire, Jane Cockayne at Ashbourne, Derbyshire, and Elizabeth Fitzherbert at
Norbury in the same county, all of whom wear the piked-horn on their effigies.

horns at which we are looking were in all probability more elegant than English ones, for, even so long ago as this, ladies' hats were made in Paris.

We have to keep this in mind, and that French ladies would wear them with more authority than English ladies. Perhaps the piked-horn was not a French fashion — could it have been of Bohemian or Polish origin ? — but it has become one of the familiar images of our world because of the traditional portraits of the Ugly Duchess — who is supposed to have been a Duchess of Tyrol — whom Tenniel and Lewis Carroll took as their model for the Ugly Duchess in *Alice in Wonderland.* She wears the piked-horn. But it has a very different appearance when worn by a beautiful young woman.

Two of the ladies in this panel of tapestry wear the piked-horn, and their fair hair is done up in a close cap or caul of network. Long veils hang from the backs of the piked-horns and trail down to their waists. Have I not said of the tapestries in Spain that ' a chapter could be written on the head-dresses ' ? And look ! Look above ! Two ladies, of the same height, preternaturally thin of waist, which makes them of an unaccountable elegance as though they must have been famous for this in their day, and they have pale features and large necklaces. Yes ! We note how pale they are of feature, and that their hair is pulled or combed back from their foreheads. It is screwed back, and we note how pale their eyebrows are ; eyebrows which need to be pencilled in, which require the faint mark of the pencil, and that then form two pretty arcs upon their fair skins. Look closely into the tapestry and you will see their blue eyes ! And now it is apparent that they are sisters, or even two portraits of the same young person. Both of them hold roses in their hands.

And we may think of the momentary, human warmth of the roses that they hold, there, in their hands.

For the theme of the *Baillée des Roses* is the giving of roses in homage, a living relic of which is the payment of a red or a white rose as rent upon quarter day, or sometimes, a red rose at midwinter and a snowball upon midsummer day which, in effect, meant nothing, no rent at all, and was an impossibility imposed on purpose. This is the English survival of a homage that the peers of France owed to the French parliament. This homage consisted in the giving of roses. The peer who was making the gift had the chambers of the parliament hung with flowers and sweet-smelling herbs. He gave a splendid breakfast, and visited each chamber in turn, having borne before him a great silver basin filled with roses and pinks, natural or made of silk, one for each person present. Here, in the tapestry, the giving of roses has been heightened into a poetical occasion, of a sort familiar from ivory mirror cases which are often carved with the Siege of the Castle of Love, and whereon you see the knights in full armour, armed cap-à-pie, knocking with their swords upon the portcullis, and the ladies raining roses down upon them from the battlements. Upon one of the tapestry panels of the *Baillée des Roses* a lady in a piked-horn has just picked a rose from a rose bush with one hand, and given it with her other hand to her knight, who carries his hat turned towards the front so that the rose given him by the lady may be seen by us.

The pair of ladies hold, each, a rose or a pink in their right hand. It is only their dresses that are different; one, of brocade with a bold pattern; the other, more simple, as though not to draw attention from her person, but, I think, the two dresses are of the sort that would be worn by young, unmarried maidens. There are no rings upon their fingers.

Look, again, into their blue eyes ! It is the same person.
Their eyes are blue pebbles, the colour of bluebells, with a
black rim as round as one of the rings of Saturn, encompassing
the iris. The soft, gentle outline of the nose shows in the
tapestry. They have the same ears ; ears that are, recog-
nizably, of the same person. Now look at the high-domed
forehead ! Both young women wear a little band or loop
coming below the line of the caul or net cap which frames
their arched foreheads. You can feel the shape of their heads
rising above that, and almost the warm touch of their hair
that is so carefully hidden, into the complicated and extraordinary structure of their headdresses. You can guess the
colour of their hair from those faint eyebrows and eyelashes
that need darkening.

But their hair is not pale at all. Indeed, it is the colour of
the firebird's wing, concealed under that fantastic pair of headdresses that are exactly alike in every detail, that we can describe as one, amalgamating their dual persons, headdresses
that are two heads in height, of starched linen, rising up in
front like an enormous tower or gateway, falling behind with
many pleats and folds, and the whole edifice of it, of linen
white as snow, like a poetical image for an iceberg, or a
mediaeval city upon a hill, or a snow mountain, or a great
sailing vessel lying becalmed below the cliffs. It seems to rise
high above the forehead in a pair of folded peaks, and a pair of
outer folds, higher and larger still, at which height and bulk
it is the snowy turbans of all the Grand Turks, all the Grand
Signiors, in one ; and it has a last pair of folds, behind that,
higher and wider still, which trail down their ends at the level
of her neck, but far out from that, far from all the snowy
structure, like the last sail of a seven-masted sailing ship ; and
the whole headdress on the head of this young girl is of an

incredible complexity and importance and you can scarcely believe that it has been prepared and fitted by her sewing maids. I think that such a headdress would only have been worn by young, unmarried girls, being in the nature of an emblem or confection of virginity.

The high headdresses have something in them of the Kirghiz or the Turcoman. The women of the round felt Kibitkas wear headdresses as fantastic of dimension in the endless plains. They, too, belong to the century of the Grand Turk. But I would wish to open the tall cupboard and feel into its darkness, which is as real as the warmth of the rose held in that hand, and find the high starched structure of linen, and lift it (I think it would be put upon some sort of hatstand in the cupboard in order not to spoil its edges) and carry it out into the light, and turn and see the young girl of the tapestry standing with her thin waist near to her brushes and combs and little boxes, and to everything that belongs to her, as in that moment of entering the room of someone with whom one is in love — and be known, as I would be, for it is the same person — and hold the high headdress to the head of this young girl who died five hundred years ago, and yet knows me, and fit it upon her head so that you do not see the colour of her hair, which would betray her, and lay the wraith of the red-haired fishergirl out upon the wet rocks, but now in her own person in the high room up the rush-strewn stair. Looking down the long folds of her dress, it is she, beyond a doubt, if I only knew her by her thin wrists, and I see her once more as in the tapestry turning round in her high headdress to show it to me, and immediately have a vision of her in the henning or high steeple hat with hanging veil, which was the fashion of a few years later, and that sounds Northern French in the mere noise of its two syllables, all for this

288

miracle of a few moments in the high room, up the steep stair.

Look, for a last time, at the young women in the tapestry! Note how tall they are, and see the long folds of their dresses! This lady, and her own double or phantom who wears the henning, is a duchess or princess, and you must bow and stand back against the wall when she comes by. They wore the long train so that, whatever happened, you could never catch sight of their feet or legs. When they rode, side-saddle, upon a milk white mule or jennet the long folds of their gowns all but touched the ground.

But it is travesty. It is all artifice. It is Titania, by the white tree-poppy, the Californian poppy, cutting dead roses from the grey stone wall, but a day or two after Midsummer Night was past ; Titania, before the hand of Oberon, her husband, squeezed the juice of Love-in-Idleness, " a little Western flower ", upon her eyelids, lying asleep in " another part of the wood ", and she was still a maiden.

It was that day a feather of the firebird was put into my hand. And, at once, the rose garden and the room, itself, are transformed into the stage of a theatre and a dressing-room, and we have a dual vision of the high linen headdress and a long train of white lace, as it might be, the long train of the white peacock among the white rose bushes, leaving her legs unencumbered for the figures of the dance, when she sheds her cloak and long train, a dance which consists in the giving of roses into her hands by her suitors or cavaliers, the pressing of the roses to her face to smell them as in the Rose adagio, and the throwing of the rose bouquet at the climax of the dance, or the giving of it into her mother's hand. And the ballerina runs out into the wings. But the metamorphosis gives us her, also, in her own person, and in the shades of that, between the goddess upon the altar and the living being. It is a magical duality, with as much of poetical fire in the differentiation of its dual lives as when I said, thinking of Isola Bella, an artificial or stage island floating like a pleasure galleon in the lake, that Italy was a land of sunlight and of the theatre.

As we grow older we should become stronger in our determinations. Half a lifetime has not made the music of *Il Seraglio* sound less beautiful, though I have never heard it played again. I am more, not less, certain now of my prejudices. But there are mysteries and questions that are left unanswered. Who is to decide between the tiger lily and the lily of the valley? Both are flowers of nature, but the mind that loves the one will find it difficult to admire the other. For myself, I do not want a rose that has no scent. The lily of the valley and the tiger lily are two different characters ; they are nations or civilizations in opposition, as unlike in their theory of life as the Greeks and Persians. But the scentless rose is a race living in its own ruins. The lily of the valley is not a lily, but a fritillary. But it never called itself a lily. That name was given to it because of its look of virgin innocence and the way it hides itself in its green leaves. Its beauty is its chastity, and this is the beauty of the camellia. But if the camellia had scent it would lose its chasteness which, yet, is not entirely innocent.

A gardenia has no innocence at all. It is a night succubus ; never more so than when unpacked out of its cotton wool, with wired stalk wrapped in silver foil, and I must give the scent of it in a sentence in order to paint its wickedness. The flower is lying on its face in a wooden box on its dark leaves that make the curtains of its bed. It is of an unbelievable and ivory pallor. No blush could ever come upon that tainted cheek. Put down your hand and lift the gardenia to your nose! The integument of the petals is aphrodisiacal in its ravishment of the senses, but not as music ravishes the senses, for invitation and consummation are soft-spoken in its breath. Now smell the gardenia ! It is an oily, ivorine nard, or an ointment, rubbed upon or exuding from the limbs. If you open the petals, and part them, the scent comes so strongly that it goes up to the brain. Now draw another breath of it, for the flower is not sated ! Like the succubus, it lies naked and never sleeping all night through until the morning. It is but more ivory in pallor. It has yellowed. It is like yellow ivory. The ghost of the gardenia has been ravished as you breathed in the scent. The petals are now browned and brittle and the gardenia scent is cloyed and heavy. By the night it is nothing and must be thrown away.

Little, indeed, has been done to improve the lily, and lily hybrids compared with the hybrids of other flowers are not lasting. The lily is emblem of innocence ; but what has innocence to do with its tigered and parded forms ? The lily-white Madonna lily is sister to the golden-rayed *auratum*. Even the martagon nodding its Turk's caps and seemingly indifferent to whether they are red, like sealing-wax, or wine red, or pure white like a turban,[1] is brother to *L. amabile*, grenadine red and spotted black, and *L. nepalense* which is a greenish lily stained red purple.

There is the leopard or panther lily as well as the tiger lily, *L. pardalinum* of California and Oregon, orange red with darker tabs or blotches ; while the tiger lily, orange spotted with black, comes from Japan. Who is to choose between them ? *L. candidum*, the white Madonna lily which grows

[1] The word 'martagon', according to some authorities, may be derived from the Turkish *martagān*, a form of turban adopted by Sultan Muhammed I ; cf. *Lilies of the World*, by H. D. Woodcock and J. Coutts : London, *Country Life*, 1950, p. 73.

beside the cottage door and waits in the still summer for the wedding and the funeral, is an emblem of virginity, and yet a rod of flowers, and a thyrsus for the hand of a teetotal Bacchus teaching the cultivation of the earth, and the manner of making honey, but not the use of the vine, to the dark Indians. Such are the upright spikes, or tall spires of the Madonna lily, with many long buds and open flowers of lily flesh among the light green leaves.

What could be lovelier than *Lilium japonicum*, washed pink or pinkish cyclamen, with slender stem and long leaves, but nearly scentless, a lily known in the native tongue as ' Sasa-yuri ', " the dweller amongst the bamboos ", and that must be of particular adaptation to the impenetrable, but unsubstantial glades ? *Lilium regale*, white, and reflexed or backed with pinkish red, is nearly impossible to believe to be so recent of discovery, and to have been found only along a fifty-mile reach of the Min river valley in Szechwan, in Western China. How different are the yellow lilies, *L. ochraceum*, and another with a name that I refuse to bring into a sentence ; [1] the first, of the type of a Turk's cap or martagon, but yellow, greeny yellow, and heavily marked and stippled reddish brown, as though fly-blown, but by some celestial insect ; and the other, yellow and beautiful, a light, almost a lemony yellow, with thick, twisting leaves, and flowers that are like drooping bells, with recurving petals, lightly dappled, and the orange red pistils protrude and dangle ! This yellow lily comes from the Caucasus, the ancient Colchis ; and the more sinister yellow lily is from Burma.

The pink martagon of Kingdon Ward, another Burman lily, is of the kind that breathes of spices. The lily flesh sparkles as though with little crystal points that make the

----

[1] *Lilium szovitsianum.*

spicing of the lily ; and it becomes an intoxicating gale if you approach the pistils and let them rub their pollen upon your nose or cheek. When the pollen blows from other lilies and stains the petals it is in sign that they are in maturity, or waning, and the scent will have hardened and lost its sugary spiciness. Not that the sweet distillation in the scent of lilies is suggestive of any sugarcane whatever, being more of the nature of a nectary exudation or an inflorescence upon the flesh of the lily, but it seems to me that the scent is sweeter and more spice-laden in a lily the shape of *L. wardii*, the pink martagon, for the particular reason that the martagon, instead of being shaped like a trumpet with flanged petals, as in other lilies, has its petals bent back and turned nearly inside out, curved back to form the folds of a Turk's cap or turban, with all the pistils protruding in a knot or bunch. The spottings and tabbyings of the martagon, its panther or leopard markings in which the scent resides, which are the spice islands of the lily, float on the open air and you can come near to them. For the turban, be it remembered, shows the face of the wearer. The Madonna lily is more retiring. It grows in a nunnery, and holds up, but hides, its face.

The martagon, and all the Turk's caps, have few leaves and hang out their crowd of heads. Human skill has coloured the Turk's caps ; but the double tiger lily, flecked and spotted, comes from the hand of nature and trembles its stamens from the salmon-red trumpet mouth. This is the most beautiful of the double lilies. But the doubling of the lily is a work of supererogation and it must be accounted among the improbabilities of nature that it should have been most successful, of all lilies, with the tiger lily. I prefer the single tiger lily and the golden-rayed *auratum* of Japan, particularly if it be the variety which has a band of vermilion down the centre of the petal and spiced, scarlet tigerings.[1] In that, it seems to me, we have the innocence of the lily transcendentalized, just in the same way that certain qualities or talents can be carried to extraordinary lengths in human beings. Here, in this lily, it is an instance of peculiar and transcendental colouring marking it as the most brilliant and dazzling of all the " lilies of the field ". It has, as it were, personal advantages which set it apart, as well as talents ; and the only trouble with this lily, as in the case of human beings born to this predicament, is that the excess of qualities can be an obstacle, almost, to their recognition. This ' painted ' lily is too beautiful to be quite credible. It has scent, form, lily flesh, the delicacy of the lily, the tiger or leopard blood, and flaunting colouring. Another variety of *auratum* is white, pure white, and flecked or studded with white spots ; tigered in the same colour, marked white on white, and I would describe this as the white peacock of the lilies. I would not care to choose between them. One lily is the colourless negative of the other, but in that variety you have the shape and purity of the lily, and the lily scent, and just when you are thinking it is the most beautiful of all lilies you may see the same lily, of which this is but the lovely wraith, in all its vermilion and scarlet colouring. Then, indeed, it is impossible not to prefer painted to pale innocence.

[1] *L. auratum* var. *rubro-vittatum.* The variety of *auratum* mentioned below is *L. auratum* var. *virginale album.*

V

Ricordanza

ALL my life I have been a lover of the rare and curious, alike of the slum kennel and the tent of Tamerlane. The Great Khanum, coming from her enclosure, " with a thin white veil before her face, which appeared to be entirely covered with white lead or some such cosmetic, the effect being to make it look as though she was wearing a paper mask ", reminded me of the paper husk of the iris. It made me think of the iris, so lovingly wrapped and veiled, hiding in its parchment integument or covering which, later, is discarded and hangs down like a mask, after the unmasking. This was at the tournament and banquet of *Koumiss* or fermented mares' milk, where the Mongol ladies sat, unveiled, and watched the knights boasting of their warlike deeds, kneeling on one knee. The device of Tamerlane was three moons or circles set in a triangle $^o_o{}^o$ and, himself a Mongol or Kalmuck and the greatest destroyer of the human race until modern times, he employed the finest Persian architects and craftsmen of the day upon his buildings at Samarcand. I am aware that there is something transcendental in such comparisons and that it is far-fetched to be reminded by an Oriental iris of the encampment of Tamerlane, and it is not without forethought that the title for this chapter has been taken from one of the *Douze Études d'exécution transcendante*. In so doing I know that I have laid myself open to criticism in more than one direction.

295

The *Douze Études* were published in their final form in 1854. They are, therefore, the work of Liszt's middle period. But they first appeared as his Opus 1 in 1827 when he was sixteen years old. They had, in fact, occupied much of his attention for a quarter of a century. In their earlier version they are often more extreme than in the final and revised edition, and though rarely played, by that much the more interesting and characteristic to his admirers. Both in subject and in technique they were something new in music. They were transcendental, alike in technique and in material, as is evident in *Mazeppa, Feux Follets, Wilde Jagd,* and *Chasse-Neige,* which are the titles of a few of them. *Ricordanza* is but another. The *Douze Études* as a whole, now, nearly a hundred years after they were published, are still most ardent and extraordinary in imagination. They have, also, a strongly marked poetical flavour which is manifest in what I can only call their ' touch ', irrespective of the pianist who is playing them, in the same sense that with an aria in classical Italian style by Bellini you can ' feel it ' in your throat. I have tried to make some episodes in this book ' sing ' after that manner, and if I could believe that I had transferred some of their quality into prose I would be flattered.

Now the meaning of *Ricordanza,* the Italian title of this chapter, is ' a little remembrance ', or, even, some object or keepsake of memory, and it will be recalled that it is the name given by Liszt to the ninth of his *Douze Études d'exécution transcendante,* which are probably the most perfect of all his original works for the piano. Ferruccio Busoni said of *Ricordanza* that playing its notes was like turning over the pages of a bundle of yellowing love letters. Perhaps its meaning is, more strictly, something done or made in memory, and of course I have been influenced in my choice of a title by the secondary meaning or implication hiding within the two last of its four syllables. Its import, then, is to be understood rather as though you were guessing the syllables that make up the keyword to a charade.

But the termination of the Italian word is a form of diminutive, or even a diminutive more in the nature of an endearment. It is a sort of affectionate belittlement on the part of the person speaking, in the same sense that *una speranza* means rather more than the mere expression of a hope. Even more, if it be politeness and good manners on the part of the writer, the word *speranza* implies that this is a hope affectionately clung to. And in the same sense, and to a like degree, *una ricordanza* is more than a mere record. It is an impression or a memory set down with care and trouble, and of which the result must stand by itself, in a little world of its own making. Perhaps that portion of the title which is a diminutive may even be taken for an understatement. If this be so, it is but in order to draw attention away from the first person and fix it on the scene and subject.

Various episodes in this present work have been approached and treated in transcendental manner, and it is not, therefore, so much a piece like *Ricordanza*, in itself, that I have had in mind as the personality and technical powers of that composer and that piece of music when applied to themes that in other hands would have received a different treatment. I am wondering if I have made my meaning clear. I am thinking of the transcendental quality of Liszt's own music, purged of its fustian, and possessing or inhabiting the music of another. Or, more simply, of his musical fire and intelligence performing other music. I have attempted to give various passages and episodes in this work a transcendental fire and quality in the sense that you could say of certain music that you had never heard it played like that before.   The promise of a chapter which has the title *Ricordan₂a* must, owing to the necessity of meaning, be retrospective.   It looks back to the past, not to the future.   And the nature of a piece of music that lasts for a few moments must be different from that of a book three or four hundred pages long.   For the title could have been transformed and enlarged in order to cover a whole series of episodes and their connecting passages, alike in one of the ' openings ' called *August 1915* and in those of which the ink and the implementation are not dry, or even not yet written on the page. *Ricordan₂a,* used in this sense, is an intangible, not factual autobiography, the record of a part, not of the whole.   But it is, as implied in its name, something complete in itself ; or it could be an account of certain strains or facets of sensibility which are in harmony with one another and recur throughout a lifetime.

For an instance the white peacock.

The first couplet of a street song : " The little boy was crying to his hyacinth that was dying ", has more of beauty in its humble words than is to be had from gasworks and town hall, from suburban villa and mid-Victorian stained-glass window ; in spite of Messrs. Piper and Betjeman who could never argue me into agreeing with them that a mid-Victorian village railway station or Methodist chapel is a work of art. The ' squiffer ' accompanies the song — the same ' squiffer ' (concertina) that is played outside the public-house door ; or it is the cracked violin of the wet pavements ; or there is no accompaniment at all.   But, at least, it is not the harmonium. Those are the words of poverty in stark ugliness ; they are wrung from sad faces in dirty windows ; and are not sung in order that the victims of the Victorian age should see the ' fun ' in their surroundings.

The blue hyacinth in the window is as lovely and rare a sight as when the peacock spreads its tail and dances. It has meaning for all, for young and old alike, for those who can scarcely read and those who have read a lot. It belongs to the same rule of beauty as Blake's little black boy and his little chimney-sweep. The geranium by the frowsy curtain is as artificial a thing as the stone galleon, with ten terraces for decks, afloat in the long waters. It is as unnatural as a bunch of primroses upon the chimneypiece; but not more artificial than a coral island. We know what flowers grow, of themselves, on bombed sites in London, and that pink willow-herb is orchid or lily of the loud ruins. There would be no mercy in the cold air for plants that are put in windows. It is unnatural that human beings, in contrast to the rest of the animal world, should live in houses. But they live in houses because it is their nature; and once that is admitted, in theory, it is not far from the caverns of Altamira to the boxes of red bricks along arterial roads.

It is no further than from the painted rock walls of the Dordogne to shack towns built of whitewashed petrol tins, by-passing, to use a phrase loved of our times, all the works of art that there have been, between. I do not disdain the Gypsy caravans or the waggons of the Mongols. The ten-wheeled waggon of Jenghis Khan had wheels eight feet in diameter, an axle like a ship's mast, and was drawn by twenty oxen. The tent upon it was scarlet in colour; and the Tartar rolled forward in that to the conquest of Asia and a part of Europe in midst of a band of Gypsy and Jewish musicians who played in open carts before him. Perhaps his waggons did not sway more than the golden coronation coach of our Kings and Queens of which the supports are tritons, in the phrase of Horace Walpole " not very well adapted to land carriage ", but of which the import was to signify British dominion over and upon the Seven Seas. The most curious collection of the gilded carriages (at Lisbon) suggests nothing so much as that the god Neptune has left his sea chariots stranded upon the shores of Tagus. It is a miracle that these heavy but fragile vehicles should have survived at all and come down to us out of the past. They must, certainly, be accounted among the greatest artificialities of all the ages, beside the false beards worn by the Queens of Egypt, and for that matter, the periwigs, full-bottomed wigs, tie wigs, and all the powdered hair worn in the Age of Reason.

Be it remembered that the clean-shaven faces, whether of the Age of Reason, or of our own day, are as complete an artificiality. It is not for us to laugh at people wearing wigs ; and a motor-car is as unnatural, and quite as improbable, as a coach carved like a golden seashell. The most complete artificiality of all is music, which is as useless as the science of astronomy. But it is necessary and indispensable like alcohol, and that part of the population which can do without it is to be pitied, but half-heartedly, as in the case of prisoners who we are told suffer less than their companions in misery because they are non-smokers. There is less of a loss implied in something of which you have not experienced or understood the benefits.

But the roses open their buds. The voice of the dove rings in the high branches.

L'ESCARPOLETTE

A YOUNG girl rides on a swing.

She swings high and low, riding on a swing that is tied to the branches high above her head.

We will have music, music of light comedy, of which the phantom in the swing is momentary embodiment. And since music is the art which is not always contemporary, but looks forward or harks back, it is theatre music played by the theatre orchestra. She swings high into the air and comes down again backwards, and the rhythm of her swinging communicates itself into the music.

It is the moment when she is at the height of her trajectory and has kicked off her slipper.

The slipper is made immortal ; the white or rose pink slipper in that blue hortensia air. But, in fact, it is a flat-heeled slipper more resembling a ballet shoe, companion to the slipper " thrust round a corner of the door as though to keep the door ajar ", and that, once again, " has left its imprint on the paper of this page ".

Why the ' blue hortensia ' ? It is for a reason that will be apparent later on.

But the season is important, and it has to be the month when the flowershops are full of huge blue hydrangeas — hortensias, I prefer them called — it must be in early May when the shops and flowerstalls have the blue hydrangeas which cannot have been as magnificent of size as now, but we will credit them with enormous, blue-faceted flowerheads, like the facets of a huge blue crystal, in fact, blue as a hortensia, or even the facets of some huge revolving globe that glitters as it turns.

And now there is a blue mist. Look up into the feathery trees ! It lies like a blue cloud, if clouds were blue, between, and in and among, the boughs. And the blue cloud fills the spaces in between the leaves.

We are in a hidden place in some great park. Not near the house. It is more likely to be close to a little pavilion.

But I do not believe it to be in the park of a château. I think the scene is in the garden of some villa, some bagatelle.

There are trees and boughs and blue mist ; and a statue of Cupid kneeling with his finger to his lips.

But I would like to describe the shafts of sunlight that slant between the trees. For they are rose-coloured. They are the colour of pink roses. Or is it that the dust that dances in the sunbeams is a different colour from the dust we know ? A paler sun than the sun of Italy, of the Mediterranean ; while the lime tree in young leaf is a bubbling, green fountain.

Not one of the blue-and-gold mornings of the Mediterranean which mean that classical antiquity is not far away ; but a rose and silver morning of the Ile-de-France. I smell roses and white lilac.

Not the goat under the olive tree : not the cuttlefish in the rock pool. But flocks of sheep, clear bells of copper at their throats, and rows of poplar trees.

And vineyards. Not the tall, tented vines, as tall as tapestries, where they dance the saltarello in the trellised shade, and a volcano smokes in the distance, or you hear the siren sea.

But the vines are low vines, no longer than faggots. Have you ever made a fire of vine branches ? Have you put vine boughs upon a fire ? For they lift and feel like hollow bones. And the blackened bones sprout into green leaves.

Those are the vineyards.

There are garden rakes that are stage properties upon the ground, and a stone group of Cupids and a dolphin nearly hidden in roses. A gardener or a valet pulls the swing, and there is a young man lying back on an elbow in the thicket of roses and looking up into the swing.

It is leaves and blue mist and rose leaves, and the young girl in the swing. Did I not say that it would be a rose and silver morning ?

Look again ! Look at the elbow of the young man lying in the roses and his outstretched arm that parts the leaves and points towards the swing ! And he holds his *tricorne* in that hand. Look at the excitement in the fingers of that hand, fingers stretched out wide with pleasure at the beautiful but living phantom above him, and just out of reach !

He has thrown himself down at the foot of the stone Cupid in order the better to see her. But first there was the lovely moment when he lifted her with both his hands upon her waist and put her into the swing. Since I am a writer of prose and not a painter, she can stand there before us, laughing, about to be lifted into the swing, and then we will see in the style and length of her dress, and her little straw hat of wanton brim, how the fascination of what was admired in 1766 has become traditional, as it were, stage costume for a lovely milkmaid.

But no more delay. The young girl rides on the swing. And the young man lies on the ground to look at her !

He pushes down the rose briars with one hand in order to do so. The curving line of his waistcoat and cravat — indeed of his upraised knee and his whole body and inclined head, looking at her — makes the diagonal of the composition, along his arm and up his pointing hand, that holds the *tricorne*. And so, along the leg of the young girl, from her foot that has kicked off the slipper, and up one or both ropes of the swing, up and up into the boughs. The other line of the pyramid to make the picture comes down the pair of ropes into the hands of the gardener or valet who pulls the swing, and keeps in the shadow. In more senses than one he is stage hand of the scene.

Her slipper is high in the air over her lover's head. But he does not turn to look at it. He does not follow the flight of the slipper. For she looks down at him. This is the true line of the composition. It is in his upward glance at her, and in her downward glance at him.

The beauty is in her floating form, riding upon the swing. And the brim of her shallow summer hat of straw echoes the whole line of her body ; it echoes the line of her arms, one lower and one higher, holding to the ropes of the swing ; it imitates and parallels that line, curving and tilting in the space between. The hat has a curved brim and shallow crown. It is of enchanting beauty, with a silk ribbon, and she wears a matching ribbon at her throat. But that curving brim has another echo, too, for it follows exactly the line of her bosom, coming down from that to her thin waist, preternaturally thin, let us have it, in evidence of the person, and following along the line of her leg that has kicked off the slipper.

She wears her summer hat of straw as lightly and easily as she rides the air. And all the time she is pushed forward and pulled back again by that stage hand in the shadow ; up and down, up and down ; one moment into the green grotto of the leaves, with a creaking sound of the ropes, high up, where they are tied to the boughs, high up, deep into the green cavern

and coming out from that into the full limelight ; the misty-
blue sunlight, blue as a hortensia, and blue as the near distance
in between the trees. And just where she passes low enough
for you to stop or touch her with your hand the swing gains
height and she goes right up in a steep climb sheer above our
heads all for the benefit of the young man lying there to see
her legs.

The mossed trunk of the great old tree is a wonder to
behold, and so are the cloudy branches. Up above they are
as twisted as forked lightning ; and the leaves that clothe the
tree stem are hardly to be distinguished from rose leaves, as
though the painter must have known the difference, but did
not care. His theme was rose briars, the rose and silver young
girl in the swing, and the blue sunlight.

Out in the middle of that blue haze, which is of the sort
that hangs above a lake in a park where there are great old
trees, there is another tree stem, slanting at an angle, between
the flying slipper and the statue of Cupid kneeling with his
finger to his lips. It leans in rhythm to the movement of the
swing. It is met at the top by the jagged lightning of the
branches coming from the main tree stem and framing in
the scene.

A green grotto into which the swing retires. You see her
drawn up, up, into its glaucous shade, up, up, as though she
will vanish into the high branches. And before you could
believe it to be true, down, down again ; and then, the steep,
thrilling lift of the swing, its climb, and its dart out into the
sunlight. Higher and higher, each time, until it can climb no
higher without danger. Impossible not to see a swing and
mark the place in your mind where it goes highest. Here,
that point is the leaning tree stem. She touches it with her
foot. That is to say, she does not touch against it, but her

foot or the toe of her slipper goes as high as that upon the painted scenery.

But, mostly, from where we see her she is climbing ; or it is as though she is, at once, leaping and reclining along the blue sunlight, ricocheting, that is it, along the blue light, with a wonderful and graceful motion : carried along, skimming the surface and hardly touching it, not falling, there is nothing falling in her movement, but borne along, scudding in her new element of blue air, lighter than the nymph who rides the wave and turns over upon the crest of it, and rolls over again as if holding to the blue mane of the wave and dragged with it, now seen carried upright, as though standing in it, as it curls and breaks ; but this flight of the swing is a new ' display ' altogether or a ' courtship dance ', as though in the language of the race of birds, to be swept, over and over again, near and nearer to him, coming down to him out of the high branches, and drawn away again, high up, into the tree heart, and let down, poured down, thrown down into the light, then climbing, banking over him, but never in any attitude but that of riding lightly and beautifully upon the saddle of the swing, holding to the ropes, and looking down at him while he looks at her in ravishment and ecstasy.

This is the most beautiful of all scenes of gallantry. And, as in the case of the picture by Watteau which was our opening, Fragonard did two versions of the painting. There are slight, very slight, differences in the rendering. The one which is immortal, if anything so beautiful and transitory can have immortality, is in the Wallace Collection. The other is best known from the engraving by Delaunay, which is in reverse.[1] The difference is in the way the young girl is dressed. In the

[1] The original painting is, or was, in the collection of Baron Edmond de Rothschild, Paris.

one painting her hat has bows and feathers, and her dress and skirt are heavier. She does not ride so lightly upon the swing. In the other version (in the Wallace Collection) her dress is slighter and more becoming. She rides the swing more gracefully and wears that summer hat of straw with the curved brim.

In its day *Les Hasards heureux de l'Escarpolette* was considered very daring. Now, it shocks not at all. There is as much, and more, of libertinism in the opening bars of Mozart's Symphony in G minor ; or in the light blue and silver mirror room of the Amalienburg, and in its bedroom and hunting room which are in silver on a yellow ground. The particular air of gallantry of *L'Escarpolette* would not have been possible in a century previous to that. We have only to consider how absurd the protagonists would have looked wearing the great periwigs and voluminous feminine clothing of the reign of Le Roi Soleil ; or how quaint and ridiculous in terms of the men and women of Lukas Cranach who painted his naked Venus, lyre-hipped, with flaxen hair, wearing a little feathered hat.

This is the first time in history that such a spirit was possible, unless it be in a poem by that most improbable of country vicars the Rev. Robert Herrick, whom we know from the engraved frontispiece to his poems, a bust upon a pedestal in the classical manner, with whiskers and mustachios and curled hair, in the open landscape of Devon with the head surrounded, poetically, by a swarm of bees ; Herrick, who only printed his *Hesperides* when he was already fifty-seven years old, in lesson to young writers. He is the poet, of all poets, who would have loved the subject of *L'Escarpolette*. It is in his spirit.

But this is our own rendering of it and we do not wish to tie it down in time. We have already done this to some little extent in speaking of hydrangeas as hortensias, for that name pins down the scene to the time of La Reine Hortense ; daughter of the Empress Joséphine by her first husband ; wife of Louis Bonaparte, King of Holland ; mother of Napoleon III ; and I want this to be earlier in date than that, but as though it could be happening this last summer, or now, this moment.

As, for instance, the dress of the young girl.

She wears the *tutu*, most beautiful and becoming of all ballet costumes, and which has been well described as " a curving plate of cloud on which rest the hips and torso of the ballerina ".

The *tutu* has become shorter and shorter, rising higher, and becoming lighter and flatter year by year ; each frill a fraction wider than the one below it, forming the petals of the *tutu*, the underneath of the *tutu*, seen when the dancer is lifted or stands in arabesque ; two wider frills making the edge of the *tutu*, and between those a light, crinoline-wire hoop to keep it rigid and sticking out ; four layers of frills on top of that, the circumference of the *tutu* ; and the eye travels over the top skirt to " the glove-tight bodice ".

Those are the secrets of the *tutu*.

It is the rose pink and silver *tutu* of Princess Aurora when she runs out from the colonnade into the garden ; the black and gold *tutu* of Odile when she enters with her magician-father to the fanfare of trumpets ; the *tutu* of Swanilda with whom, long ago, I planned to walk by the edge of the corn-field, in a corner of the golden harvest. " Swanilda, in her short ballet skirt, walking birdlike, in the convention of the ballerina, in her satin shoes. Not, really, Swanilda : still less, Coppélia," I quote. " Only the girl who mimed that rôle ; but who walks with you down the summer evening. For whom you could break off a sheaf of corn," I continued, " And with your own hand hold it to her ear, lifting her hair to do so."

But, as with the little flowerseller, that would betray her.

And we change the lighting.

It is in the theatre.

She walks on before the curtain rises and gets into the swing, settling herself into it in her white tights, and smoothing the frills of her ballet skirt which are those, precisely, of the rose Belle Isis, a flat or ' quartered ' old gallica rose, described in the catalogues as " a clear, soft flesh-pink flower, neat and double ". Anyone who has grown the rose Belle Isis will agree that the folds of its petals are the frills, exactly, of a *tutu* : Belle Isis, rose of Saturn : daughter of the Golden Age : sister and odalisque of Osiris : moon of the rose-bed : rose of rose and silver : night-rose and rose of Cybele : rose of the theatre : rose of the fountain and the colonnade : and, as well, the rose of day ! And we leave her for ever in the swing : the same person, or the shades of her, through all time.

CUPID AND THE JACARANDA

In nearly every composition or work of art there is a Cupid, if it be only to fill in a corner or populate a cloud ; and Cupid, we are told, " is generally represented as amusing himself with some childish diversion. Sometimes he appears driving a hoop, throwing a quoit, playing with a nymph, catching a butterfly, or trying to burn with a torch ; at other times he plays upon a horn before his mother, Venus, or closely embraces a swan, or, with one foot raised in the air, in a musing posture, seems to meditate some trick."

That is what Dr. Lemprière has to say of him.

His, indeed, are directions for the placing of Cupid in classical compositions of any and every sort, and in obedience to that instruction here is our picture of him. If it has no other merit, it brings our fantasy born of fact and of imagination to an appropriate end.

I must explain that in the early summer of 1949 I was in Lisbon, and that in one respect there is a difference or an improvement since I was there before. It is a matter of the jacaranda. I am inclined to believe that upon previous visits to Lisbon, the earliest was in 1926, the jacarandas were not old enough to flower. Since then, many of the wider streets and avenues have been planted with them, and they grow in many gardens.

The jacaranda is a Brazilian tree and was probably brought to Europe from Madeira. The wood is of splendid quality. But the beauty of the jacaranda tree is when it is in blossom.

Then, it is one of the most wonderful sights of nature. It may be the loveliest of all the flowering trees. I must further explain that I had been ill, and that I have never before seen a jacaranda tree in blossom.

The first that I saw was upon a steep hill, one of the seven hills of Lisbon, climbing abruptly to the British Embassy. It stood in a walled garden, to the right-hand side of the road, and was about as big as a fair-sized oak tree. Rather smaller than beech or sycamore, and with a smooth stem. Not a leaf to be seen. For the blue jacaranda was in flower. But I had little time for it. I was so late for luncheon. Coming out, I saw it again, but with difficulty because of the high wall.

This must have been one of the earliest jacaranda trees to flower in Lisbon. A morning or two later, on waking and looking out of the open window, a tree at the back of some houses opposite the hotel, had broken into blossom. The tree had been of little significance and no interest; it had shown no sign of it the day before. It had not even occurred to me that it was a jacaranda. Now, in one night, it had become a blue tree.

That morning, or the next, there were any number of jacarandas in full flower along an avenue down by the harbour, where you take the train to Estoril. But they are not seen at their best, there, because the houses in the background are washed or painted blue, and because they climb too high above the jacarandas and enclose them. Also, they are tall, dull tenements. What are wanting are the tilted roofs of Lisbon; curving eaves that give to the old houses of Lisbon the touch of Macao or Canton; walls washed with bright colours, or lined with china tiles.

One of the most beautiful of the jacarandas grows outside the Museum of Artillery, which is in an old palace of the eighteenth century along the Tagus. The Museum is a two-storey building, of just the right height, and the jacaranda is about as high as that, or a little higher, and about as wide as a plane tree or a sycamore. Here, you can walk all round the jacaranda and look at it from every angle. You can see it against the façade of the palace, or against the sky, or distant buildings ; or stand right under it and look up through the boughs. Or, again, move away a few steps until you can take in the whole of the blue tree with your eyes.

And now it is time to describe a jacaranda tree in flower.

It is a blue you have not seen before. Like the blue helio-trope, in substance, that is to say, the whole head of flower, the entire jacaranda taken in at a glance, has something of the soft outline of a heliotrope. It is of powdery texture like the heliotrope, but only at the first sight of it, and only at a distance. For the individual flowers of the jacaranda have no resemblance at all to the florets of the heliotrope. It is only that they are in the same key of blue ; that they strike the same note of blueness. The little separate flowers, indeed, are trumpet-shaped. We shall see that one of the flowers, by itself, can become the horn that Cupid plays while Venus listens.

I would call the flowering jacaranda powder blue, if it were not that powder-blue china is of another and darker colour altogether. Neither is it the powdered blue of the heads and necks of certain pigeons ; a pale silvery blue ; or a paler, more distinct blue frosted with silver ; or as if powdered with flour ; or a little like very fine dew or hoar frost upon blue. The jacaranda has no undertones. It strikes the note and holds it. I think the moment of first seeing it is one of the memorable sensations of a lifetime. What it evokes is a new civilization and a new music, borne to one upon the soft Brazilian airs, " the *modinhas* that Beckford loved, that Beckford wished to learn . . ." and other, newer measures of that huge sub-continent where race mingles with race but there is no enmity or persecution of minorities. I do not believe the jacaranda in Burma or in South Africa, or wherever else it grows, could evoke a civilization of its own. It could be only, and nothing but, Brazilian, for the jacaranda, as we have said, is a Brazilian tree.

I have not seen the flamboyant, which is another tropical flowering tree. But I am not prepared to think that its vermilion flowers could evoke a whole new world before you, an architecture and a music, and inhabited streets and houses. The jacaranda tree in front of the Museum of Artillery at Lisbon does all this for you, and more. It is a sensation approaching the miraculous to stand a few feet away from it and look up at the blue flowers — again I am bound to say that it has something of the heliotrope, but with the black or purple of the heliotrope left out of it, and keyed brighter, softer, clearer ; or perhaps it is that the black in the heliotrope is altered to a base of red in the jacaranda. The blue note of the jacaranda is incomparable ; a marvellous mid-blue, but neither mauve, nor violet ; not like the plumage of any bird, nor the colour of any sky ; and with the property, it seems to me, that you forget your worries and sorrows, and how old the world is, or how new and augmenting are its troubles, and have time only for the jacaranda during the few days it is in blossom.

I had seen the blue paulownia, which grows in Tuscany at the same season as the blue wistaria, but it is as nothing to the jacaranda. So I thought ; at which moment the whole blue tree shook and trembled in the wind, and I saw a few of the blue flowers lying on the ground. Above them, the dove-soft boughs lifted and danced in the wind. I wondered, what would a jacaranda look like by night ? Would it keep that colour, which is the promise of music not yet written, and of a harmony and a civilization as yet unborn ?

Upon the evening of that same spring day we walked along the square of the Rossio with its striped pavement, up the Praça dos Restauradores, and into the long tree-lined avenue beyond it ; which is a public promenade up a hillside, with bars and band kiosques on the sidewalks, and shops and cinemas. It was near midnight, and very warm. Too lovely a night, indeed, for an early bed.

So we wandered, on the left of the avenue, to a place where there were bright lights, and paid for admission at a stile and found ourselves in an enclosed space into which people were streaming out from a theatre upon one side and a cinema on the other, and taking up all the empty seats in one or other of the cafés. We were lucky to find a table and two empty chairs.

The café was half in the open and half inside, and we were sitting in the open part of it, nearly, but not quite, under a magnificent jacaranda tree. A band played in the restaurant, but for the first few moments one could do nothing but admire the jacaranda, for night made no difference to the beautiful blue flowers. Now and again they danced in a breath of wind, and as in the morning a few of the blue flowers lay on the ground.

Soon, we began to take note of the other persons in the café and it was not long before we noticed they were all young. There were a good many young men who must be students and four or five young women, sitting by themselves, at first, but who before long exchanged glances with their neighbours or recognized old admirers. A little later, two or three of the young men came and joined them at their table.

At this point the prettiest of the young women detached herself from her companions and went to sit alone. She was tall, with a thin waist ; with dark eyes, dark skin, and dark, dark hair ; and in Brazil would have passed for a Brazilian. In fact, more Brazilian that a native of Portugal ; and with, who knows, the touch of Angola or of Mozambique ? Or of the black fishing quarter of Bahia, in Brazil, where they dance the conga and the samba, and other tropical dances under the jacaranda. And, evidently, she wished to sit alone.

Now it so happens that in cafés and restaurants in Portugal, that is to say, in Lisbon and in Oporto, which are its only cities, there is often a little page boy to take your hat or run with messages. There are some horrible children in a restaurant in Lisbon who wear large Eton collars, several sizes too big for them, but the child in this café wore the ordinary page's clothes, pale blue, with a pale blue pillbox hat. He was a fair child, ten or twelve years old, who should have been sent to bed hours ago ; a pretty child, and not unlike a Cupid. Only he looked so tired, which gave him a sinister air of dissipation. For a moment, it looked in the shadow as if his eyes were painted. But it was no more than the dark circles of fatigue. Lisbon is without the wickedness of other cities.

The child hung about with nothing to do, walking round idly, or leaning upon a balustrade, while the prettiest of the young women sat near him at her table, still alone.

The May night grew warmer, and more warm. The blue jacaranda had never looked so tropical by day.

Soon, one of the older students beckoned to Cupid and sent him on an errand. I was shocked with the import of it ; but I need not have worried about his messenger. Cupid, before running to her, stooped to pick a fallen jacaranda flower from the ground, and making the blue calyx into a little horn or trumpet, blew into it between his fingers, and so playing, ran to Venus and whispered into her ear.

THE END

PRINTED BY R. & R. CLARK, LTD., EDINBURGH